D1084321

THE ARMY OF CHARLES II

STUDIES IN SOCIAL HISTORY

Editor: HAROLD PERKIN

Professor of Social History, University of Lancaster

Assistant Editor: ERIC J. EVANS

Lecturer in History, University of Lancaster

For a list of books in the series see back endpaper

THE ARMY OF CHARLES II

John Childs

Department of History
University of Newcastle-upon-Tyne

LONDON: Routledge & Kegan Paul
TORONTO AND BUFFALO: University of Toronto Press

First published in 1976
in Great Britain
by Routledge & Kegan Paul Ltd
and in Canada and the United States of America by
University of Toronto Press
Toronto and Buffalo
Set in Monotype Bell
and printed in Great Britain by
Ebenezer Baylis & Son Ltd
The Trinity Press, Worcester and London

RKP ISBN 0 7100 8301 7

UTP ISBN 0 8020 2180 8

To Ann and my parents

Contents

PART THREE

Preface

THE need for a study of the British Army 'post Firth' has long been apparent, and hopefully this volume will fill the vacuum. Initially the topic was suggested to me by Professor J. P. Kenyon of the University of Hull, and throughout he has been a constant source of encouragement and advice. Originally, this book formed the essence of a doctoral thesis for the University of London, and whilst in that condition it was presided over by Dr Ian Roy of King's College. My debt to him is immense, particularly with regard to my style and presentation. These he made more coherent and manageable.

The transition from thesis to book was undertaken during the tenure of a Sir James Knott Research Fellowship in the University of Newcastle-upon-Tyne. The relaxed atmosphere of the university helped greatly in bringing the work to a speedy conclusion.

I am grateful to Mr E. C. L. Mullins of the History of Parliament Trust for permitting me to make use of the Trust's abundance of unpublished biographical information. I doubt if Chapter 2 would have proved feasible without access to this source.

JOHN CHILDS
University of Newcastle-upon-Tyne

Abbreviations

BM	British Museum, now the British Library
PRO	Public Record Office, London
Add. MSS	Additional Manuscripts, BM
CO	Colonial Office Papers, PRO
CO 279	Colonial Office Papers relating to Tangier, PRO
PC 2	Registers and Minutes of the Privy Council, PRO
SP 29 and 30	State Papers Domestic, Charles II, PRO
SP 44	Domestic Entry Books, PRO
SP 71	State Papers Foreign, Barbary States, PRO
SP 77	State Papers Foreign, Flanders, PRO
SP 78	State Papers Foreign, France, PRO
SP 84	State Papers Foreign, the Dutch Republic, PRO
SP 89	State Papers Foreign, Portugal, PRO
WO	War Office Collection, PRO
CSPD	*Calendar of State Papers Domestic*
CSPV	*Calendar of State Papers Venetian*
CSPC	*Calendar of State Papers Colonial, America and the West Indies*
CJ	*Commons' Journals*
LJ	*Lords' Journals*
HMC	*Reports of the Royal Commission on Historical Manuscripts*
SR	*Statutes of the Realm*
APC	Acts of the Privy Council, Colonial Series, vol. 1, 1613–80

JSAHR	*Journal of the Society of Army Historical Research*
EHR	*English Historical Review*
TRHS	*Transactions of the Royal Historical Society*
DNB	*Dictionary of National Biography*
Regt	Regiment

Note on dates

All dates referred to in the text and appendices are given in the English Old Style (O.S.) which was ten days behind the continental New Style (N.S.) in the seventeenth century. As in modern usage, the new year has been taken to begin on 1 January and not 25 March.

Introduction

THE first standing army in England during time of peace was that of Charles II. Since the earliest times kings of England had raised temporary armies in time of war, but the concept of a force which was not disbanded on the conclusion of hostilities was a radical departure. Cromwell's New Model was a standing army but it differed in some important respects from the Restoration army. It was a political force with an interest in and an effect upon politics acting both as a 'king maker' and an instrument of coercion. For many Englishmen the Interregnum was not a period of peace but a continuation of the Civil Wars and the new government had to rely upon the army for its very existence. Richard Cromwell fell from power because he lost the favour of this all-powerful machine. Sixteen sixty-one witnessed the formation of a new type of standing army: a non-political body concerned solely with the execution of the civil authority's wishes regarding national defence and the preservation of internal law and order. Not only was the army neutral in politics but not once did it attempt even to enter the theatre. Such qualifications were sufficient for this force to be regarded as the foundation of the modern regular army rather than the New Model.

Three strands were woven into the fabric of the new army of 1661: the exiled royalist army fighting with the Spaniards in Flanders, disbanded officers and men from the New Model, and old royalists who had endured the Interregnum in England. Following the flight of their monarch in 1649 a number of ardent royalists sought employment in the French army. This came to an end in 1655 when Cromwell signed an alliance with Louis XIV forcing Charles II to vacate France and seek refuge in the Spanish Netherlands. Here, on 2 April 1656, he made an agreement with Spain whereby he undertook to raise some troops of his own to fight against France in return for a promise of armed support should an opportunity arise of regaining his throne. Initially three regiments were recruited; one of English Guards under Henry Wilmot, Earl of Rochester, a Scottish formation under the Earl of Middleton, and an Irish unit commanded by the Duke of Ormonde. A further three regiments were added in the first half of 1657; a Scottish regiment under the Earl of Newburgh, and two Irish regiments under the Earl of Bristol and the Duke of Gloucester. Nearly all the officers and men were exiled royalists who were destitute and desperately in need of paid employment having been either forced to leave England by the Cromwellian government, or loyal volunteers. Lists of these regiments read like a roll-call of the principal royalist soldiers of the Civil Wars; Edward Sackville, Charles Wheeler, Thomas Ashton, William Carless, and Thomas Throckmorton. Reluctantly, the Duke of York assumed command of this corps and formed a small Life Guard of fifty horse under his life-long supporter, Sir Charles Berkeley, to bring the army up to a strength of seven regiments by April 1657.[1] The brigade first took the field under the Spanish flag in June of that year.[2]

The existence of this force was common knowledge in England where Cromwell was preparing to step into continental land warfare. In return for the possession of Dunkirk and Mardyke the Lord Protector agreed to send an expeditionary force of 6,000 men to fight for France under the command of Turenne who was instructed to campaign during 1657 and 1658 with the specific objective of taking these twin towns. Only a quarter of this brigade was drawn from the regiments of the New Model, the remainder being fresh volunteers. Sir John Reynolds, commissary-general of the Irish army, was given command with Major-General Thomas Morgan as his deputy. The four other regiments were directed by Samuel Clarke, Roger Alsop, Henry Lillingston, and Bryce Cochrane. Interestingly, the French requested that all the soldiers were to be English without any Irishmen or Scotsmen. After landing at

Boulogne in May 1657 the six regiments took the field with Turenne in June.

Not until September did the French commander-in-chief turn his attention to the promised goal of Dunkirk and Mardyke, but when he did the latter fell rapidly and was handed over to the English. Reynolds's troops took up winter quarters in and around Mardyke but suffered dreadfully from the unhealthy conditions. Already action casualties had cost them 2,000 men, but even after these had been replaced the brigade emerged from the winter with only 3,000, half their official establishment. Reynolds himself was dead having been drowned whilst sailing to England in December 1657. He was succeeded by Sir William Lockhart.

With the valued English reinforced, Turenne invested Dunkirk in May 1658. Almost immediately the Spanish marched to relieve the town, forcing the French to meet them in open combat at the Battle of the Dunes on 4 June. All Lockhart's regiments were present as a separate corps, whilst all Charles II's units were with the Spanish army although so weak in numbers that they could only form three battalions. The battle was decided by the Cromwellian regiments decisively defeating the royalists, driving them off the field. After the action Charles could muster only 800 men.

In the wake of the victory half of Lockhart's troops remained to garrison the twin towns whilst the rest fought in the French field army. Then, in April 1659, a truce was arranged between France and Spain which allowed all Lockhart's command to retire into the two fortresses, a sensible precaution as both France and Spain had their eyes fixed in that direction. At no time after the battle did the brigade have more than 3,000 men, as Dunkirk was extremely unhealthy, and the ranks were thinned still further when three regiments were recalled into England in the wake of the panic caused by Sir George Booth's uprising in 1659. During the ensuing political strife in England Lockhart and his men were able to achieve nothing and so they acquiesced in the Restoration as the only possible solution to England's instability.

From the time of the Dunes to the truce Charles was unable to effect much with his tiny, demoralised army; he could not afford to pay them, food was in short supply, and the troops lacked nearly all basic necessities.[3] Cromwell's death revived hopes of an armed restoration and this so assisted recruiting that Charles again possessed 2,500 soldiers by July 1659. Booth's uprising provided another boost to morale and resources, but following this failure Charles had no more use for his army and it survived as best it could in Flanders. After the Restoration it was drawn little by little into Dunkirk and gradually dissolved.

Part One

I

The New Royalist Army

WHEN Charles II landed at Dover in May 1660, two professional armies existed, both owing him allegiance: the New Model in England and the army of exiled royalists in Flanders and Dunkirk. Neither force was very healthy, being in arrears of pay, and although the New Model was still technically formidable it was broken in spirit and thoroughly demoralised. John Lambert had led this force north in an effort to halt Monck's victorious Scottish regiments but it had disintegrated through desertion before even coming into contact with them. At the Restoration it was Monck's troops quartered in and around London which represented the remains of the New Model, with the additional support of Lockhart's brigade in Dunkirk. If there was to be a military danger to Charles's return it was likely to come from across the Channel.

Whatever its condition the mere existence of the Cromwellian army was a grave threat to the sovereign, standing as it did for an alien theory of government and society. Moreover it was politically experienced in achieving its constitutional aims having served as the keystone of English politics since the end of the Civil Wars. At the Restoration the army stood aside and did not oppose but it could never be said that the military actively supported the return of Charles Stuart. As the new monarch reviewed 'his' troops on Blackheath his reception was at best unenthusiastic, for these were men who had built and run the country without a king and were quite capable of repeating their actions. That they did not was largely due to the power and influence of General George Monck. In his sane and practical manner he had removed all the odiously republican officers and men before Charles set foot in England, and one of the king's first duties was to appoint loyal colonels to all the Cromwellian regiments.[1] One of the most curious factors of the Restoration was this seeming about-face by the army, 'which if it had captured Charles II in 1659, would assuredly have demanded that he should share his father's fate', yet meekly accepted his restoration twelve months later. Monck was one of the few men, along with Cromwell and Fairfax, able to impose his will upon his soldiers. As a military administrator and disciplinarian he has had few equals, and these abilities absolutely swayed the New Model.[2] He earnestly believed that the military should be subordinate to the civil power,[3] and with his immense prestige and bearing he was able to carry the army with him. If the army did not actually approve of the Restoration, Monck was able to ensure that it did not actively oppose it. Charles's debt to him was huge.

Quiet and passive though they were, the rank and file could not be relied upon, and it was certain that the ultra-royalist Convention Parliament would never consent to a continuation of the New Model army. Before Charles came over to England he was undecided as to what policy to adopt towards the Cromwellian armed forces and he toyed with the idea of taking the entire army into the royal service. The Declaration of Breda offered to adopt the army and, 'to consent . . . [to] the full satisfaction of all arrears due to the officers and soldiers of the army under the command of General Monck, and that they shall be received into our service, upon as good pay and conditions as they now enjoy'.[4] However, once in England Charles opted for the disbandment of the army. One of the most pressing causes of this alteration in policy was the appearance of the spectre which was to haunt him all his life—shortage of money. The Cromwellian legacy of a war with Spain swallowed Charles's meagre funds at the rate of £6,000 a day, the upkeep of the New Model amounted to £55,000 a month, whilst Dunkirk drained the Treasury of £73,868 between December 1660 and July 1661.[5] A substantial reduction in the armed forces was urgently required and over this king and Parliament found themselves in complete accord. With his revenue unsettled, Parliament against any form of standing army, and the New Model posing a potential threat to both himself and his nation, Charles had to disband the army.

Sir William Doyley reported a systematic programme for the disbandment of the New Model to the House of Commons from the Committee for the Army on 30 August 1660.[6] Under this scheme all the officers and soldiers who were in pay on 25 April 1660 and had not deserted since that date would receive their full arrears and be paid off with a bonus of an extra week's pay from the king's own purse. This was accepted by Parliament and shortly afterwards two acts were passed which sealed the fate of the old army. 'An Act for the Speedy Provision of Money for Disbanding and Paying Off the Forces of this Kingdom both by Land and Sea',[7] continued the hated monthly assessments for a further two months at the rate of £70,000, whilst a Poll Bill was raised to yield £210,000. With these sums it was hoped to be able to pay off the arrears of the army and keep it in full pay up until the time of its disbandment. A second act, 'for the Speedy disbanding of the Army and Garrisons of this Kingdom',[8] arranged for the army to be broken up three regiments at a time the order of which was to be chosen by lots drawn by the Privy Council. Exceptions were made of the regiments of the Dukes of York and Gloucester and those commanded by Monck, now Duke of Albemarle,[9] all of which were to be disbanded at the very end of the proceedings. Likewise, companies guarding the arsenal at Hull and the Scottish border at Carlisle and Berwick were also retained in pay until the completion of the disbandment. These relevant acts received the Royal Assent on 13 September 1660.

The disbandment commenced immediately with Albemarle in overall charge. This fate was accepted quietly and calmly by the army, a mentality no doubt assisted by the inclusion of a clause in the Act for the Speedy Disbanding which withheld the arrears from any man who attempted to jeopardise the operation. The full payment of arrears amounted to a considerable sum of money and this must have served as a weighty bribe to ensure the good behaviour of the troops and the smooth running of the disbandment. Parliament's wisest precaution was in relaxing the laws relating to apprenticeship permitting disbanded officers and men to practise a trade in their own towns or counties without having to undergo the rigours of an apprenticeship.[10] This must have greatly eased the return of 40,000 men into civilian life. The king and his wealthier subjects did their best to employ disbanded soldiers on building houses and gardens, the canal in St James's Park being constructed by ex-soldiers.

It cost the country £835,819 8*s* 10*d* to disband the army. The Poll Bill and the monthly assessments raised £560,000, but the king had to find the balance from his own resources.[11] The disbandment went more slowly than had been hoped, as the money from the Poll Bill did not materialise very quickly and even the monthly assessments had to be hurried along by a proclamation from the king.[12] On 6 November fifteen regiments of foot, four of horse, and twenty-two garrison companies had been dissolved, leaving three of foot, nine of horse, and eleven garrison units. By Christmas 1660 the New Model army had ceased to exist except for Albemarle's foot, the 'Coldstream Regiment', and his own regiment of horse. Ludlow was deeply incensed at the death of this magnificent fighting machine:

The Army which had so long stood in the way of the Court, was now wholly disbanded, except only Monck's Regiment of Foot; and that was balanced by a Regiment of Horse under colour of being a guard to the King. This together with the payment of their arrears and a liberty of trading in corporations was the reward they received for their services, notwithstanding all the fair promises of Monck and the King. And thus these men who had accumulated treachery upon treachery, were dismissed with infamy.[13]

Burnet was of a more reasoned opinion:

The Army was to be disbanded, but in such a manner, with so much respect, and so exact an account of arrears, and such gratuities, that it looked rather to be a dismissing them to the next opportunity, and a reserving them till there should be occasion for their service, than a breaking them. They were certainly the bravest, the best disciplined, and the soberest army that had been known in these latter ages: every soldier was able to do the functions of an officer.[14]

Whatever the political rights and wrongs of the disbandment the actual process was a great success with little record of disturbance by the soldiery. Pepys, writing in 1663, leaves the impression that the old soldiers settled down into civilian life with ease:

Of all the old Army now you cannot see a man begging about the street; but what? You shall have this captain turned a shoemaker; the lieutenant a baker; this a brewer; that a haberdasher; this common soldier a porter; and every man in his apron and frock etc, as if they had never done anything else . . . the spirits of the old Parliament soldiers are so quiet and contented with God's Providences, that the King is safer from any evil meant him by them one thousand times more than from his own discontented Cavaliers.[15]

For the majority of the New Model this return into trade and commerce was natural as it had been from these employments that they had originally been recruited.

Whilst only the two regiments of Monck and a few garrison companies remained in England at the end of 1660, the entire Dunkirk brigade was unaffected by the general disbandment. Charles appointed Sir Edward Harley to the governorship on 14 July 1660 in place of Sir William Lockhart. Harley had originally fought for Parliament during the Civil Wars but fell foul of Cromwell over the disbandment of the New Model in the late 1640s. As in England, the Cromwellian regiments in Dunkirk were purged of their republican officers and royalists commissioned in their stead, whilst some supernumeraries were paid off. The new governor was given a warrant for £5,000 to pay off 200 horse and 400 foot as they were 'unserviceable', but whether these men were politically or physically unserviceable is a matter for conjecture.[16] Given the generally high standards of the New Model these men were probably political undesirables. One thousand men were sent over to Dunkirk to fill these vacancies from the pool of disbanded men in England. Once under the command of Harley and the royalist colonels the discipline of the garrison deteriorated so that on 30 December 1661 Secretary Nicholas was forced to write to Lord Rutherford, who had succeeded Harley in May 1661, complaining that there was too much drinking and debauchery within the garrison and that the officers were never present with their commands but spent all their time in London.[17]

For the two years which Charles retained Dunkirk the garrison numbered 6,000 foot and 600 horse, half of which were stationed in the fort at Mardyke. The only non-Cromwellian troops in the garrison were the remains of Charles's army of exiled royalists. At the Restoration the survivors of this corps were taken into Dunkirk and formed into a single regiment of foot guards under Lord Wentworth and the few cavalry later amalgamated with the Duke of York's Troop of Life Guards.[18] The enforced coexistence of these two forces, the Cromwellians and the royalists, in one confined garrison town might well have accounted for the loss of discipline. Two years before they had fought one another at the Battle of the Dunes; one clause in the new articles of war summed up the tension between the two factions:

> No man shall presume by word or deed to transgress against His Majesty's Gracious Pardon in the Act of Indemnity, or to utter any reproachful words to the disrepute of the Three Nations, or the inhabitants of this garrison, or of any person in them, for former actions, on pain of punishment as an Incendiary.[19]

Wentworth's Guards were soon in a miserable condition having received no pay for six months, and in a petition to the king in October 1660 the officers stated that they were 'daily constrained to sell one thing or other of clothes, as some already have to the very last shirt they had to put on'.[20]

Without sufficient money to maintain this garrison Charles realised that the only possible solution was evacuation but this conveniently coincided with another reason for wishing to be rid of the place. Dunkirk was full of republican troops and was viewed with the deepest suspicion in England, for it was both strong enough and correctly positioned to invade across the Channel. Negotiations were opened for the sale of Dunkirk to France. In October 1662 England parted with her colony for 5 million livres and the English and Irish troops dispersed. Prior to this Lewis Farrell's and Edward Harley's regiments had been sent to Tangier late in 1661, and on the sale the three troops of horse went to serve with the British brigade sent to fight in Portugal, Wentworth's Guards sailed for England, and the Duke of York's regiment entered the French army as a mercenary unit, whilst Rutherford's, Falkland's and Taafe's regiments were disbanded in Dunkirk. The policy was to permit only Wentworth's to return to England as a formed unit, all the Cromwellian formations being broken up abroad so that the men came back to England as individuals or were sent into foreign service *en bloc*. In this way no political danger developed from the Dunkirk garrison and the dispersal of the last reservoir of the New Model passed off without any serious incident.

The old army had virtually disappeared by the end of 1660 and yet by March 1661 Charles had founded the nucleus of a new army. He was certainly no opponent of a standing army, provided that it was controlled by him and not by Parliament, having been very proud of the little army which he had raised to fight with the Spaniards in Flanders. Ludlow stated that the king was in favour of establishing a new army,[21] and, according to Burnet, Clarendon held similar views:

> And there was a great talk of a design, as soon as the army were disbanded, to raise a force that should be so chosen and modelled that the King might depend upon it; and that it should be so considerable, that there might be no reason to apprehend tumults any more.[22]

However, the scheme found an opponent in Lord Treasurer Southampton as 'they had felt the effects of a military government, though sober and religious, in Cromwell's Army: he believed vicious and dissolute troops would be much worse: the king would grow fond of them: and they would quickly become insolent and ungovernable'.[23] Southampton's fears were soon justified even though the new army was minute in comparison with that of Cromwell:

> They go with their belts and swords, swearing and cursing, and stealing; running into people's houses, by force oftentimes, to carry away something, and this is the difference between the one and the other.[24]

The military defeat of his father and the harrowing time which he had endured in exile left deep scars on Charles II, so that one of the guiding principles of his reign was the avoidance of having to go on his 'travels' once more. Security was all-important. In the experience of the king this was impossible to achieve without armed force of some kind. This did not mean that Charles ever planned to govern the country by a standing army as Southampton feared, for even during the final years of his reign when he managed affairs without the assistance of Parliament the army did not significantly increase in size. Indeed it was only swelled by the return of the Tangier garrison in 1684 but this made the total number of troops barely 6,000. Any fears that Charles would attempt to rule by an army should have been quashed by the appointment of Albemarle as Lord

General. Already he had demonstrated his desire for the military to be subordinate to the civil power, for this had been the direct cause of his entry into politics in 1659 and 1660. Unfortunately England was in a slightly hysterical condition in the early 1660s and did not see the army for what it was: a weak and often poorly run police force. Neither did Parliament appreciate the king's real motive in establishing a standing army, which was to secure his throne and his own position in relation to Parliament and not to overawe the Lords and Commons. It was Charles who suffered from political weakness after 1660 and not Westminster. He had been forced to accept both his crown and his financial settlement on the terms of Parliament, but, even so, Parliament delighted in the masochistic idea that it was they who were being threatened by a pro-monarchical and popish standing army. Parliament and the king held opposite views upon the nature and value of an army in England.

The period from 1660 to 1663, and for some years afterwards, although to a lesser degree, was filled with plots and rumours of plots. Some of these conspiracies were real, others imaginary, but most possessed an element of fact surrounded by mystery and exaggeration. Nearly all were supposed designs by ex-Cromwellian soldiers and politicians to overthrow the restored monarchy and many were connected with Ludlow, Lambert and Desborough. To both the government and the people this threat must have seemed very real indeed.[25] Carolian England was ripe for plots at any time[26] and during the first three years of the reign there were a huge number. During his speech to Parliament at the dissolution of the Convention Lord Chancellor Clarendon urged the houses to consider the state of the militia and settle it as soon as possible due to the uncertain mood of the country, for already 'many suspected and dangerous persons' had been 'clapped up'.[27] When the Militia Bill reached the upper house on 18 July 1661 Clarendon informed their lordships that the measure had become essential for the safety of the kingdom as yet another plot had just been uncovered. In this one hundred and sixty officers of the New Model intended to instigate a nation-wide rebellion at the end of January 1661, seizing Shrewsbury, Coventry and Bristol.[28] Excitement had reached such a pitch by the end of 1661 that a joint committee of both houses was summoned to sit through the Christmas recess owing to the 'apprehensions and fears that are generally abroad'.[29] For the security of the nation a small, permanent army was necessary, if only to gain some public confidence for the new order.

The conspiracies in the last two months of 1660 were followed by the formation of a regiment of foot in England, the 1st Foot Guards. John Russell was commissioned colonel on 23 November 1660[30] and his regiment consisted of twelve companies each of 100 men. Russell, the third son of Francis Russell, the fourth Earl of Bedford, had fought throughout the First Civil War as colonel of Prince Rupert's Guards. During the Interregnum he was active for the King's cause, being a member of the 'Sealed Knot', the secret organisation founded in 1652 which worked for the restoration of Charles II. He suffered imprisonment in 1659 for his part in Sir George Booth's abortive uprising. Russell was forty-eight years of age in 1660, well past the prime of life, but this was a failing common to most royalists who gained office after the Restoration. No sooner was the regiment formed than an incident occurred which illustrated the wisdom of organising a new army. On Sunday, 6 January 1661:

About 50 Fifth Monarchymen at 10 of the clock came to Mr Johnson, a bookseller, at the north Gate of St Pauls, and there demanded the keys of the Church, which he either not having, or refusing, they broke open the door, and setting their sentries, examined the passengers whom they were for, and one with a lantern replying that he was for King Charles, they answered they were for King Jesus, and shot him through the head, where he lay as a spectacle all the next day. This gave the alarm to the Main Guard at the Exchange who sent 4 files of musketeers to reduce them, but the Fifth Monarchymen made them run, which so terrified the City that the Lord Mayor in person came with his Troop to reduce them. But before he arrived they drew off, and at Aldersgate, forcing the Constable to open the Gate, and so marched through Whitecross Street, where they killed another Constable, and so into the woods near Highgate; where, being almost famished, on Wednesday morning about five of the clock fell again into the City, and with a mad courage fell upon the Guard, and beat them; which put the City into such confusion, that the King's Life Guard, and all the City Regiments advanced against them. These 40 men beat the Life Guard and a whole Regiment for half an hour's time. They refused all quarter, but at length, Venner, their Captain, a wine cooper, after he had received three shots, was taken, and nine more and twenty slain. . . . The Duke and the Duke of Albemarle with 700 Horse fell into the City, but all was over before they came.[31]

Burnet thought Venner's party closer to twenty than fifty, making the impotence of the City Militia even more apparent. The insurrection came as a climax to a series of supposed conspiracies and the government was so alarmed that Russell's Guards were almost immediately expanded into a standing army by the addition of three new regiments. Albemarle's Foot had still not been disbanded but under the regulations of the disbandment procedure all the units of the New Model had to be officially broken up. On 14 February 1661 the regiment was drawn up on Tower Hill, disbanded by the commissioners, and then re-engaged in the service of Charles II as the 2nd Foot Guards, the 'Coldstreamers', with Albemarle as colonel.[32]

These two infantry formations had to be balanced by some cavalry. Charles had possessed a Life Guard of eighty gentlemen during his exile under the command of Charles, Lord Gerard of Brandon, and when the king left Holland for England in 1660 this force had increased to 600.[33] These attended Charles at his coronation but then 200 were 'retired' and the remaining 400 sent to Dunkirk where they were known as the Duke of York's Life Guard of Horse.[34] After the defeat of Venner this force was withdrawn from Dunkirk, augmented to 500 men, and then formed into three separate troops; the King's Own, the Duke of York's, and the Lord General's. Although these three were distinct from each other they were looked upon as one regiment with the captain of the King's Troop ranking as the colonel of the Life Guard. Cromwell's Life Guard of Horse was disbanded simultaneously with Albemarle's Foot, but again the majority of the soldiers were retained in the king's service to form the basis of a new cavalry unit, the Royal Horse Guards, known later as the 'Blues'. Aubrey de Vere, the 20th Earl of Oxford, was commissioned colonel and he recruited his regiment from loyal volunteers to augment the Cromwellian Life Guard during February 1661.

Venner's insurrection was not the sole reason for the foundation of the army. An 'intended establishment' had been drafted as early as August 1660, five months before Venner's uprising, allowing for two regiments of foot and two of horse at an annual cost of £118,529.[35] The intention of forming a standing army was in the minds of Charles and Clarendon long before Venner acted as a catalyst. The first official establishment appeared on 26 January 1661 providing for the 1st and 2nd Foot Guards, the Life Guards and the Royal Horse Guards, at the overall charge of £122,407 15*s* 10*d* per annum.[36]

It was to be a ceremonial, household army of royal guards based on the model of the French armed forces under Louis XIV. Such a tiny army was able to guard the king's person, present itself on state occasions, execute police duties, and act as a trained cadre for a rapid expansion in time of war. In addition to the four standing regiments there were a number of independent, non-regimented companies of foot stationed as garrison troops in the forts and castles which occupied England's strategic points. At the Restoration these units were Cromwellian, but their officers were then removed and royalists who had business or landed interests in that particular region replaced them.[37] An establishment for the garrisons appeared in June 1661 with the twenty-eight stations costing £67,316 15*s* 6*d* a year. This made a total charge for the Guards and Garrisons in England of £189,724 11*s* 4*d*. For a monarch who was saddled with debt and whose annual revenue was only £1,200,000 this was a considerable sum showing the reliance which he placed on the army as the only sure means of securing his own future.

This charge accounted for the standing army in England, but by the Portuguese Marriage Treaty of 1661 England gained the city of Tangier in North Africa. To use this port as either a naval station or a commercial post for the Levant trade a large garrison was required to protect it from the Moors of Barbary.[38] In effect the acquisition of Tangier cancelled out the sale of Dunkirk.[39] Two regiments from Dunkirk, Farrell's and Harley's, were transferred to Tangier late in 1661, whilst two foot regiments and a troop of horse were raised in England by the Earl of Peterborough, the first governor of the new colony.[40] Farrell's men were old royalists from the exiled army in Flanders whereas Harley's were republican to a man, but political sympathies mattered little in the far-off lands of Africa. The troops recruited by Peterborough came from the pool of soldiers disbanded from the New Model, for their performance against the Moors in 1662 and 1663 suggested that they knew their duties very well, whilst their discipline was tight and of a sort that could not have been achieved with raw levies. The Tangier garrison was part of the standing army of Charles II forming a permanent reserve of action-trained men ready to return to England on any emergency, or that was the sinister motive which Parliament attached to the maintenance of forces in Africa.

Likewise under the terms of the Marriage Treaty Charles was bound to send 2,000 foot and 500 horse to assist Portugal in her long struggle for independence from Spain,[41] and this was used as another opportunity of retaining Cromwellian veterans in abeyance outside England. Charles benefited greatly from this arrangement as the Portuguese undertook to pay the British brigade, enabling him to maintain his overseas military reservoir at no cost to his over-worked Treasury. Later in the reign regiments were hired out to France and Spain under similar agreements. Perhaps the primary advantage to the king in all this was that Parliament's anti-military sensibilities were not upset for the troops were out of the country and did not burden the nation.

Another reason for the foundation of an army after the Restoration was the necessity of satisfying the horde of place-hunters, reward-seekers and unemployed royalists, all of whom sought some material recognition for their services to the king and his father. This was an important factor in the perpetual shortage of money which hamstrung the Restoration government, as Parliament considered it the king's duty to reward his supporters and no business of theirs. The foundation of an army was one method of providing places, with the addition that men thus employed fulfilled a useful role in society rather than sitting in some parlour in the maze of Whitehall taking fees for doing nothing. During his exile Charles had raised his army as a convenient means of employing many of the vagrants who followed him around Europe and this ploy was used again in 1661. So the new army was officered by old royalists or their sons, with the exception of the Coldstream Guards. All the Cromwellian officers were retained in this regiment as Albemarle had purged it before marching out of Scotland ensuring that all were loyal to himself and his beliefs. Out of defence to the Lord General Charles did not interfere with this regiment at the Restoration but permitted it to remain intact.

There were not nearly enough places in the new army to

accommodate all the military office-hunters, and it became normal to find men who had headed regiments for Charles I during the Civil Wars holding a captaincy or a lieutenancy in the army of his son. Numerous petitions flowed in to the king and Privy Council from old royalists but there were far more petitioners than there were vacancies.[42] Parliament made one effort to assist the king in his endeavours to deal fairly with the impoverished cavaliers when they passed an act in 1662 designed to raise £60,000 on a Poll Bill, which sum was to be distributed amongst all the officers of the royalist armies of the Civil Wars who had been unable to find any means of support since the Restoration. A list of the men who were eligible to receive succour from this statute was printed by order of Sir Henry Bennet and it contained the astonishing number of 5,353 commissioned officers.[43] The money was not divided equally but was issued on a graded scale according to the arrears due to each officer from his actual time of service. Only 107 of those on the list were field officers, so that the real hardship fell on the lesser men who had been subaltern officers. To such men as these the new army offered very little assistance as the commissions went to those who held senior positions in the Civil Wars and were able to exercise some influence over appointments in 1661. The new army did no more than explore the surface of this huge problem.[44]

The army of 1661 was not a political thoroughbred, for republican elements were not entirely excluded. A conspiracy amongst some of the disbanded soldiery of the New Model in late 1661 involved some members of the new army including some men of the Coldstream Guards.[45] Three extra cavalry regiments were raised under the earls of Lindsey, Cleveland and Northampton, supported by two of foot commanded by the Earl of Craven and Sir William Killigrew, in September 1662, as the diversity of political persuasions within the four original regiments made their loyalty suspect in dealing with internal security.[46] There was intelligence of a republican rising in London in November 1663 which implicated men from both the Coldstreamers and the Life Guard.[47] It was inevitable that a few dissidents crept back into the ranks but these were few and there is no evidence to suggest any positive dissatisfaction in the Restoration army and no mention of any mutiny.

From its birth the army of Charles II was unpopular as it broke with historical precedent. Before 1661 the kings of England had always retained a bodyguard of 'Gentlemen Pensioners' and 'Yeomen of the Guard', who were ceremonial troops of no military value. Charles followed this tradition but became the first monarch to maintain field regiments in peacetime. These units he referred to as 'Guards', and in the establishments the land forces were always termed 'the Guards and Garrisons' so as to avoid the emotive name of 'army'. However, as was pointed out in a debate on the state of the nation in 1678, the King of France had 16,000 Guards which constituted a fair-sized army in those times. But, whatever its name, the new army was neutral in politics and always remained subordinate to the civil authorities. It was an excellent precedent for the future.

II

Officers and Men

MILITARY life was relaxed and relatively attractive in the days before British involvement in continental wars. There were abuses in the pay system but these were minor compared with the corruption in the early eighteenth century; the soldier was never rich, in fact he was one of the worst-paid men in the land, but with the advantage of unofficial free quarters his economic status was equal to that of men from similar social backgrounds who remained in civilian life. Foot soldiers were always more poorly paid than cavalry and dragoons, but they were without the burden of having to maintain a horse from their army pay. It was no disgrace for the sons of yeoman farmers or artisans to enter the ranks of the Royal Horse Guards or the Tangier Horse, but neither was it an ideal career.

The military calling has never been much respected or popular in England, but in the days of the Restoration there were less agreeable careers for a young man. A general guide to the popularity of an army as a vocation is the availability of recruits, and there was no obvious shortage for service with the standing regiments between 1660 and 1685, although the press gang had to be employed to fill the mass levies of 1673 and 1678. Service in the colonies or on foreign service was universally loathed, and, whenever possible, expendable Scots and Irish lives were sent out in place of native Englishmen. To recruit English soldiers for foreign service implied the automatic use of the press.

Whether a man volunteered or was forcibly impressed his service was for life. Occasionally a discharge was obtained, for ill-health or physical disability, but this was rare, the exception rather than the rule. Poverty, unemployment, debt, all caused men to enlist as private soldiers, although in an age of violence the army offered all that a young thug could desire in the way of legalised brutality. However, for the first few years of its life the Restoration army did not have to search for personnel.

The Coldstream Guards started their new existence in 1661 with the same troops who had served Cromwell, whilst the unfortunates sent out to Tangier, Portugal, and Bombay, came from the huge pool of disbanded soldiers from the New Model. The Royal Horse Guards were raised around the nucleus of Cromwell's disbanded Life Guard, and the new Life Guard was composed of cavalier gentlemen. All this was straightforward and natural using readily available material to create a new army, merely taking the necessary precaution of ensuring that all the professed changes of allegiance were genuine and reliable. This was only temporary for these men could not endure for ever. Many had fought with the armies of Parliament and the New Model for over a decade before they entered the royal service, and although the army received a transfusion of younger men with the return of the Dunkirk garrison in 1662, the veterans soon retired. From the mid-1670s onwards the military authorities were faced with the problem of manning the army. In peacetime there was little apparent difficulty. The army was small and compact and the absence of fighting kept wastage to a minimum, but when the country went to war expediency was the only possible method of enlarging the ranks. The Trained Bands were the most obvious target for the recruiting officers.

Technically the militia was totally separate from the standing army and none of its troops could be pressed into full-time service, but there were no regulations preventing militiamen from volunteering to fight with the regulars. These part-time soldiers of the Trained Bands were used to handling arms and knew something of the workings of martial discipline. They were in fact ideal for the short-term levies of 1666–7, 1672–4 and 1678–9, as they required little or no training. In return this military service did no harm to the militia as the men were disbanded immediately upon the conclusion of a war and their experiences with the standing army might well have improved some of the slack methods of Parliament's private army. That great armchair general, the Duke of Buckingham, recruited his new regiment from amongst the Yorkshire Trained Bands in 1673 after volunteers had failed to come forward due to their fears that the duke was a papist. Even after he had publicly said the Oaths at York the rural population was not entirely convinced and so Buckingham took the easy, but accepted, way out.[1]

The press was not used to fill the standing regiments in England but was reserved for manning the colonies, the foreign service stations, and the occasional mass levies in England. In an effort to induce more volunteers to join-up for the expansion of 1678 'levy-money' of £1 per man was introduced.[2] In theory this meant that each volunteer received a bounty on his enlistment, but the money was paid directly from the Treasury to the captain of each troop or company and it was then up to him to strike the best bargain that he could with each man. This resulted in a considerable profit for the captain. On the three enlargements of the army recruiting parties scoured the length and breadth of the country. Each group consisted of a captain, a sergeant, a corporal, a drummer, and two privates. They would halt in a suitable village, plant the captain's flag, and then summon the inhabitants by beating the drum. With the villagers assembled the captain mounted an improvised rostrum and delivered a speech, couched in properly heroic and glamorous language, enticing the able-bodied men to come to the drum-head and enlist for a bounty of five shillings. This was recruiting by 'beat of drum', a practice permitted anywhere except in the City of London.

The precise identity of the soldiers in a regiment of foot is almost impossible to describe. That they came from the lower social orders is beyond doubt, and most probably they were discontented agricultural workers, vagrants, unemployed apprentices and journeymen. Criminals seeking to avoid arrest regularly enlisted in the army, as did debtors hoping to escape the clutches of their creditors.[3] The army offered a fairly safe haven from the law. Within the six standing regiments the turnover in personnel was slow. In 1673 it was noted that many of the soldiers in the two regiments of foot guards were, 'by reason of age or wounds', no longer fit for service in these élite formations. Rather than discharge them eighteen such men were transferred into non-regimental garrison companies who were in need of replacements.[4] The same problem reappeared in 1679 when Sunderland sent a circular to all regimental and garrison commanders commenting that many of the non-commissioned officers and soldiers were no longer fit for duty 'by reason of old age or weakness'.[5] Some foreigners served with the standing army, mostly Germans and Dutchmen, and one of the former, Melkar Gold, was trumpeter to the King's Troop of the Life Guard throughout the reign.

Without sufficiently detailed evidence it is impossible accurately to portray the typical foot soldier of Charles II's army, but an impressionistic picture is valuable. He was unmarried, could not be a householder,[6] could not run a tavern, had no permanent home being continually on the move from quarter to quarter, and carried all that he possessed on his back. If he swore or got drunk he could be cashiered, and if he wished to leave the service then he had to seek the approval of his commanding officer, which was rarely ever given.[7] On the remarkable chance that such permission was granted, the soldier then stood in danger of being 'encouraged' to settle in Jamaica or some other outlandish colony.[8] Surprisingly the education of the private soldier was high. At Tangier sixty-two out of 150 non-commissioned officers and men could write their own names.[9] Perhaps this was atypical, for the Tangier garrison contained a very large number of Cromwellian veterans whose previous service had paid some attention to reading and writing.

The Life Guards and the Royal Horse Guards, the two regiments of cavalry, were composed of an utterly different class of soldier. Even within these two formations the Life Guards stood above the Horse Guards; their pay was higher, their privileges greater, and they were not designed for the everyday police work of their colleagues. This was a school, 'for young gentlemen of very considerable Families, who are there made fit for Military Commands'.[10] The men of the Life Guards came from the poorer gentry and from amongst the old royalist officers who had been unable to acquire other employment or commissions in the new army.[11] In all probability the Royal Horse Guards were manned by a similar type of trooper; younger sons of the poorer gentry who hoped that experience in the Horse Guards would fit them for commissions in later years. There is little else that can be said of the private soldier. No one was interested in recording facts about so humble a being; he was never included in portraits or engravings so we have no clear idea of how he looked in uniform, and his exact identity and background can only be guessed. Of the officers we know a great deal more.

Most of the officers commissioned into the army of 1661 were either old royalists who had followed Charles I, or officers of the New Model who had successfully attached themselves to the cause of George Monck and the Restoration. Some of the former were catholics. Seventeenth-century Englishmen regarded catholics with much the same suspicion and hatred that Americans held towards communists after the Second World War. The English detestation of catholics was partly emotional but there was also a real basis for fear. Everything in England relied upon the Reformation Settlement of the sixteenth century; education, the monarchy, the law, land ownership, and the entire social order, were all embodied in the protestant Church of England. Catholicism was the one force which could overthrow all this, and so Parliament was continually on the watch for any insidious advance by popery into high places. Catholics in the army were just such a threat.

At its foundation the Venetian Ambassador had noted that many of the new army were followers of the Bishop of Rome.[12] Five years later the Commons typically discovered that the catholics had probably been implicated in starting the Great Fire of London and insisted that the king should enforce the Penal Laws against Dissenters and Papists. In response Charles published a proclamation on 10 December banishing all priests and Jesuits from the country and ordering the lords lieutenant to disarm all popish recusants and other suspected persons who refused to take the Oaths of Allegiance and Supremacy. All military personnel had to take the Oaths within twenty days, and the Privy Council reinforced this by instructing the commissaries that no new officer or soldier could be mustered into the army until he complied with the regulations. These attempts to purify the army proved fruitless. Albemarle advertised these orders to all company commanders on 17 November 1666, but in the following April the Privy Council relented and allowed each officer and soldier one year's grace in which to acquire all the appropriate certificates.[13] After twelve months of masterly inaction the government was again pestered by the Commons to act against the supposedly large bodies of catholics infiltrating the executive. Lord Keeper Sir Orlando Bridgeman directed that any catholics found in the army after the next muster-day were to be dismissed. Charles took notice and a purge of the standing army commenced.

On 28 September 1667 all catholic officers and soldiers were turned out, but Parliament must have been disappointed as their witch-hunt produced very few victims. Those who were cashiered promptly petitioned the king for relief,[14] and in 1668 the Privy Council ordered that all those who had been reformed but who had served either Charles I during the Civil Wars or Charles II in his exile were to receive half-pay from the army establishment.[15] Sir Stephen Fox produced a list of these gentlemen in December 1668 and from this the rough number of catholics who had been serving with the army can be deduced.[16] From the 600 men of the Life Guard eighty-seven were dismissed, but the Royal Horse Guards lost only two lieutenants, a reflection of the large Cromwellian element in the regiment. Major John Legge and Captain Edward Charleton of the Admiral's regiment, Captains Mathew Wise, John Gwillims, Thomas Howard, Sir Edward Scott, and Thomas Panton of the 1st Foot Guards, all had to leave the service and go on to half-pay. In all seventeen officers from the four foot regiments and eighteen from the garrison companies were cashiered. Precisely how many private soldiers lost their places is impossible to estimate accurately. No financial provision was made for these unfortunates and many applied to the king for permission to go overseas and seek employment as mercenaries. Perhaps as many as eighty were dismissed from the 1st Foot Guards, but in any event the numbers were very small when compared to the total size of the army.[17] Those officers lucky enough to be granted half-pay were attached to their previous units as reformadoes, but many had done no previous royal service and had to search for employment abroad. Sir George Hamilton sailed to France where he formed a troop of 'Gens d'Armes' for Louis XIV composed entirely of refugee English military catholics. Others went further afield into Germany and Austria.

For those who found themselves on the half-pay list this did not mean that their military careers were at an end. Sir Edward Charleton reappeared as major of John Fitzgerald's Foot in 1672, Sir Edward Scott was lieutenant-colonel of Buckingham's Foot in the same year, whilst Thomas Howard outshone them all by regaining his place as a captain in the 1st Foot Guards rising to become lieutenant-colonel by 1676. Even Sir George Hamilton was permitted to raise an Irish regiment for the brigade which went over to France in 1673. After allowing tempers to cool the catholic officers crept back into the army almost unnoticed.

This situation might well have endured had Charles acted with circumspection in expanding the army for the Third Dutch War. Colonel John Fitzgerald was Irish and catholic, Buckingham was suspected of popery, and a number of the junior officers were known to follow the Church of Rome. Parliament grew alarmed and both houses jointly addressed the king, 'that no Popish Recusant be admitted into employments of trust and profit and especially into military commands over the Forces now in your Majesty's Service',[18] adding that the Oaths of Supremacy and Allegiance be again tendered to all the army and those not complying be immediately dismissed. Charles neatly side-stepped this by explaining that all the catholics in the army were going to serve overseas and were not intended for home duty.[19] This was plainly unsatisfactory to Parliament and the First Test Act followed very shortly, but again the king was one move ahead of the politicians. To avoid his soldiers having to take the Tests, Charles sent over eighty companies to serve with the Fleet thus keeping his catholic soldiers at sea well beyond the reach of Parliament.[20] The king's order to the commissary-general of the Musters on 13 March 1673 indicated that he interpreted the Test Act as applying to soldiers 'serving at land'[21] and not to those at sea. Certainly the military authorities had quietly forgotten about the provisions of the Act by the end of May with Secretary Coventry informing Lieutenant-Colonel Edward Villiers of the Earl of Ogle's regiment that 'no oaths are now to be put upon the foot soldiers'.[22] Over military matters the king was free to do very much as he pleased.

However, such evasion could not continue indefinitely although the general disbandment of the home army in 1674 and the retention of most of the catholic officers in France postponed a recurrence of the problem until 1678. In this year the British Brigade in France was recalled into England only to discover that the Second Test Act barred its personnel from finding employment. Charles was obliged to support his soldiers against the wishes of Parliament. On 28 July he used his Dispensing Power to allow several catholic officers of the Royal English regiment to continue in service in Monmouth's Foot,[23] but as the year progressed and the excesses of the Popish Plot came before the public Charles had no option but to strengthen the anti-catholic machinery within the army. A reminder went out to all regimental and garrison commanders on 1 November instructing them to dismiss all known catholic officers and men as well as those who had not taken the Oaths. A printed order was circulated from Whitehall on the following day offering a reward of £20 to each informer who could expose any military man who, having once taken the Oaths and the Sacrament, had been perverted back to the Romish persuasion. Compared to the situations in 1667 and 1673 that of 1678 contained a genuine catholic problem, Monmouth's Foot having to dismiss ninety-one soldiers and sixteen officers.[24]

One of Parliament's greatest fears was that the hated standing army would develop into a catholic institution. This apprehension was totally unfounded. There were catholics in the army amongst both the officers and the men, but in relation to the overall strength of the six standing regiments their numbers were minute throughout the reign. Out of a sample of 300 officers who served with the standing army between 1660 and 1685 only thirty were known to be catholic. In Tangier and foreign service stations the proportion of catholics was much higher. Tangier was governed by John Fitzgerald, John Lord Bellasise, both of whom were staunch catholics, and the Earl of Peterborough who was 'converted' in 1687. In France between 1673 and 1678 there was a succession of catholic colonels: Sir George Hamilton, Lord George Douglas, Justin Macartie, and Thomas Dongan. The Portuguese Brigade was free of this difficulty as its personnel were drawn from the Cromwellian regiments in Scotland. As a general rule, where the forces were predominantly Irish then a large percentage were devoted to Rome. When the professional soldiers returned to England to serve in the levies of 1667, 1673 and 1678, the number of catholics on the English establishment appreciably increased, but within the six permanent regiments the catholics composed but a tiny section and the army was 95 per cent protestant. A few of these catholics held commissions all through the reign—Charles Godfrey, Humphrey Orme, Ralph Widdrington, and members of the Bellasise family—but their numbers were so small that they presented no problem to the standing army. Parliament's complaint was with the enlarged catholic contingents in the officers' corps of the three mass levies.

A recent study of the catholic officers in the armies of Charles II and James II arrives at no precise figures.[25] Only seventy commissions are known to have been granted to catholics by Charles II, but this includes places at Tangier, in Portugal, and in the brigade which fought in France in the 1670s. Without any accurate lists or exact evidence we can only say that the number of catholic officers in the six standing regiments was minute, probably little more than 1 or 2 per cent of the total number of officers commissioned into those regiments between 1661 and 1685. Such a figure corresponds with the catholic population in England which was approximately 1.2 per cent of the whole.[26]

Charles II's army offered a career to a young man and was a genuine alternative to the navy, the law or the church. Almost without exception the officers came from amongst the gentry and the peerage, and the majority were younger sons. The first sons inherited the family titles and wealth leaving the other sons as liabilities unless they married well or secured sinecures like army commissions. Competition for places in the six standing regiments was tough as the number of vacancies was small. In 1665 there were 210 officers in the regiments with a further 134 stationed in the garrisons, but by 1684 this had increased to 463 with the regiments and 150 in the garrisons. From 344 officers the army expanded to 613 by the end of the reign. This appears to indicate a doubling of the number of army officers between 1665 and 1684, but this was not the case. The difference over the nineteen years is accounted for by the adoption of the Tangier garrison and the Royal Scots by the English establishment; only one new regiment was created, the Royal Dragoons. In fact, the available commissions rose by a mere thirty between the end of the Second Dutch War and the death of Charles II. During the levies for the French and Dutch Wars, the officer corps was temporarily increased: in 1667, 796 officers belonged to the English establishment, with 491 in 1673, and 925 in 1678.

Army life in England was relaxed. There was little or no fighting and the possibility of being required to serve overseas was remote. Any officer could volunteer for foreign engagements, but normally when a force was required to operate abroad it was specially recruited. An officer of the standing army fulfilled his untaxing duties in garrison and ceremonies and little else, but entry into these privileged places required certain social and political qualifications. In 1665, 65 per cent of the officers had fought with Charles I or had accompanied his son into exile, 25 per cent were ex-professionals who had returned from the Anglo-Dutch Brigade, whilst only 10 per cent had seen service with the armies of the Protectorate. Nearly all of the latter were in the Coldstream Guards. Other old Cromwellian soldiers, John Rumsey, Henry Pearson, Tobias Bridge, Roger Alsop and Nathaniel Fiennes, had to seek employment in Tangier and Portugal. Advancement in the army in England depended upon being either a royalist or the son of a royalist and being well connected with the twin centres of patronage, Monck and the Duke of York. Of the 10 per cent of Cromwellians in the army, only Samuel Clarke gained any real importance and he was a close associate of Monck.

In England there was no officer corps,* although there was an officer class, hence no man was ever given specific military training or aspired to anything approaching professionalism. He was expected to gain knowledge for himself by serving overseas as a mercenary or a gentleman volunteer, but as England was not seriously involved in a land war during this period young men with martial ambitions had to fight with the Dutch, the French, or the armies of the Holy Roman Emperor. An alternative was a period of service in Tangier. When Lord Plymouth went out to the colony in 1680 he took with him Lord Mordaunt and Lord Lumley as well as a gaggle of aristocratic friends who desired some military experience.[27]

There were three types of officer in the Restoration army: professional soldiers who earned their living by the sword, usually on foreign service; the 'Gentlemen Officers' of the six

* I use the term 'officer corps' throughout this chapter for convenience, but it should be understood in the sense of an 'officer class'.

standing regiments in England; and the garrison officers whose work was part-time and not taken too seriously. These divisions were fairly rigid, but there was some movement as professional officers found places on the English establishment and garrison officers took commissions in the standing regiments. Further confusions occurred when officers from the standing regiments went on foreign service to France in 1672 and Flanders in 1678. However, the three varieties of officer were distinct enough for us to be able to discuss them separately, bearing in mind the inevitable overlaps.

The career, or professional, soldier hired his services to foreign governments or fought for Charles II in the colonies or foreign service theatres. Mostly they were gentlemen, occasionally noblemen, without great lands or resources who were forced to look to their swords in order to earn a living. From a sample of forty-three professional officers, eight were the sons of peers, ten were born to knights and baronets, twenty to ordinary gentlemen, and five came from poor backgrounds. Within this quota only eleven were sons and heirs, the remainder being younger offspring with little hope of an inheritance. In short, the majority of professional officers came from the poorer families of the upper classes who were without important political connections. John Churchill and his brothers turned to the sword after their family had suffered financially during the Civil Wars, whilst Andrew Rutherford, Earl of Teviot, came from a cadet branch of a great Scottish family but was without means being the fifth son. The professionals were always to be found on active service. For them peacetime service in England was dull and profitless so they turned to Tangier, Portugal, France, and the Anglo-Dutch Brigade. Moreover, the professionals were not usually well enough connected to be able to enter the select ranks of the army in England, or were too poor to be able to afford a commission.

Sir Abraham Shipman and Sir Gervase Lucas, two impoverished cavaliers, were only too glad to take up the outlandish office of governor of Bombay as they were without any other means of support. Fairborne at Tangier had been a career soldier since his boyhood; Teviot had fought with the French and achieved the rank of lieutenant-general; Norwood was an old Cromwellian officer; and Bridge had fought for Parliament all through the Civil Wars. In Portugal, John Rumsey, Sir Thomas Morgan, Sir John Talbot, Henry Pearson, and Lawrence Dempsey, were all career officers. When sent home in 1668 many of them were forced to go into the Spanish and French armies as they could find no alternative means of earning a living. It was essential for the professional to remain abroad as there were no vacancies for him in England. On their return from Portugal Rumsey and Dempsey had to wait until 1672 before they could find places in the English standing army, and in the meantime they had to exist off royal pensions, having no other income.[28] This was not unnatural for soldiers who had led a military career throughout the Civil Wars and the Interregnum, as they had experienced no other way of life. Out of our forty-three officers, nine were old royalists, eight old Cromwellians, nine were life-long mercenaries, and seventeen were young men who first turned to the military after the Restoration. Whereas the first three groups consisted of older men too set in their ways to change, the last was composed of younger sons of gentlemen who had been ruined by the twenty years of strife in the British Isles. As Charles's reign advanced more and more younger men turned to the military life abroad: Percy Kirke, the Churchill brothers, and the Trelawneys. These were the men who were to officer the vastly expanded army of William III.

Some professionals, particularly those who fought for the Anglo-Dutch Brigade, settled abroad permanently. Philip Babbington, a lieutenant-colonel in the Dutch service, sold all his lands in England in 1677, as did John Beaumont, another Anglo-Dutch officer, in 1684. Professional soldiers were employed on the English establishment after 1665. In that year the Anglo-Dutch Brigade was disbanded and the Holland Regiment was formed in England almost entirely out of the officers and men who were forced to vacate the service of the United Provinces. Colonel Robert Sidney, Lieutenant-Colonel Thomas Howard, Alexander Bruce, and Sir Thomas Ogle, can all be regarded as career officers, but from 1665 they were Gentlemen Officers in the English army. There were other officers from the Anglo-Dutch Brigade who successfully transferred into the standing army; Sir Walter Vane commanded the Holland Regiment after 1670, whilst Sir William Killigrew was Colonel of the Admiral's Regiment after 1664.

The majority of the senior officers in England knew their business thoroughly and can be regarded as professionals. Feversham was the nephew of Turenne,[29] the Earl of Oxford came from the long line of the de Vere family whose military heritage dated back to the days of Elizabeth and Leicester,[30] he himself having learnt the art of war with the Dutch between 1644 and 1650. William, Earl of Craven, fought with the Elector Palatine during the Thirty Years' War, whilst Sir Charles Littleton had fought in Flanders in the 1650s. The commanders of the army were mostly seasoned soldiers as a result of their earlier, unofficial training on active service, but throughout the army, both in England and in the colonies, there was a solid core of professional officers who formed the backbone of the entire force. In peacetime they went abroad to fight for their livings, but when war threatened England they returned home to take up the vital senior commissions when the army prepared for active operations.

In addition to the two regiments formed out of the evicted soldiers of the Anglo-Dutch Brigade—the Holland and the Admiral's—the Scottish regiment of Lord George Douglas,[31] which was professional to a man, was recalled from France into England in 1666 in readiness for the Second Dutch War. The following year witnessed the return of a large number of career officers to man the new regiments: Walter Vane, Francis Lovelace, Sir Arthur Bassett, John Mill, Guy Molesworth, and John Rumsey, who was specially withdrawn from Portugal due to the shortage of good officers. The time between the conclusion of the Second Dutch War and the commencement of the Third in 1672 was a lean period for the career officers. The Anglo-Dutch Brigade was in abeyance, there was no British corps in France, the war in the Iberian Peninsula ended in 1668, and even France and the United Provinces enjoyed the luxury of five years of peace. However, in 1672 the English army was expanded both for home service and for a brigade to fight under the banner of Louis XIV. Nearly every officer able to make any claim to military ability was able to gain a commission, but once more the central positions went to the experienced professional soldiers. John Fitzgerald, Prince Rupert, Sir William Lockhart, Lord Bellasise and the Earl of Mulgrave all received colonelcies, whilst Sir John Talbot, Edmund Andros, Sir Lionel Walden,

Edward Villiers, Thomas Howard, Henry Pearson, Henry Lillingston and Robert Scott all took lieutenant-colonelcies and majorities. On the conclusion of the war in 1674 the enlarged army was disbanded, but the brigade in France remained on active service until 1678. It was to this theatre that the majority of the professionals gravitated, with Sir Samuel Clarke, Robert Scott, Percy Kirke, Charles Trelawney, John Churchill, Sir Thomas Daniell, John Lanier, Thomas Dongan, and Roger Langley all taking commissions in this force. However, in 1674 the Anglo-Dutch Brigade was reconstituted, providing another source of work. Into this service went Sir John Fenwick, Henry Lillingston, Molyneux Disney and Alexander Collyer. Most of these itinerants returned to England to take up senior commissions in the mass levy for the projected French War of 1678.[32] The Duke of Monmouth's Regiment of Horse was a good example of how the professional core operated within the English standing army.

This unit first saw the light of day as the English Regiment of Light Horse in France under the command of Sir Henry Jones in 1672, but after the death of this officer at the Siege of Maestricht in 1673 the command passed to the Duke of Monmouth. The regiment fought under the colours of Louis XIV until it was recalled into England in 1678 to form part of the English army for the projected war with France. It was disbanded in France and then reformed in England with virtually the same officers in the same ranks. Early in 1679 it was disbanded but was reconstituted in June as Colonel Charles Gerard's Regiment of Horse to fight in Scotland against the Covenanters. Again, apart from the alteration in the colonelcy, the officers of the unit were almost identical with those of its previous formation. Gerard's was finally disbanded late in 1679, but three of its captains, Thomas Langston, John Coy and Charles Nedby, retained their troops and took them out to Tangier as part of the general reinforcement of 1680. On their return from Tangier in 1684 these three troops formed the spine of a new, permanent regiment, the Royal Dragoons.

This process was repeated frequently during the reign. Few good, experienced officers existed. When the army was founded in 1661 most of its officers had seen warfare in the Civil Wars in England, but after 1667 the number of old royalists rapidly diminished. The replacements were young men who knew nothing of the conditions of war and were simply 'Gentlemen Officers'. Clearly when the army prepared for war men of knowledge and ability were vital and these were acquired in one of two ways; by recalling the professionals into England, and by summoning retired and superannuated royalists back to the colours. Officers who knew what they were about regained commissions right up to the final mass levy in 1678. When Monmouth led the expedition to Flanders in 1678 he relied heavily on the few good officers at his disposal: Fenwick, Charles Wheeler, Henry Sidney, Edward Villiers, Samuel Clarke and Charles Littleton.[33] More significantly, the battalions which went over to Flanders were those commanded and officered by the professionals. Those manned by the courtiers and the ignorant gentry were left in England.

Edmund Mayne had just turned twenty at the Restoration. Coming from a poor background he volunteered for service with the Portuguese Brigade and was commissioned as a cornet in Schomberg's Horse. After returning to England in 1668 he had to wait until the expansion of the army in 1672 allowed him to become a captain in Sir Henry Jones's Light Horse fighting in France. Mayne fought at the Siege of Maestricht and then campaigned with Monmouth's Horse on the Upper Rhine theatre throughout the war. By 1678 he had reached the rank of lieutenant-colonel. When the regiment came back to England Mayne was commissioned major of Monmouth's Horse, and afterwards lieutenant-colonel of Gerard's Horse. He was fortunate enough to transfer into a regular army commission in 1680, becoming guidon and major in the Duke of York's Troop of the Life Guard. Mayne proceeded to the rank of lieutenant and lieutenant-colonel in the Third Troop of the Life Guards in 1686, and eventually rose to become a lieutenant-general in the reign of Queen Anne.

Henry Lillingston was a detached professional soldier who cared little for politics or religion. His career started in earnest when he was commissioned major of Syler's Regiment in Scotland in the early 1650s, and in 1657 he commanded a regiment in Lockhart's expeditionary force in Dunkirk. Unable to find a place in England after the sale of Dunkirk he sold himself into the Anglo-Dutch Brigade where he fought until the disbandment of that force in 1665. Lillingston's military career is lost after 1665, but he reappeared as lieutenant-colonel of the Earl of Mulgrave's Foot on the English establishment in 1673. This regiment was disbanded in the following year and Lillingston returned to Holland to receive a commission as colonel of one of the regiments of the new Anglo-Dutch Brigade. He was killed at the second Siege of Maestricht in 1676. His son Luke served with his father as an ensign in Mulgrave's and as a captain in the Anglo-Dutch Brigade, and after his father's death he continued in Dutch pay coming over to England with William of Orange's invasion force of 1688. Once in England he transferred to his native army and rose to the rank of colonel in 1693. Luke had little option but to remain in the profession of arms as Henry Lillingston possessed few lands and little wealth.[34]

Although its aristocracy was not noted for its military bearing, England did possess some military families, or at least families which directed a considerable proportion of their male offspring into the army. Before the Civil Wars England had possessed no regular army and so these families had found that their chosen careers led them abroad into the service of the Dutch, the French, or the many factions involved in the Thirty Years' War. Here were found the Cravens, the de Veres, the Russells and the Sidneys. After 1660 a new type of military family arose which trained its children in the new standing army as well as overseas. Into this category fell the Churchills, the Darcys, the Sackvilles, and the Trelawneys of Cornwall. Sir Jonathan Trelawney's first son, John, entered the regular army only to be killed at the break-out from Charles Fort at Tangier in 1680. His fourth son, Charles, also went into the standing army and fought as a captain in the French Brigade, as a colonel in Tangier, and finished his career as a major-general and governor of Dublin in 1690. The seventh son, Henry, joined the Admiral's regiment in 1678 and rose to become a brigadier under William III. Two other brothers, Edward and Francis, served as captains in Schomberg's Regiment of Horse in Portugal, even Sir Jonathan himself took a temporary commission as lieutenant-colonel in the Duke of York's Horse in 1678. This family suffered severely under the Protectorate, losing much land and wealth, and it was this factor which directed so many of Sir Jonathan's sons into the army.

Similarly, another family ruined by the Protectorate sent its sons into the army after 1660, the Wrays of Cornwall. Sir Chichester Wray, the third baronet, served as lieutenant-colonel of the Admiral's Regiment from 1665 until his death three years later. His first son, Sir Bouchier, served with his father in the Admiral's and achieved its colonelcy in 1690, whilst the second son, Chichester, followed the family tradition in this regiment but finished his days as lieutenant-colonel of the 1st Foot Guards. Generally these new military families were royalists who had suffered sequestration and deprivation during the Interregnum. For such families the army, or the navy, offered a rare chance of providing for their male children and as a consequence they took the army in England seriously, seizing every opportunity to gain experience at Tangier or on foreign service stations. They were in the army to earn a living and not just to fill in time like the 'Gentleman Officers'.

These 'Gentleman Officers', the majority of the regular officers on the peacetime establishment of six regiments, were more politicians than soldiers. From a sample of 188 who served at some time between 1661 and 1685, thirty-nine were the sons of peers, seventy-three were the offspring of knights or baronets, fifty-eight came from the untitled gentry, and only eighteen were of low birth. Within these categories, eighty were first sons, fifty-eight were second sons, thirty-three were third sons, ten were fourth sons, and only seven were from further down the family hierarchy. This was the opposite of the social status of the professional soldiers, the minority of whom were first sons and the majority second and third. Amongst the Gentleman Officers 60 per cent were untitled gentlemen, 25 per cent were knights or baronets, 12 per cent were peers, and only 3 per cent were from the middle classes. After 1674 the number of knights and baronets began to decline and the untitled gentry correspondingly increased, reflecting the gradual elimination of the old royalist officers. From this time onwards the subalterns and middle ranking field officers of the army came from the untitled gentry, although the senior commissions remained in the hands of the peerage and the knightage.

Military experience was not a necessary qualification for a commission in the standing army, but rather places were granted as rewards for particular services to the Crown or to a political faction. Commissions were court appointments. There was no social mobility within the officer corps, in direct contrast to the army after 1689 when continental wars forced the army to draw its officers from outside the narrow confines of the aristocracy and important gentry.

Some money could be made from commissions both legitimately and illegally, but the pay of an officer was not high and certainly inadequate for a courtier. Gone were the days of Cromwell when an army officer could live off his pay. Modest men could have survived quite comfortably on a captain's salary, but the officers of Charles II were not artisans and tradesmen, they were wealthy men accustomed to a high standard of living. Indeed, they had to be men of means as the cost of buying a commission in one of the six standing regiments was alarmingly high, often as much as £1,000 for a place as a captain in the Foot Guards.

Out of our 188 officers, eighty-nine held seats in the House of Commons at some time during the reign,[35] and sixty-one members of the House of Lords also served with the standing army. In addition, fifty-four professional soldiers sat in the Commons and a further fourteen in the Lords, so that both the regular army and the military profession were well represented in Parliament. During the first of the two critical periods of civil–military relations, the Third Dutch War, thirty-six officers sat in the Commons, and in the second, the projected French War of 1678, forty-one members of Parliament held commissions in the standing army. Most of these gentlemen were loyal supporters of the court as commissions were given to Members of Parliament as pensions, turning them into 'placemen'. In this way the king built a loyal voting block of some size in the Commons with an equally efficient unit of support in the Lords at times when the army required Parliamentary assistance.

A wrong vote by an officer in the Commons often meant the end of his military career. Sir Thomas Armstrong left the Life Guards in 1679 to fight with the Anglo-Dutch Brigade as his support of Exclusion cost him his commission. James II removed Richard Bertie and Charles Fitzwilliam from the army after their votes had not pleased him in the Parliament of 1685. Some officers did oppose the court and support the Earl of Shaftesbury during the Exclusion Crisis, but as Monmouth was then captain-general they had good reason for their actions. The number of political renegades in the standing army was small and 85 per cent of the army officers remained loyal to the Crown and the succession of the Duke of York.

Philip Sherard was a lieutenant in the Royal Horse Guards and for this he was regarded as a placeman in the Commons. Sidney Godolphin was another career officer who was thought of as a placeman due to his commission in the army. In the 'Sarcastical List',[36] the victims had their army commissions quoted as causes of 'bribery and corruption'. Francis Lord Hawley was not only 'Sergeant Buffoon and Commissioner for the Sale of Fee Farm Rents', but also a captain in the Royal Horse Guards. Likewise Sir John Talbot, Sir James Smith, Sir Charles Wheeler and Roger Vaughan went on to the List and were also included in the 'Seasonable Argument'[37] as court pensioners and placemen part of whose rewards were commissions in the army.

Typical of the breed of Gentlemen Officers was Roger Kirkby, the first son of the old royalist soldier Richard Kirkby. In recognition of his father's loyal services to Charles I, Roger was able to buy a commission as an ensign in the Coldstream Guards in 1670. His promotion was slow, although he secured a brevet captain's place in one of the new regiments for the projected French War of 1678, and some time after 1680 he transferred from the Guards to command an independent company in the Chester garrison. Under James II his progress in the enlarged army was more rapid, becoming a captain in Sackville Tufton's Foot in 1687 and a colonel of infantry in 1689. Kirkby advanced only after the accession of James II when the army was increased, creating more vacancies.

Whereas Kirkby was an example of the second generation of royalist gentry who found their careers in the standing army after 1660, Francis, first Baron Hawley, was one of the old royalists rewarded with a commission on the Restoration. Hawley was reputedly one of Rupert's finest cavalry officers who commanded a regiment of horse for Charles I. During the Interregnum he accompanied Charles II into exile and returned home to become a captain in the Royal Horse Guards in 1661. He retained this rank until 1676 when he retired from all his offices on account of chronic ill health. In addition to his place in the Guards, Hawley was governor of Deal Castle from 1672 and a Member of Parliament.

In an army which never undertook active service and was small an officer needed patronage in high places first to acquire his commission and second to secure him promotion. This situation was reversed in wartime when there was a shortage of officers and there was little difficulty in gaining a commission, but the tiny peacetime army offered few vacancies and these were much sought after. For the first decade of the reign the Duke of Albemarle held sway over army patronage, resulting in many of his loyal supporters being commissioned into the ranks.[38] The other principal fount of patronage was the Duke of York; after Albemarle's death in 1670 he came to dominate the machinery of commissioning officers. George Legge, John and George Churchill, Sir Allen Apsley, Sir Charles Wheeler, Thomas Dalmahoy, Philip Howard, Sir Charles Littleton, James Graham, Thomas Dongan, Justin Macartie and Henry Jermyn all owed their professional advancements to the future James II. The Duke of York controlled the ranks above captain and nearly all the field officers in the six regiments were his protégés. Other centres of patronage were varied depending upon family ties and political allegiances. Sir Edmund Andros was the brother-in-law of the Earl of Craven, Sir Thomas Berry was closely related to Lord Clifford, whilst Monmouth found places for his exclusionist henchmen Sir Thomas Armstrong and Silus Titus. Arlington supported Sir Robert Carr, Roger Whitley relied on Lord Gerard, and Sir William Maynard worked under the influence of the second Duke of Albemarle. In their time Danby and Shaftesbury used what resources they could to obtain commissions with which to reward their political adherents. The one exception was Prince Rupert. Although one of the major figures in the First Civil War he was completely unable to command any patronage or military power after 1660. His rift with Charles II was too deep.

Military patronage worked in a controlled manner. Within the six standing regiments the Crown exercised a rigid direction over all commissions, from colonel down to the youngest ensign, but in the three mass levies the patronage system operated more loosely. Field officers were appointed by the Crown but then these gentlemen were free to use their own patronage in the appointment of their subalterns. This was facilitated by regiments being recruited in specific areas of the country and very often being family concerns. Colonels recruited their regiments from regions in which they held considerable political and personal influence, their own estates and the counties in which they held office. If a colonel was a member of the county lieutenancy then his recruiting difficulties were quickly solved as he had direct access to the militia. Buckingham's Foot, raised in 1672, came almost exclusively from Yorkshire where the Duke was all-powerful, and his men were so attached to him that they refused to serve at sea unless he himself commanded them.[39] Friends and relatives of the colonel abounded in most of the regiments and in Sir John Fenwick's Foot of 1678 there was barely a single officer who was not related or connected to him in some way, and every man and officer in the unit came from Durham or Northumberland. The raising of soldiers was the responsibility of the colonel but the onus of actually recruiting the men fell on the captains. It was essential for the captains and the colonel to be able to gather men from the same area employing their joint influence in both the county and the militia. 'My Lord Mulgrave cannot brag of much interest in Yorkshire, where half his complement are not yet raised',[40] wrote Henry Ball to Williamson in 1673, indicating that a colonel could only raise men from an area where he possessed a real territorial, political and militia interest. Under this system it was easy for the Wrays to control the Admiral's Regiment and the Trelawneys the Duchess of York's.

All over England stood garrisons supposedly situated at key points for internal security and national defence. In fact they were mostly decayed Tudor castles of no strategic value except as convenient quarters for troops. Every garrison contained independent, non-regimented companies of foot raised locally to serve in that one station. The officers of these static and highly ineffective units came from the gentry of that region. The Arundells of Trerice in Cornwall ran the Pendennis Castle garrison where one member of the family succeeded another, whilst the Godolphins excluded all outsiders from the government of the Scilly Isles. In other parts of the country the guiding principle was similar but without the intense parochialism of

Cornwall. Sir John Reresby at York was a good example of a local gentleman being appointed to command a garrison in his own county, whilst the Tufton family looked after Tilbury and Gravesend. These garrison officers and governors were not important for their role was stationary and involved little work. Reresby found much else to occupy his time in York, and most garrison companies were commanded *de facto* by junior officers and the officers of visiting units from the standing regiments.

Officers who were Members of Parliament had one special advantage over their colleagues. No officer was permitted more than two months' leave in any one year and even for this he had to obtain a special leave pass from the king. However, if the officer was also a Member of Parliament then he was allowed unlimited leave of absence during such time as the Houses were in session without having to seek the prior approval of the sovereign.[41] A further regulation required that no more than one-third of all the officers of a regiment be on leave at any one time, and so the Parliament men with their involuntary vacations were able to fill most of the leave places to the exclusion of their brother officers. In practice liberty of leave was grossly abused by all the officers, whether MPs or not, to such an extent that Henry Sidney found no one but 'a corporal and three files of musketeers' at Tilbury Fort, whilst 'at Gravesend there was never a commissioned officer'.[42] Four years later the king wrote to the Earl of Plymouth, the governor of Hull, stating that the previous rules had not been sufficient 'to continue our military officers with our companies in our garrison', and in future any officer absent without leave would be faced with 'absolute cashiering'.[43] Such behaviour was typical of the gentleman officers in England.

Young men of the period were noted for their disregard of the law and other people's property and the army contained its fair share of these characters. As early as 1662 four of them, Charles Sackville (later the Lord Buckhurst), Edward Sackville, Sir Henry Bellasise and John Bellasise, were pardoned by the king for 'the felonious Robbing and Killing of one John Hoppey for the killing of whom they stand convicted in our Court'.[44] Buckhurst was a notorious rake and a bosom companion of Sir Charles Sedley, but the king had no alternative but to employ the highest born in the land. Officers of wealth and social standing were able to live comfortably without their army pay and were never reliant on the army for a livelihood. In this way there was never any danger that the army would oppose its own disbandment and become a political danger. Even so, some curious gentlemen found their way into commissioned places. 'Swift Nix' was once an eminent and infamous highwayman but after receiving a royal pardon he changed his name to Swiftnam and bought the company of William Wycherley, the dramatist, in Buckingham's Regiment in 1673.[45] How much either of these knew of soldiering is open to question but they were no more ignorant than the officers who received their commissions for political services. Wentworth Dillon, fourth Earl of Roscommon, was better known as a poet than a soldier, but he commanded an Irish regiment into the French service in 1672 as well as serving as a captain in the Duke of York's horse in 1678. Ralph Widdrington was blinded in action at sea during the Second Dutch War, but he was granted a pension of £200 a year and commissioned into the army where he remained as a captain in various garrison units until 1688. Military knowledge and physical fitness were not prerequisites of entering the army:

But all men fear our officers in this army are not well picked out, for the most of them are debauched, profane persons and public atheists which they say openly they learn of the Duke of Buckingham, one yesterday publicly in company I am told saying he believed neither Heaven nor Hell.[46]

After the days of disciplined military forces under Cromwell this sort of officer did a lot to harm the reputation of the army. In keeping with gentlemanly etiquette he was high-handed, dogmatic, easily offended, and touchy to the point of stupidity over questions of honour. The Gentleman Officers of the levy of 1673 objected so strongly to being commanded by the Frenchman, Schomberg, who actually knew what he was about with a large army, that they 'daily offer him affronts',[47] and generally acted like a troup of opera singers. Soldiers of the 1st Foot Guards were encouraged to riot and cause serious breaches of the peace in Huntingdon by their captain, Thomas Stradling. For his sins Stradling was cashiered but he soon reappeared in the Guards in the same rank.[48] As captain of the King's Troop of the Life Guard, Lord Gerard of Brandon was the senior cavalry colonel in the army. To emphasise his status he and Lord Cornwallis, a junior officer in the King's Troop, beat up the sentries in St James's Park and then murdered a footboy. Cornwallis was tried by his peers and acquitted whilst Gerard spent a few months in France until the scandal abated and then quietly returned to resume his high military office.[49] Such incidents were depressingly frequent amongst the officers. Junior subalterns used their men to threaten, and sometimes kill, their civilian enemies,[50] officers of the Guards committed robberies and murders,[51] and others fought, squabbled and duelled.[52] When it came to obeying orders amongst themselves, social conventions and personal differences barred all hope of operating a real command system. Gentlemen and peers were not keen on taking orders from their social equals or inferiors:

> To show military discipline, Sir Philip Howard was suspended his employment for not obeying some orders the Duke of Monmouth gave him in which though his Grace be found in the wrong it is thought fit the other should suffer for example's sake to show that orders must be obeyed though never so foolish.[53]

All that a private soldier could hope for was promotion to sergeant or corporal, but for this he was entirely dependent on the will of his company commander who appointed his own nominees to non-commissioned rank. It was impossible for a ranker to gain a commission. In keeping with the general practice of the Restoration government all army posts were bought and sold. To gain a commission or promotion an officer had to have his request granted by the king who retained the final choice of his officers. Once approval was obtained then the matter rested with the out-going holder as it was his vacancy and his to sell. Officially, when an officer was promoted he paid a fee to the Secretary at War according to a set table of prices drawn up in 1667,[54] but this was only half the story. A vacancy occurred when an officer either retired or moved to a higher post, but his position was a property which had been bought in the first instance and was a saleable commodity. An army commission was an investment. There was some money to be made from the pay, false musters, selling licences to sutlers, and from corruption, but, more important, it was a 'place', so vital to courtiers and politicians in the seventeenth century, providing its holder with status, prestige and patronage. With the pension system in its infancy an officer had to sell his commission on retirement in order to finance his old age, and this was especially true of the officers descended from the royalist families impoverished during the Civil Wars. Promotion was supposed to be on merit and the sale of commissions was technically illegal, but the king turned a blind eye and unofficially condoned the practice. The Royal Hospital at Chelsea was partly financed by a fee of one shilling in the pound from the sales of all commissions. This deduction was diplomatically termed 'compensation'.[55]

Commissions in the temporary regiments of the three mass levies were not expensive; an officer simply had to pay the basic fee to the Secretary at War and then purchase the place from the colonel for a small sum. However, within the six standing regiments the vacancy had to be bought from the outgoing incumbent for a considerable sum of money. Vacancies were few and so the rates were high. Desperate for a regiment of his own the Duke of Buckingham paid Sir George Scott £1,500 for his foot regiment in 1672,[56] whilst Philip Darcy had to find £2,000 for his guidon's commission in the Life Guard in 1680. The highest price paid for a commission was the £5,100 paid to John Russell by the Duke of Grafton for the colonelcy of the 1st Foot Guards in 1681.[57] Information on the average price of commissions is scant, but the cost of commissions was generally very high, with a captain's place in the Guards usually fetching around £1,000. The struggle which occupied Sir John Reresby for the governorship of York illustrates the way in which commissions changed hands.

In May 1681 Reresby was pressing to be appointed governor of York as the incumbent, Lord Frescheville, a captain in the Royal Horse Guards, was seriously ill and not expected to live long. Reresby's dilemma was whether to wait until Frescheville died or to pre-empt and immediately buy the place. There were rivals for the office. Sir Thomas Slingsby had already bought Frescheville's troop in the Horse Guards in readiness, and the lords Huntingdon, Scarsdale, and Conniers were also in the field. These contenders were supported by the Duke of York, not a popular figure in 1681, whereas Reresby had the backing of the Earl of Halifax whose star at court was in the ascendant after his speeches in defence of the succession. Halifax recommended Reresby to the king who was agreeable provided that Reresby and Frescheville could come to terms over the purchase. This was achieved and in March 1682 Halifax received Charles's firm promise that his associate would have the governorship. The unfortunate Frescheville died on 2 April 1682 and Reresby was duly commissioned as the new governor of York.[58] Progress in the army was dependent upon patronage and purchase, and patronage itself rested on family and political connection, the need for money being understood.

Between the standing armies of England, Ireland, and Scotland, there was almost no interchange of officers; once committed to a national establishment an officer remained in that service. Even within the English army there was no scope for advancement unless a candidate had sufficient money and patronage to ensure that his claims overrode all others. Professional officers were financially unable to enter the standing army in England, and their sole alternative was to fight abroad until commissions could be gained for little or no money and that only happened in war. The army attracted the genuine soldiers it so desperately needed in wartime almost by accident and in spite of its methods of promotion. When the social and fiscal barriers were dropped during national emergencies the professionals were able to secure places only to lose them again on disbandment.

III

Military Life in England

1 *Pay, pensions and finance*

PARLIAMENT made very few financial grants to assist the standing army in England and what sums they did raise for military purposes were reserved for supporting the mass levies in time of war. The king had to pay, equip and meet the contingencies of the six standing regiments from his own revenues. Throughout the reign the army was a fiscal embarrassment to Charles, stretching his over-extended Treasury to the full, for the army never cost less than £140,000 a year. The Commons granted Charles an annual revenue of £1,200,000 after the Restoration, an amount which might have proved sufficient had the yield not been well below the official value. A trade depression, the plague, and the Great Fire of London all contributed to an annual shortfall on the ordinary revenue of up to £300,000. Added to the cost of the army, the deficit in the 1660s was crippling, leading to the Stop of the Exchequer in 1672. After that, matters improved with Danby's retrenchment and reforms and a more certain return from the customs and excise. When estimating the king's revenue for life Parliament had not considered the possibility that he would maintain an army and it was this factor, added to the inadequacy of his actual income, which led to the deficit spending of Charles's government. In addition to the English establishment, money had to be found for the garrisons in Tangier, Dunkirk, Bombay and the colonies. Fortunately, the establishments in Scotland and Ireland were paid for from their own national revenues. Most of the funds for the English army came from the excise. The Guards,

Garrisons, and the Royal Household devoured £59,000 from the farm of the excise in London, Surrey and Middlesex, whilst the Guards and Garrisons took a further £61,000 and Tangier £70,000 from the collection in the remainder of the country.[1] These sums just covered the minimum annual cost of the peacetime establishment in England.

In the very first year of its foundation the army caused financial problems for the government. So desperate was Charles for money that he designed to use some of the money raised on the Poll Bill of 1661, intended by Parliament to pay off the New Model, to pay his new guards. The scheme came to nothing as the yield on the Bill fell short of expectations by nearly £90,000. Charles spent £97,000 of his own money on the army during 1661 and had to borrow £36,968 7*s* 8*d* to meet the rest of the charge.[2] A deficit in the first year of its existence was a poor omen and for the next twenty-four years the government had to struggle to pay its army, discovering the only solution in long-term credit.[3]

Before any increase in the army establishment was brought about, estimates of the expected cost were worked out in great detail. This was a simple process as the only items actually paid for by the Crown were the men's pay, the contingencies, small charges like candles and firewood for guard posts, pensions and half-pay. Clothing, food and quarters were all met by the soldier from his own pay, so an estimate could be accurate to within a few pounds. Such estimates were valuable in trying to gain additional money from Parliament to support a foreign war, enabling the legislators to have a precise picture of the expected size and cost of the force. There was, however, no hope of any Parliamentary aid in peacetime. Even contemporary observers thought that the major reason for Charles's ever-increasing annual overdraft was his retention of a standing army,[4] and certainly the expenses of the army amounted to most of the deficit of between £300,000 and £400,000. Salvation for the Treasury and the army was found in the work of one man, Sir Stephen Fox, the Paymaster-General of the army from 1661 to 1679.

Born the youngest son of William Fox of Farley in Wiltshire, Stephen Fox received his basic training in book-keeping and domestic management in the households of the Earl of Northumberland and his brother Lord Percy of Alnwick. From 1654 to 1660 he undertook the running of the household of the exiled Charles, an unenviable task, but one which he executed with incredible skill, it even being claimed that he balanced the accounts and maintained the king in funds.[5] Fox's reward at the Restoration was the office of Paymaster-General of the Guards and Garrisons and a seat on the Board of Green Cloth. In politics Fox was a follower of Arlington, and although he was never a close supporter but tried to remain neutral, he was sufficiently attached to Arlington to lose his paymastership in 1676 on that minister's final fall from power. Sir Henry Puckering took over the office but this was merely a sinecure and the real work was undertaken by Lemuel Kingdon.[6] Unfortunately this new arrangement broke down as neither Puckering nor Kingdon could secure the credit which Fox had been able to acquire, and when Kingdon was involved in some very dubious dealings with the Earl of Ranelagh in 1678 Fox returned to his old post. He had not been back in this position for more than a year when he committed the unpardonable sin of voting for the impeachment of Danby; the paymastership passed to Nicholas Johnson. After Johnson's death in 1682 Fox's eldest son Charles took over, but his father was still very active in politics and finance and guided his son in army matters.

Fox's financial abilities were too obvious and necessary for the king to ignore and in 1679 he was drafted on to the Treasury Commission and subsequently served on every such commission until 1702. He was one of the financial wizards of the age, and his management of the army pay office was a model of the 'greatest exactness, decency, and frugality'.[7] Without doubt he made a great deal of money from the army, quite honestly by the standards of the times, even though the 'Sarcastical List' stated that 'at the Restoration [he] was made pay master to the Guards where he has cheated £100,000'.[8]

He procured to be Pay-Master of the whole Army, and by his dexterity and punctual dealing [obtained] such credit amongst the bankers, that he was in [a] short time, able to borrow vast sums of them, upon any exigence. The continued turning thus of money, and the soldiers' moderate allowance to him, for his keeping touch with them, did so enrich him; that he [is] believed to be worth at least 200,000 pounds, and unenvied, which is next to [a] miracle.[9]

The basic pay system of the army was fairly simple and straightforward. Following each muster the rolls were returned to the paymaster who issued the money for each troop and company on the figures presented in these documents.[10] This assumed one central fact: that the paymaster possessed the ready cash with which to pay the soldiers. If this was the case then Fox issued Full Pay to the colonel of the regiment involved and it was then up to this officer to deduct the 'Official Off-Reckonings'. This money was used to pay for the men's clothing and personal equipage. Once this was done the colonel passed the balance to his company commanders who then paid it to their men as 'Subsistence Money'. Given reasonably honest officials this system could have functioned with some efficiency but it was hamstrung by the inability of the Treasury to supply the paymaster with regular sums of money with which to pay the men. For most of the reign the six standing regiments were given Full Pay at intervals varying between six and eight weeks and so they had little to complain of, but garrison companies sometimes had to wait as long as two years for their Full Pay. Guernsey was twenty-three months in arrears by October 1665,[11] and every garrison was in arrears by at least four months in December 1667.[12] When the country was plunged into war the regularity of pay went totally awry and arrears extended to a minimum of five months for the entire army.

Arrears of pay did not mean that the soldiers received no money, as this would have been politically and socially intolerable. Arrears represented the balance owed to a soldier between his Full Pay and his Subsistence, in other words, the Off Reckonings. Fox made an agreement with the king in 1668 to pay Subsistence to all the foot weekly when they were quartered in London and monthly when in garrison.[13] The arrears, or Off Reckonings, were paid to the colonels whenever Fox could discover the funds. During Fox's tenure at the Army Pay Office the Subsistence was regularly met, but the issue of Full Pay varied between two and four months. After his departure from office the pay system fell into disarray; Subsistence was maintained but the delivery of the arrears was highly irregular. On 10 January 1680 Sir Charles Littleton, the colonel of the Admiral's Regiment, complained that the issue of only Subsistence was forcing the colonels and the captains to pay for the soldiers' clothing out of their own pockets.[14] Technically the non-payment of arrears affected only the Off Reckonings and so only the officers, the ones who could afford it, suffered. The practice, however, was rather different from the theory. When only Subsistence was paid the officers normally stopped the amount of the Off Reckonings out of the troops' Subsistence Money, reducing this meagre pittance still further. On the eventual delivery of the arrears there was no guarantee that the officers would forward this to their men, but were more likely to keep it for themselves.

From 1679 the semi-efficient pay system gradually broke up. In January Fox complained that he was quite unable to release pay in good time as the officers were tardy in sending him the muster rolls.[15] This led to a new agreement between Fox and Monmouth,[16] by which Fox undertook to forward the Subsistence for each regiment within ten days of receiving the completed rolls provided that these came to him within six weeks of the actual parade. If he was late then Fox's 'poundage', his deduction of one shilling in the pound, was forfeit for that muster period. Finally, Fox took the gamble of promising Subsistence one week in advance, and was hopeful of delivering the balance of Full Pay before the end of each muster period. The Privy Council issued a new set of regulations concerning army pay in November 1683 under which all captains and colonels had to tender annual accounts to the paymaster showing where every penny received from the Pay Office had gone. Colonels and garrison governors were reminded that they were to keep a close watch over their regimental agents, those notoriously corrupt officials who handled the regimental moneys on behalf of the colonel.[17]

Whatever the shortcomings of the Pay Office after 1679 we must not exaggerate the position. Compared to the corruption in that office in the time of the Earl of Ranelagh, Fox ran an orderly and relatively honest house. Subsistence was paid regularly to both the guards and the garrisons and the soldiers never wanted for money. Certainly the balance of Full Pay was often long delayed, but when the state of the Treasury and general government finance is taken into account the payment of the army over these twenty-five years was little short of remarkable. How did Fox attain this high standard?

Never was the Treasury able to give Stephen Fox a lump sum with which to pay the army as it could never lay its hands on a sufficient amount at the correct time; sixteen weeks' full pay for the guards came to £38,000. So the paymaster borrowed the necessary money on his personal credit from London bankers and financiers and was then repaid by the Treasury in its own time. On all the sums which he borrowed for the army Fox charged the government 6 per cent interest per annum, but this was not a profit for Fox as he in turn had to pay a similar interest to his city creditors. Clearly, there was little money to be made out of borrowing from one source to pay another, but the government allowed him certain perquisites in return for the risks that he ran. Occasionally the Treasury allowed a bonus of £2 per cent on its repayment of capital and interest[18] and this could amount to as much as £300 in every £1,000. Most important of all, he was permitted 'poundage'. In 1667 Charles allowed Fox to deduct 4*d* in every pound of army pay to cover the running costs of the Pay Office and the large number of fees payable to the Treasury. In reality most of this money represented a straight profit for the Paymaster.

When added to his official salary of £400 a year this poundage could give Fox a total income of £2,400, to which must be added his interest bonuses from the Treasury. Between 21 January 1665 and 29 September 1666, Fox advanced £221,071 3*s* 4*d* to pay the army, and on repayment from the government the interest amounted to £12,810 7*s* 8*d*. When the bonus of £2 per cent is added another £3,000 can be tacked on.[19] Clearly, Fox made a handsome profit out of the army.

His gross income was further increased in 1668 when the poundage deduction was raised from 4*d* in the pound to 1*s*, meaning that Fox personally received one-twentieth of all army pay, about £7,000 a year in peacetime.[20] At the Stop of the Exchequer in 1672 Fox was owed nearly £27,000 by the government, but the whole sum was met over the ensuing six months[21] so that neither Fox, his creditors, nor the army suffered from the national bankruptcy. Fortunately for the Treasury Fox's own credit and integrity were so high with the city bankers that he was always able to obtain the required cash for the army pay warrants, and in return the Treasury had the good sense to undertake the repayment of the Paymaster-

General as one of its first priorities. An unpaid army was a mutinous army, and in a country which was violently anti-military the maintenance of regular payments became a political necessity.

Not all army pay was issued *in specie*. During a major disbandment, as in 1674 or 1679, dismissed soldiers were frequently paid with debentures.[22] This method possessed advantages for everyone except the disbanded soldier. By paying the men with promissory notes which could be cashed for their face value at a given date on the Treasury, the government was able to stagger the financial weight of paying off large numbers of troops. As the revenue raised for these disbandments came in irregularly and normally produced less than the anticipated yield, debentures represented an admirable system of utilising such money as became available over a long period. This scheme was open to gross abuse, as Ranelagh demonstrated in Ireland. Most disbanded men were desperate for their pay and arrears and happily parted with their debentures to accomplished speculators for well under their face value. Able to wait until the required date, the speculator then cashed the notes at the Treasury for their full value. A profit of 50 per cent was quite normal in such dealings, indeed it was probably much higher as debentures had been purchased for as little as 3*s* or 4*s* in the days of Cromwell.[23] No evidence has been discovered suggesting that subsistence money was ever paid in anything other than cash, but it is possible that debentures were issued during the financial crisis of 1672.

Between pay and pensions stood half-pay. This curious institution applied only to officers taking the form of a retainer paid to them whilst unemployed. Following a reduction in the establishment or a major disbandment, the reformed officers, or reformadoes, were often given half their previous establishment pay and attached to a regiment where they served as gentlemen soldiers, often responsible for drill and training. When the army was expanded again these half-pay officers were the first to receive the new commissions.[24] Half-pay and pensions were met quarterly by the Paymaster-General.

Elizabeth I made the first grant of pensions to the military by statute.[25] These were administered out of the local poor rates by the Justices of the Peace to those who 'had ventured their lives and lost their limbs, or disabled their bodies in the defence of Her Majesty and the State, [and] should at their return be relieved and rewarded'. Every injured soldier could make a claim on the Treasurer of the county in which he had enlisted for temporary relief, or upon the Quarter Sessions for a permanent pension not exceeding £20 a year. This remained the situation until 1660 when the Commons 'discharged the maimed and disabled soldiers previously kept in the hospitals of Ely House and the Savoy',[26] and placed them on the counties to be provided for under the Elizabethan Poor Law. Ely House and the Savoy were then turned into barracks for regular troops.

Such was the position for the non-commissioned officers and private soldiers, but officers were eligible to receive money pensions out of the contingency fund included in every army establishment between 1661 and 1685. Half-pay was also paid from this source amounting to £1,143 14*s* 4*d* for thirty-six reformadoes in 1666. The establishment for 1680 contained an allowance of £1,270 5*s* 6¼*d* for pensions to various officers and soldiers,[27] and three years later there was no change except for the addition of £365 for pensions to ten reformed officers of the Royal Scots and another £260 15*s* 0*d* for 'other pensions to individuals'.

Money pensions were worth between 6*d* and 2*s* a day depending on the recipient's rank and service. Widows, children and dependants of deceased officers and soldiers normally received a lump sum as compensation rather than a quarterly pension. In 1673 the widow of Ensign James Finley was granted £20 after her husband had been killed by mutinous soldiers of Sir William Lockhart's Regiment at Canterbury.[28] Soldiers and officers wounded at sea during the Dutch Wars were eligible for pensions, whilst the dependants of those killed in that service were considered for lump-sum payments.[29] Military men who had been maimed or disabled in the service of Charles I or his son when in exile were allowed rooms in almshouses in inland counties provided that they could produce 'good certificates'.[30]

A favourite device for rewarding a soldier for faithful service or serious injury was to continue him on the muster roll of the company but permitting him to do no duty. Private Roger Foster of the Holland Regiment, lost his right arm when serving at sea in 1673. His company commander, Sir John Berry, was instructed to continue him in the company but not to impose on him 'any other duty than he can well discharge'.[31] Two elderly and superannuated soldiers, John Erwin and John Ward, were dismissed from the 1st Foot Guards on account of their age in 1674, but after petitioning the king they were allowed to take two vacant places in the Berwick garrison. When on marine duty with the same regiment, Private John Leake lost his leg, but was allowed to continue in his company and receive pay following his recovery.

A pension system which led to the retention of old and disabled soldiers in active service units was undesirable, undermining the effective strength of the army and weakening its potential. Furthermore, the awarding of pensions and compensation to old or wounded soldiers was erratic. Some were fortunate enough to receive grants or places, but others had to sell their debentures and take to the streets and beg. A combination of these evils resulted in the foundation of military hospitals. As in many social functions connected with the army, Ireland was in the van, having been the first to provide permanent barracks for garrison companies and then the first to build a hospital for old soldiers. Kilmainham Hospital in Dublin was constructed in 1681 to house old and 'unserviceable' men who had been continued in pay for want of other maintenance. In the same year Charles planned to put up a hospital in England for the 'relief of old, lame, or infirm soldiers'. He donated some acres of his own land for the building and its grounds at Chelsea and by 1684 the hospital was ready to receive the first 'Chelsea Pensioners'. Superannuated, sick, disabled, and maimed soldiers were allowed to live in the hospital under a strict military regime, supported by substantial private donations and a deduction of 8*d* from every £1 of army pay.[32] In addition Charles ordered 1*s* in the pound from the sale of army commissions to be given towards the upkeep of the hospital.[33] At first the foundation took in 100 men, so that the returning Tangier garrison, many of whom were sick and over-age, benefited immediately from the provision. The full capacity of 400 was achieved in the time of William III.

This year of 1684 witnessed one final development in the care of old soldiers. The deduction of 8*d* in the pound for the Royal Hospital was collected centrally and placed in the 'Invalid

Fund', the principal of which was to remain untouched as far as was possible and only the interest employed to provide money pensions for retired soldiers. To qualify for provision from the fund a soldier had to have fifteen years' service behind him, or a disability or illness directly caused by life in the army. A foot soldier was allowed a pension of half his former establishment pay, and a horseman or dragoon one-third of his previous wage. Scotland too possessed a similar fund devoted to the 'subsistence of antiquated soldiers'.[34] There was one major drawback to these schemes. To take a pension from the fund a soldier had to have contributed towards it from his army pay; in Charles's time, those who needed this money most urgently, the Tangier garrison, were unable to gain advantage from it.[35]

2 *Dress and uniform*

Cromwell's New Model army had been amongst the first in Europe to adopt a standard uniform, although before this in England such bodies as the Gentleman Pensioners and the Yeomen of the Guard, as well as some of the regiments of the Civil Wars, had worn standard clothing. The commonwealth soldiery based their dress upon the red coat, a trend which was basically followed by Charles II's army, and it appears that during his reign the term 'red coat' came to be used as a general nickname for the military.[36] Here the similarity between the two armies ended. Whereas the uniform of the New Model had been practical and highly functional, that of the Restoration force was Frenchified and a victim of the whims of civilian fashion, especially in the case of the officers. We are unfortunately without adequate illustrations of the precise uniform worn by either the officers or the other ranks. Wenceslas Hollar's engravings of Tangier provide some visual evidence on the nature of military vestments, but these are unreliable as Tangier was a foreign service station and both the uniform and equipment differed in some important respects from that in use in England. As the army was a vaguely unfashionable occupation for a gentleman it was not customary to have portraits composed in uniform, the reverse of the mode in the eighteenth century. The common private could not hope to be remembered on canvas, with the result that we possess no clear conception of his dress. The best that can be accomplished is to piece together the jigsaw of the written evidence:

A cloth coat lined with bayes . . . one pair of kersey breeches lined with pockets . . . two shirts, two cravats, one pair of shoes, one pair of yarn hose, one hat edged and hat band, one sash, and also one sword and belt.[37]

Such was the issue to each man of the newly raised garrison companies of 1677, and the clothing of a non-commissioned officer was identical but with the addition of 'a cloth cloak lined with bayes'. A soldier had to pay for his uniform out of the Off Reckonings on extended hire purchase. Only when the total of his Off Reckonings equalled the original sum laid out by his officer did the soldier consider his debt paid. In fact this debt was never met. An infantryman's uniform cost *53s*, and so it took approximately one year for this amount to be paid back at *2d* a day. By that time the clothing, not of the best quality in the first instance, needed replacing and so the process continued. Cavalry and dragoons enjoyed higher pay but also wore more expensive uniforms so their overall situation was comparable to that of the foot.[38]

Of all the little army the most gorgeously dressed were the three Troops of the Life Guard. Their trumpeters and kettle-drummers wore ceremonial uniforms which cost *£58 3s 6d* each,[39] their coats and cloaks covered in yards of lace and embroidery. The coats of all three troops were red; the King's Troop's were faced with royal blue and richly ornamented with gold lace, the Duke of York's were the same but with silver lace, and the Queen's Troop was without lace decoration. Over this basic uniform the accoutrements and accessories were very grand. The King's Troop sported blue velvet carbine belts edged with gold and silver, red breeches and stockings, pistol holsters embroidered with the royal crown and cipher, and broad-brimmed hats adorned with white feathers. Similarly attired was the Queen's Troop except that the basic colour was sea-green, the colour of the Braganza family, whilst the Duke of York's were in yellow, the Duke's favourite colour.[40] It is not possible to offer a more accurate description than this, for there is no information available on the cut and design of the dress, whether boots were worn, and other points of detail. The other horse regiment, the Royal Horse Guards, wore blue coats faced with red, blue breeches and stockings, topped with buff carbine belts edged with red and laced with gold.

In comparison with the splendour of the cavalry the foot soldiers were quite dowdy. Of the 1st Foot Guards we can only say that they wore red coats faced with light blue, although in 1669 their pikemen wore silvery coats lined with blue. However, by 1684 this regiment was totally dressed in red coats, blue breeches and stockings, with white waist sashes fringed with blue. The Coldstreamers had their red coats faced with green, and their breeches and stockings also of green, although their pikemen had worn green coats with red facings in 1669. Another of the standing units, the Holland Regiment, was one of the few to alter its colours radically during the reign. In 1669 their red coats were seen lined with yellow, but by 1684 their facings had changed to a buff or flesh colour.[41] Other than these, the Royal Scots had red coats faced with white, light grey breeches and stockings, and white sashes, whilst the Admiral's wore yellow coats with red facings.[42]

The style of uniform changed according to the tastes of civilian fashion. At the beginning of the reign coats were short and hats high-crowned, but as the years progressed the insidious influence of the French introduced long coats, baggy breeches, periwigs, and an abundance of lace. Around 1680 a regimental officer must have dressed in a broad-brimmed, low-crowned, black hat, with a white linen shirt and cravat. Over this would have gone a cassock-shaped coat buttoning at the front as far as the waist, with streams of coloured ribbon at each shoulder. A silk sash would have been wound around the midriff, and the hands covered with buff gauntlets decorated with gold or silver lace. Breeches were voluminous ending just below the knee, the lower part of the leg being covered by stockings of fine worsted. High-heeled shoes topped with a buckle or more ribbons completed the outfit. Adjutants and field officers possibly wore jack-boots when on duty. Dress for the other ranks was little different in style although a good deal less grand.

At Tangier such a uniform must have been unbearably hot and uncomfortable, so here officers wore a special service uniform of light grey with many of the trimmings removed.[43] However, the foot regiment of the second Duke of Albemarle, raised in 1673 for the Third Dutch War, also wore grey coats.[44] Whether this was merely a peculiarity of this one regiment or whether a grey coat and breeches was normal service wear, the red outfits being reserved for ceremonial purposes, is not clear. Certainly the rank and file only paid for one uniform out of their Off Reckonings which they used for both fatigue and official duties, but it is possible that the officers dressed in grey when on garrison or field duty reserving the scarlets for full dress occasions.[45]

Besides the obvious difference between officers and men, the grenadiers formed a separate entity as far as their dress was concerned. Their first appearance in the English army was in 1678 when they created quite an impression on John Evelyn:

Now were brought into service a new sort of soldier called Grenadiers, who were dextrous to fling hand grenadoes, every one having a pouch full, and had furr'd caps with coped crowns like Janizzaries, which made them look very fierce, and some had long hoods hanging down behind as we picture fools: their clothing being likewise pyebald yellow and red.[46]

These fur caps were similar to the later hussar busbies but with the addition of a long conical bag the point of which flopped back over the man's shoulder. To complete their weird appearance the grenadiers wore cravats made from fox tails hung round the neck on a ribbon.[47] Evelyn's reference to 'pyebald' clothing is not supported elsewhere; perhaps the usually precise diarist was for once mistaken.

Non-commissioned officers sported basically the same uniforms as privates, except that sergeants had different coloured sashes, usually red, and carried a halberd. Also, the coat of a sergeant was bound with wide lace and that of a corporal with narrower lace. Drummers ranked as non-commissioned officers and their uniform was very distinctive; their hanging sleeves were the same colour as the regimental facing and were ringed and edged with lace. The royal cipher, or coat-of-arms of the colonel, was embroidered on to the back and breast of their coats.

Before 1684, the officers of a regiment, from the colonel down to the most junior ensign, wore almost identical clothing, making it difficult for the soldiers to distinguish one rank from another. This muddled state of affairs was corrected by a circular order 'for the better distinction of our several officers serving us in our Companies of Foot'.[48] All foot captains were ordered to wear gold-coloured gorgets, lieutenants black ones studded with gold, and ensigns gorgets of a silver colour. A captain was to carry a partizan, a lieutenant a pike, and an ensign the company colours. Whether a similar system was extended to the horse is uncertain.

For the six standing regiments, clothing was wholly a regimental concern. Like so much else in the Restoration army the regiment ran itself and conducted its own affairs in clothing. When new coats or breeches were needed by these permanent units the colonel contracted for them himself with private tailors and then recouped his financial outlay from the Off Reckonings. However, there were two exceptions to this generalisation which enabled the headquarters staff to exercise some control over the dress of the army. When the Foot Guards were formed in 1661 their uniforms were ordered in bulk and paid for by the Paymaster-General. In turn he stopped the soldiers' Off Reckonings in his own hands to meet the bill of £1,928 17*s* 4*d*.[49] After this initial issue of clothing the regiments then proceeded to order and contract for their own replacements. Similarly the new levies of 1667, 1673 and 1678 had their clothing supplied by the central staff, and again Fox retained their Off Reckonings to cover the cost.[50] All these units were temporary wartime levies and unlikely to be on foot long enough to cover the cost of their own uniform. To have asked the officers to have supplied clothing would have resulted in almost certain financial loss for them, whereas Fox had the assurance that any of the clothing fund not met by the soldiers' Off Reckonings would be made up by the Treasury. In none of these instances were single contractors employed by the army. Tailors and suppliers were hired when and where they were required on a temporary basis: John Allen, Josiah Print, Edward Reddish and Monsieur St Giles Vannier were all used at one time or another to make items of army clothing. Ceremonial uniforms for the Life Guards were ordered through the Royal Wardrobe.[51]

This era has been pictured as one of military splendour with puppet-like soldiers dressed in exotic creations of all the colours of the rainbow, but the facts do not bear out this popular fantasy. No common soldier had a change of coat or breeches for years at a time, and after a short while he must have looked ragged and dirty. His coat was made from cloth which was not pre-shrunk so that the first shower of rain must have made this, and his felt hat, badly misshapen. The romantic vision of the 'red coat' was far removed from the reality.

3 *Weapons, drill and tactics*

Weapons and equipment differed little from those which had been in use during the Civil Wars. Muskets were still of the matchlock variety, although they no longer required a forked rest when fired, whilst the unwieldy pike continued as an important infantry weapon. Neither had the efficiency of the musket improved; it remained inaccurate, of short range, with a very slow rate of fire. As if these disadvantages were not sufficient, the quality of these arms was poor, costing little to manufacture and consequently breaking very easily.[52] A report of 30 September 1674 listed 403 muskets of the 1st Foot Guards as defective and in need of repair,[53] approximately one-half of all the firearms belonging to that regiment. These muskets must have been of appalling quality. Sir Palmes Fairborne estimated that between fifty and sixty arms were ruined every day at Tangier during the sieges of 1680, whilst, during the suppression of the conventicles in Southwark in July 1670, the Coldstream Guards broke sixty-seven muskets and twenty-seven pikes.[54] Some of the trouble was due to the nature of the matchlock. With such a slow rate of fire it was often impossible to reload the gun in time after its first discharge, so the soldier used it as a heavy club. This accounted for some of the breakages.

In concert with his musket the soldier carried a 'collar of bandoliers', a shoulder baldric from which were suspended twelve narrow, metal cylinders each containing a charge of powder and shot, and a sword or 'dagger for their muskets'.[55] This was the first reference to the bayonet in England, a weapon which was just beginning to be adopted by some of the continental armies. At this time the bayonet was of the 'plug' variety, a hopelessly inefficient attachment as the blade had to be inserted into the actual muzzle of the musket. Once in place the device effectively prevented the gun from being fired, and, if the bayonet was used offensively, the pressure tended to split the barrel. During 1678, when grenadier companies were added to the British regiments, the bayonet became a regular piece of equipment replacing the outmoded pike. Vauban has been accredited with the invention of the 'socket bayonet', a vast improvement over the plug type as the blade was screwed around the outside of the muzzle permitting the gun to be fired with the bayonet in place, some time around 1678. In this same year Charles II paid a special bounty to John Gibbons and Philip Russell 'for his invention of a new sort of bayonet'.[56] Probably these two gentlemen pirated the idea of the French. The bayonet superseded the pike which was made of ash and was not less than sixteen feet in length, although the soldiers normally cut them down for ease of handling.

Life Guardsmen had to provide their own horses, horse furniture, swords and pistols, whilst the king issued armour and carbines. This defensive armour consisted of a pot helmet, and back and breast plates, making both the Life Guard and the Royal Horse Guards, who also wore this equipment, into heavy cavalry or cuirassiers.[57] Their carbines were short-barrelled flintlocks which could be fired from horseback and slung over the shoulder on a buff belt when not in use. Only the Life Guards and the Royal Horse Guards had the advantage of this weapon, all the other horse regiments raised during the reign were armed only with a sword and a pair of horse pistols with fourteen-inch barrels. Dragoons, as befitted their status, carried a mixture of infantry and cavalry arms. From the foot they borrowed muskets and bayonets and took pistols from the horse.

All through the reign the infantry carried both pike and musket in the ratio of two firearms to every pike. These years witnessed the progressive decline of the pike in favour of the musket fitted with a bayonet, all over Europe, but this movement did not gather real momentum until after the introduction of the socket bayonet in 1678. Pikes were still used in the British army during the War of the Spanish Succession. There was one radical change in weaponry in the British armed forces after 1678; flintlock muskets started to replace the matchlocks. Flintlocks were more accurate, had a quicker rate of fire, were smaller, lighter and more manœuvrable, and were more reliable with fewer misfires. Horse carbines had always been fitted with a flintlock, but adoption by the foot was much slower. The

Admiral's Regiment had been armed with flintlocks from its formation in 1664, for sea spray was unkind to lighted matches and pikes were useless on board ship.[58] On 10 December 1680, 127 recruits were sent to Tangier; one-third were armed with flintlocks, one-third with matchlocks, and one-third with pikes.[59] The entire Coldstream Guards were rearmed with pikes and flintlocks in 1683, and one year later even the lesser regiments received a quota of the new guns.[60] Total evolution was slow and the flintlock did not wholly replace the matchlock until after 1702.

English military theory, such as it was after 1660, was based on past precedent and experience. The leading figures in the army, York, Craven, Rupert and Oxford, had all studied the arts of war either during the Thirty Years' War in Germany or in their own Civil Wars. The younger men who saw modern active service in France, Holland and Tangier did not rise to martial prominence until the late 1680s and 1690s, and so the Restoration army was steeped in heritage and the lessons of England's own little wars. This was not the disadvantage that it might appear. Differences in the military theory of 1640 and 1660 were minimal; weapons altered but little, drill and tactics were much the same, and no important innovations had taken place within the realm of minor tactics. In strategy, Turenne, Condé, Louvois, Louis XIV and Montecuculi were rapidly altering the whole conception of warfare, but this did not concern the British. The fact that Richard Elton's *Complete Body of the Art Military*, originally published in 1650, could be republished, unaltered, in 1668 speaks volumes for military development in England. Until the flintlock and bayonet became standard at the end of the century there was no real incentive or requirement to adjust drill and minor tactics.

The principal British military theorist was Sir James Turner. He saw active service in both the Thirty Years' War and the English Civil Wars, ending his career as lieutenant-colonel of the Scottish Foot Guards under Charles II. Turner's thoughts reflect his limitations,[61] sound, sane and sensible, but his conclusions look backward rather than forward. Another important writer was Roger Boyle, Earl of Orrery,[62] but he was more parochial than Turner, basing his ideas upon his own limited experiences in the Civil Wars in Ireland. With judgments founded upon the miserable and disorderly skirmishes which passed for battles in Ireland, Orrery's work does not possess great weight. It is further hindered by the fact that Orrery planned to write a second volume containing 'the greatest, most useful, and the most intricate parts of the Art of War'.[63] The book was politically useful to Charles II. Dedicated to the king it indirectly supported the concept of a standing army, arguing that the best way to prevent war was to ensure that sufficient preparations were taken to deter others. As a part-time soldier, Orrery had more right to express such a view than England's numerous 'armchair strategists', but the army was regarded as politically and socially evil and it needed a more competent apologist than Orrery to make it acceptable.

The Restoration army never fought together as a single unit, most of it never saw active service in twenty-five years, and it rarely drilled in formations above company size. There was no opportunity of experimenting with martial theories. Regardless of this the first official drill manual of the English standing army was issued in the early 1670s. During May 1674 a circular letter addressed to all colonels and garrison governors informed them of a new drill manual about to be issued,[64] containing the revisions resulting from the lessons of the Third Dutch War. Thomas Newcombe, the king's printer, set about publishing the initial 100 copies of this *Abridgement of English Military Discipline* late in 1675,[65] to be followed by a further 1,500 in 1676. Late in 1679 the *Abridgement* was adopted by the Scottish army, for Charles was determined to have

> one method established for the exercising of his forces, in all his Dominions, [and] he hath already, upon that consideration, appointed An Abridgement of Military Discipline to be made use of by his forces in his Kingdoms of Scotland and Ireland.[66]

This manual gave a uniform system of drill, words of command, and minor tactics for cavalry, dragoons, grenadiers and foot. Such standardisation was badly needed:

> The King saw the Scots Regiment exercise the French Way, and it pleases so well that the King says he likes it far better than ours, which the Prince, Coll. Russell, and all the English officers almost do not, and I know not if we shall be ordered to change.[67]

Buckingham further confused the issue in the following year when he exercised the Blackheath Army,

although not at all to the officers' satisfaction, who say he is too much Frenchified in all he does, and brings new terms amongst the soldiery which they have not been used to.[68]

France dominated European military fashion in the same way that Prussia was to do in the eighteenth century. Buckingham, an early convert to the wonders of France, and Monmouth, a protégé of Turenne and the army of Louis XIV, succeeded in making the 'Frenchified' drill victorious over the old, native system. The *Abridgement* was in strict accordance with contemporary French manuals to the subsequent advantage of the British army, for France could teach much to the rather ponderous and amateurish soldiers of England.

Whether the drill methods in the *Abridgement* were ever put into practice is a matter of conjecture. Although the great age of linear tactics was just around the corner, the reign of Charles II witnessed only the birth of this system. For such tactics to be effective each soldier had to be trained into an automaton, but it is doubtful if such vigorous training went on in England. There was a training ground at Barnet and the army was permitted to exercise on the Artillery Ground at Moorfields, but training was not a fashionable pastime, being considered largely unnecessary amongst garrison companies and field regiments. References to troops exercising are few and far between in Charles's reign when compared to the mass of such to be found in the reign of his brother. Drill and training were synonymous. Parade ground movements were precisely the same as those performed on the battlefield, giving ceremonial marching and display some genuine significance. The six standing regiments drilled and paraded quite often in public, so their efficiency must have been reasonable.

To make it even better Solomon de Fobert optimistically presented the king with plans for establishing a military academy in London. This scheme was nodded at favourably and then quietly shelved by the Earl of Essex and the Duke of Monmouth:[69] in a country scared by the Popish Plot, 1679 was not the ideal time to contemplate such designs. Had Fobert's proposals for a school where young gentlemen could receive a thorough basic education with a military bias come about, England might have been provided with an officer corps in her future years. The ultimate rejection of the project left England reliant on her officer class without professional training or specialist knowledge.[70]

4 *Peacetime service in England*

Being so small, there was a limit to the duties which the army could perform. More important, it was so unpopular with both politicians and public that it was thought best to restrict its activities to the minimum and render it as harmless as possible. Thus the army spent most of its time sitting idly in quarters, occasionally being called upon for some special task, or taking part in ceremonial duties connected with the king and the court.

The foot regiment which was stationed nearest to the City of London supplied the guards for the Tower, the palace at St James's, and Whitehall.[71] It fell to the Life Guards personally to escort the king wherever he went. Each of the three troops was divided into four squadrons, or divisions, each of fifty men, commanded by one of the principal commissioned officers of the troop. Two divisions from each troop did one day's duty in every six, attending the king and queen, or the Duke and Duchess of York when they went 'near home'.[72] If all four royal persons left London then they were escorted by detachments from all three troops. One of the captains of the Life Guards had the tedious duty of always walking next to the king sporting an ebony truncheon with a gold head engraved with the king's cypher and crown. Before the Restoration and the Interregnum it had been the tradition for the Band of Gentleman Pensioners to be in constant attendance on the king, with their captain marching next to the monarch. The usurpation of this role by the military was bitterly resented by the Pensioners,[73] causing a running feud between them and the Life Guards. These ceremonial functions required that portions of the army were permanently stationed in and around London; the Life Guards were at Westminster and Whitehall, whilst two companies of the Foot Guards were posted in Scotland Yard. Two companies of the Coldstreamers were quartered in St James's Park and Palace, and one troop from the Royal Horse Guards was permanently on duty in Southwark. Such an arrangement also gave the king a solid phalanx of troops to quell any political riots or disturbances which might spring up in London.

Connected closely with the duty of guarding the king were the reviews of the army in their full, uniformed splendour for the benefit of visiting dignitaries. The Russian Ambassador was received by the army in 1662,[74] and in the following year the French envoy, Cominges, was treated to a display in Hyde Park.[75] When the army was rapidly expanded for the projected French War of 1678, the units camped on Hounslow Heath were inspected by the king on 22 May and again on 29 June.[76] The most famous parade of the reign was in 1684 involving the majority of the army being reviewed on Blackheath, and permitting Nathan Brooks to record his detailed accounts of uniform and equipment.[77] Some formation drill was performed at these gatherings for they were virtually the only occasions when regiments came together as single units.

During the spring it was the custom of the king to travel to Newmarket for the horse racing and selected units of the army had to accompany him all along the route from London. This was accomplished in prearranged stages so that each detachment travelled a short distance with the royal party and was then relieved by another. This function was performed by the horse as the foot were too slow, but once the sovereign reached Newmarket there were always some companies from the Foot Guards posted near at hand. The Duke of York was subjected to similar attentions whenever he left London.

One of the great events of the age was the siege of Maestricht by the French in 1673. Here the great Vauban had first matured his system of three parallel trenches[78] to capture one of the largest and most formidable fortresses in Europe in just three weeks. This aroused some enthusiasm in England, for not only was England allied with France but many of her noblemen, Monmouth amongst them, had been present at the siege as volunteers in the French army. On 21 August 1674, a replica of Maestricht was built at Windsor and detachments of the English army tried their hand at a reconstruction of the siege:

There was approaches and a formal siege, against a work with Bastions, Bulwarks, Ramparts, Palisades . . . Hornworks, counterscarps, etc: in imitation of the City of Maestricht, newly taken by the

French . . . defended against the Duke of Monmouth (newly come from that real siege) who (with the Duke of York) attacked it with a little army, to show their skill in tactics; so on Saturday night, they made their approaches, opened trenches, raised batteries, [took] the counterscarp, shot, mines sprung, parties sent out, attempts of raising the siege, prisoners taken, parleys, & in short all the circumstances of a formal siege to appearance, & what is most strange, all without disorder or ill accident, but to the great satisfaction of a thousand spectators, when being night it made a formidable show, and was really very divertisant.[79]

Another elaborate war-game had taken place three years earlier in 1671, when a mock battle between the 'Loyalists' and the 'Mutineers' had been fought on the Artillery Ground before the Lord Mayor of London.[80] These weird events were the equivalent of modern manœuvres, and as the army did no serious fighting throughout the reign these ersatz battles assumed some importance.

On 14 February 1669, soldiers accompanied the king to the state opening of Parliament for the first time, a development not viewed with favour by contemporaries as it represented 'a sovereign entering upon the exercise of the legislative power under the awe and influence of the sword'.[81] The ceremonial aspects of military life must not be taken too lightly for during the troublesome years of the Popish Plot, the Exclusion Crisis, and the Rye House Conspiracy, the army as a bodyguard for the king was a political necessity, whilst its very existence served as a stabilising influence on the more extreme politicians.[82] Without the indirect threat of the standing army, London could well have been seriously troubled during the Exclusion Crisis.

England had no organised police force in the seventeenth century, most of her roads and countryside being left to the mercy of robbers and highwaymen. The parish constable offered some security but his effectiveness was limited to say the least, and the only body which could execute the more robust police duties was the army. In the countryside the bulk of the work fell on the Royal Horse Guards, with occasional assistance from the Life Guards. One of their most frequent assignments was to escort bullion to and from London; a troop of horse often had to convoy money from the Navy Pay Office in Broad Street to the dockyards at Harwich or Portsmouth.[83] Money raised from taxes and assessments, as well as the revenue from the customs and excise, had to be brought to London under military guard.[84] So insecure were the roads that wagons belonging to long-distance tradesmen had to be escorted by troops, although this more lowly role was usually allotted to foot soldiers.[85]

When not guarding specific convoys the cavalry were frequently used to patrol the highways apprehending robbers and highwaymen. There were not enough troops to maintain continuous patrols on all major roads, but when an area suffered a severe epidemic of highway robbery then assistance was requested and a troop of the Royal Horse Guards was sent to assist the local constables and magistrates.[86] Sometimes lawlessness became so general that troopers of the Royal Horse Guards were instructed to ride around whole counties in groups of five or six in an effort to reduce the number of offences.[87] None of these patrolling expeditions was over-successful as new orders for similar operations occur repeatedly amongst the War Office records.

The people of Gloucestershire and Worcestershire constantly attempted to grow their own tobacco, and when the problem became too large for the sheriffs to handle a troop of horse was summoned to aid the Surveyor-General of the Farmers of the Customs to destroy the crops.[88] Herefordshire, Monmouthshire and even Oxfordshire were all affected by this desire to cheat the customs and no amount of intervention by the military was able to cure them of the habit. In the absence of a police force the transfer of prisoners from one part of the country to another fell to the army. A commanded party from the Plymouth garrison moved Major-General John Lambert from his prison in Guernsey to Plymouth in 1670.[89] The army had to operate as police in the town, as well as in the country, preserving the peace and maintaining law and order when this duty became too much for the local magistracy. Two companies of the Coldstream Guards and a troop of the Royal Horse Guards were sent to Southwark in May 1670 'to be assisting to the Lord Lieutenant, deputy lieutenants, and Justices of Peace of the said Borough for the preservation of the peace'.[90] In such cases the army detachments came under the direct command of the civil authorities, being the servants of the Crown and its deputies.

During the troubles of 1683 the military were frequently called upon to help apprehend wanted men and search properties.[91]

Following the declaration of war on the United Provinces in 1672, the navy was rapidly increased to a war footing by the use of the press gang. Many of the more unwilling volunteers soon deserted from the fleet, and the army was ordered in to prevent deserters coming ashore near Rochester and Chatham, thus assuming the role of modern military police.[92] Two years later the press was still rounding up recruits for the navy, but the merchant seamen of Wapping and Shadwell received them in such a manner that a company of foot had to be sent to preserve the peace and allow the press gangs to operate freely.[93] Even the actual dockyard at Chatham had to be guarded by troops late in 1678.

'Seditious Conventicles' occurred in England from time to time and when they did it was the army's task to disperse them and break up the meetings. Colonel John Frescheville of the Royal Horse Guards suppressed 'dangerous attempts at seditious conventicles', near York in 1663, whilst the Life Guards and 'some foot' broke up meetings of Quakers, Anabaptists and Presbyterians around London during 1670.[94] These were years of unusual turbulence in England and large-scale riots and disturbances of the peace were fairly frequent in London and the larger towns. When these broke out the government had to employ the army in force. Easter Monday in 1668 saw the London apprentices start a huge affray aimed at the destruction of the brothels around Moorfields. The Life Guard was sent in and the ensuing struggle became a straightforward fight between the civilians and the hated red coats, with the latter hard put to quell the mob.[95] When the Lord Mayor of London refused to lower his ceremonial sword on entering the College of the Templars in 1669, a riot broke out which was only stopped by the intervention of the army, and even then it took all night.[96]

In 1676 it was found necessary to have some soldiers on duty at the theatre in Dorset Garden 'to keep the peace there . . . so that no offence may be given to the spectators, nor no affront given to the actors'.[97] In its function as a police force and general kill-joy the army was odious to the public, being seen as the instrument of coercive authority, but it was one of the only organised bodies of men in England and had to undertake tasks which are now executed by specialist groups. One of these was fire-fighting. Fire was the major danger to urban life but also the one with which the community was least able to deal. One hundred and ninety-one men of the 1st and 2nd Foot Guards shared £25 from the king 'for hindering the spreading of the fire in Southwark', on 26 May 1676. Three years later £39 was divided between 297 soldiers for 'working at the fire in the Temple', but £42 2*s* was granted to the seven gunners who assisted at the same blaze.[98] The usual method of halting a serious fire was to create fire-breaks by blowing up selected buildings and for this service the Ordnance Office had to supply gunners and powder. 'A very dreadful fire' in the Waterhouse at the lower end of York Street consumed the whole building and several others near it, but was stopped by the timely assistance of the Foot Guards and the blowing up of two houses.[99]

The cavalry were kept well occupied with their police and ceremonial duties, and, when quartered in large towns, the standing foot regiments could play a useful role. The same cannot be said for the independent garrison companies which stayed in their stations all the time. For these men life must have been indescribably boring and monotonous, and it is difficult to establish how these men filled in their time apart from guarding their strong-point. If Colonel Hutchinson is to be fully believed then these soldiers were fit for little else:

When he came to the castle, he found it a lamentable old ruined place, almost a mile distant from the town, the rooms all out of repair, not weather proof, no kind of accommodation for lodging or diet, or any conveniency of life. Before he came, there were not above half a dozen soldiers in it, and a poor lieutenant with his wife and children, and two or three cannoniers, and a few guns almost dismounted, upon rotten carriages; but at the colonel's coming thither, a company of foot besides were sent from Dover to help to guard the place, pitiful weak fellows, half-starved and eaten up with vermin, whom the governor of Dover cheated of half their pay, and the other half they spent in drink. These had no beds, but a nasty court of guard, where a sutler lived, within a partition made of boards, with his wife and family, and this was all the accommodation the colonel had for his victuals, which were bought at a dear rate in the town, and most horribly dressed at the sutler's. . . . The captain of the castle, one

Freeman, had all this while a chamber which was a little warmer, and had a bed in it, but this he reserved, intending to set a rate upon it, and this too was so dark that one could not have read by the fire or the bedside without a candle at noon day.[100]

Life in a garrison, Sandown Castle in Kent in this instance, was not pleasant. Most of the independent companies were composed of pensioned or superannuated soldiers, a place in a garrison often being given as the reward for a lifetime's devotion to the army. So arduous was the life.

A final and universally detested duty for the army was service on board the fleet in the capacity of marines. Naturally horse regiments were exempt from this service, but the burden was otherwise shared equally between the standing regiments of foot. In time of war all the regiments furnished a detachment to fight with the fleet, and this practice continued into the reign of Queen Anne when a separate Marine Corps was founded.[101] During the Second and Third Dutch Wars it was the Admiral's Regiment which first embarked,[102] followed by companies out of the other infantry regiments. Normally about two companies from every foot regiment were serving at sea at any one time[103] and these were rotated during the year.[104] Even newly levied units had to send their quotas for sea service, and such unlikely formations as the Irish Foot Guards, and men from the garrisons of Newcastle, Dover, Rochester, and Deal. A special marine regiment was raised under Prince Rupert in 1672 for the duration of the Third Dutch War solely for marine service, but it was disbanded in 1674. In peacetime the fleet was not regularly manned by the army, but when certain punitive expeditions were undertaken then an army detachment was sent on board. Men of the Coldstream Guards accompanied the squadron of Sir Thomas Allen to the Mediterranean when he went to check the activities of the Algerian pirates in 1670,[105] whilst Sir Robert Holmes's expedition to Guinea in 1664 took with it fifty men of the same regiment.[106]

5 *The medical service*

As the army of Charles II undertook very little fighting, the methods and organisation of its medical service did not come to the fore and were largely still untried in 1685. The casualties from the two Dutch Wars caused the navy to look to its laurels in this department, but not the army.

The Flanders Expedition of 1678 was an example of the army administration operating on active service, even though the corps did not fire a shot in anger, but virtually no mention is made of any medical service in any of the extant papers relating to the arrangements for the campaign. No ambulances were provided, there were no proper field or base hospitals, and the system was quite incapable of dealing with sickness amongst the soldiery let alone action casualties. Sick men were taken to Bruges, the unofficial base hospital, housed in whatever lodgings the local people could offer—convents, private houses, tents—and, when recovered, were taken to Brussels and then sent back to their regiments.[107] As late as 1692 British casualties from the Battle of Steenkirk were taken into Brussels and left to the goodwill and charity of the population as the army could not cope with them. At Tangier the hospital was built on marshy ground and was mostly full of soldiers and women suffering from venereal disease.[108]

However, the total lack of a medical corps was of little real significance. Medicine in the seventeenth century was primitive. The curing of disease relied on guesswork and good luck whilst the treatment of physical injury was more in the hands of the Almighty than the surgeon. Even with sufficient hospitals, doctors and ambulances, little could have been accomplished with the sick and wounded without antiseptics and anaesthesia. Bleeding, purging and blistering were the main weapons of the physician, although quinine, the 'Jesuits' Bark', had recently been introduced into England, whilst amputation was practically the only method available to the surgeon.

Every regiment, whether of horse or foot, possessed a surgeon, or 'chirurgeon', who received a commission from the king and was thus an officer of the unit. Each troop of the Life Guards had a surgeon paid at the rate of *6s* a day with the addition of a further *2s* for a horse to carry his medicine chest.[109] One surgeon served the whole of the Royal Horse Guards and each of the standing foot regiments had one surgeon assisted by a mate. Regiments raised during the emergencies of the Dutch Wars and the French War of 1678 were similarly manned.

Then, as now, physicians and surgeons regarded themselves

as two separate professions and this division was echoed in the army. The physician-general was a post specially created to assist with the rapid expansion of the army in 1678, but there was always a physician serving the Guards in peacetime.[110] Little importance was attached to this office and it was one of the first to be retrenched in financial crises. More important was the surgeon-general who was responsible for all the regimental surgeons. He had to oversee the care and attention given to sick and wounded soldiers in England and Wales, examine and appoint regimental surgeons, 'ordering all other surgeons to obey his directions', as well as provide and distribute medicines.[111] In this last task he was aided by the apothecary-general. This official issued 'internal medicines' to the regiments whilst the surgeons were responsible for the 'external medicines'.[112] For this the apothecary-general was allowed *6d* per man every year from the Contingency Fund held by the Paymaster-General, and the regimental surgeons were permitted a similar amount for their requirements.

To be in hospital was a serious matter for a soldier. Not only was there a grave risk of not coming out alive, but whilst he was incarcerated he received no pay. Fourpence out of his subsistence was sent directly to the surgeon-general to cover the cost of his nursing and food, and the balance of *2d* or *4d* was given to the sick man's company commander to pay for any clothing or equipment which might be found necessary when the soldier left hospital.[113] This vicious system whereby a soldier had to pay to be ill was used in England and on foreign service stations.

A surgeon's commission was not one of the more lucrative posts in the army and was little sought after. When the army had been expanded for the projected French War of 1678 there was an acute shortage of surgeons for the new regiments, and financial inducements had to be offered in order to obtain men from civilian life for even temporary commissions.[114] It was a dirty and ill-rewarded task and in a community which had a low regard for the medical profession and hated the army the lot of a military surgeon was not a happy one.

IV

Discipline and the Law

THE precise legal status of the army of Charles II was ill-defined and confused. The sole piece of legislation which gave any guidance to contemporaries was the Petition of Right of 1628. Although this was not a statute of Parliament but merely a statement that existing grievances were illegal according to the law as it then stood, it did receive the royal assent thereby forcing the judges to interpret the law in the light of its requests. The petition did not create new laws but simply emphasised certain aspects of the standing law which Parliament considered were being ignored by the king.[1] Much of the petition was concerned with martial law and the quartering of troops on civilians, issues which arose from the serious friction between soldiers and civilians during the preparations for the expedition to relieve La Rochelle in 1627. Charles I and Buckingham had given commissions for the operation of martial law amongst the levies, resulting in a number of soldiers and sailors being imprisoned or executed without recourse to the proper channels of the common law.[2] Infinitely worse, many of the military received light punishments from the courts martial when they would have been severely dealt with by the civilian courts:

> Also, sundry grievous offenders by colour thereof, claiming an exemption, have escaped the punishment due to them by the laws and statutes of this your realm, by reason that divers of your officers and ministers of justice have unjustly refused, or forborn to proceed against such offenders, according to the same laws and statutes, upon pretence that the said offenders were punishable only by martial law.[3]

The Commons saw this declaration of martial law as a potential threat to their position as the supreme legislature of England. Accordingly, martial law was declared to be 'wholly and directly contrary to the said laws and statutes of this your realm . . . and that hereafter no commissions of like nature may issue forth to any person or persons whatsoever'. On the basis of this precedent, martial law in England was illegal, apparently in either peace or war.

Before embarking on their futile voyage for La Rochelle the soldiers and sailors had been quartered on private families all over the south of England 'against their wills [having] been compelled to receive them into their houses, and there suffer them to sojourn, against the laws and customs of this realm'. Such action undermined the liberty of the subject and so the petition demanded of the king 'that your people be not so burdened in time to come'. Thus, the quartering of troops on civilians without their consent was illegal.

Between the petition and the raising of the Restoration army intervened the armies of the Civil Wars and the Interregnum, all of which ignored the law and billeted their men on civilians as a matter of course.[4] By the time of the Restoration the very ideas of army quarters and martial law had become utterly repugnant to the population, yet it was these two questions which were to remain at the heart of civil–military relations over the ensuing twenty-five years.

What was martial law? In a time of war or national emergency the monarch had the power to suspend the workings of the common law and replace it with a written code of regulations enforced by the military, which applied to both civilians and soldiers alike. This meant that the harsh rules which governed soldiers temporarily covered civilians as well, thus removing their basic liberties under the law. During the reign of Charles II, martial law was never brought into England; to have done so would have been contrary to the Petition of Right and political suicide. In foreign service stations—Tangier, Dunkirk, Portugal, Flanders in 1678—martial law was accepted as the only possible method of ruling a garrison far from home, so these forces automatically lost their common law rights the moment that they left England. At Tangier the 'Articles of War' applied to both soldiers and civilians alike until a Court of

Record was established to take care of civilian offenders. Under martial law the arbitrary code was administered by a court martial, a panel of military officers guided by no jury and with little provision for legal representation. Declaration of martial law was a prerogative of the king, no reference to Parliament being required.

Only once in his reign did the king have the temerity to even consider the introduction of martial law into England, and then it was only supposed to apply to the soldiers and not to the civilians. As the army for the Zealand Expedition assembled on Blackheath during the summer of 1673, it was thought best to operate martial law over the army in order to control such a large body of men. Immediately, the Lord Keeper, Sir Orlando Bridgeman, objected that this was directly contrary to the Petition of Right, but his boldness merely resulted in his being dismissed and replaced by the Earl of Shaftesbury as Lord Chancellor.[5] By 13 June the Articles of War, the written code for martial law, had been printed and were ready for publication to the troops,[6] and a court martial had been erected and was ready to proceed with the administration of the new justice. At this point the authorities were overcome with caution. The Articles had still not been published by 18 July, no one having discovered the courage to put them into effect. The excuse for inaction was that the 'horrid oath' contained in the Articles forced a man to swear to obey the king's commands in all circumstances, but no one was precisely sure of what the position would be when martial law was revoked. Would those who had acted illegally under the umbrella of martial law become liable to prosecution under the common law? In addition, many Members of Parliament grew seriously worried about the possibility of the declaration of martial law, but their concern was ultimately groundless for the Articles were never put into operation: 'Parliament men and lawyers do not care to hear of martial law; and, without that, I do not see how an army can be governed.'[7]

The maintenance of discipline in the Blackheath Army was a serious problem for the higher officers without the weight of martial law to support their authority. All that could be done was to apprehend offenders and send them before the local magistrates for trial under the normal process of law. When the army landed at Great Yarmouth, Schomberg complained bitterly of the trouble he was experiencing in keeping the men in some sort of order without recourse to martial law, especially when his officers set such a terrible example.[8] He was unable to execute a soldier or order any capital punishments without the official suspension of the common law within the army, and his officers were afraid to take matters into their own hands for fear that Parliament would call them to task for it. Quite a number of the officers were actually Members of Parliament themselves and hence suffered from divided allegiance, making Schomberg's task yet more difficult. Fortunately, Schomberg was a resourceful and well tried commander, who, although only able to govern by 'menacings', managed to maintain reasonable discipline at Yarmouth. Many of the soldiers complained that his methods were too severe and that his French discipline was far harder than the English even without the help of martial law.

There was one other type of law connected with the army: military law. This was not law in the sense of the common law and martial law, but a collection of rules and regulations for running the army issued by the king. This military law was no more than a code of professional conduct, although it was intended to form a separate justice for the army in England in peacetime. The theory ran that the army, which was the property of the king and not of Parliament, was to be answerable to this prerogative law issued by the monarch and not to the common law. Viewing itself as the keeper of the peace and an impartial dealer of justice, the army thought itself to be exempt from the common law and responsible only to its commander, the king. In effect, military law was the will of the sovereign passed on to the senior officers.[9] These orders were codified into various sets of Articles and Rules of War,[10] and the principle of the co-existence of the common and military law was clearly laid down in the Articles of 1666:

> No magistrate of a town or county shall imprison an officer or soldier in our pay unless it be for High Treason, or impression of treason, or being an accessory thereunto, or for killing or being an accessory unto the death or robbery of any person not being an officer or soldier.[11]

By the Petition of Right and past precedent there was only one law in England, that as represented by Statute of Parliament. From 1666, the year in which the first codification of military law appeared, the Commons insisted that soldiers should come under the terms of the common law like everyone else, whilst the king and his army were adamant that the military should be governed by their own special articles of war, being answerable to the common law only in cases of murder, treason and felony. There was little that the Commons could do. The army was as much a part of the accepted Royal Prerogative as was the King's Household, and it was within the power of the monarch to run them both as he wished, provided that neither the common law nor the privileges and position of Parliament were infringed. This was Parliament's only substantial case; by operating under a prerogative law the army formed itself into a separate class outside the known law of the land, undermining the authority of the Lords and Commons.

With such a diversity of opinion, a compromise had to be reached. On 4 September 1663 Sir Orlando Bridgeman wrote to Clarendon about two army officers who had resisted the civil power when accused of felony, claiming that it had no power to arrest them. Bridgeman, always an advocate of the dominance of the common law, remarked that acceptance of such a principle would be very damaging to the king.[12] The Government tried to have the 1666 Articles of War brought before Parliament as a bill, but after one reading the Commons rejected the proposal.[13] Gradually, a balance between the two conflicting systems was evolved, although it was always unofficial. If a soldier or officer committed a major crime against a civilian then he was answerable to the law of the land, with the proviso that it was normal to ask the permission of the offender's commanding officer before making an arrest. Once this was obtained then a military man could be dealt with by the common law in the same way as a civilian.[14]

Michael Hale of the Life Guard was arrested in 1675 on the suit of one, Henry Richards, without the permission of his commanding officer. The case went before the Privy Council for a ruling. In the following year this protocol was broken when Private Anthony Weston of the 1st Foot Guards was arrested and incarcerated in the Marshalsea on the suit of James Colmore without the prior permission of his captain. In both instances the substance of the complaint was not the fact of the arrest, but that it had been done without first seeking the senior officer's permission. Mostly these matters were dealt with amicably, as in 1684 when Captain Hutton wrote to William Blathwayt about one of his corporals, William Wisdom, who had been recaptured after deserting. Hutton was uncertain whether Wisdom should have been dealt with under the common law or the military law, and neither was Blathwayt who passed the case on to the attorney-general for his opinions.[15]

There were many exceptions to the rule of peaceful settlement as there were bound to be when legal demarcation was so ill-defined. Soldiers were jealous of their privileged status under military law, whilst Parliament was equally jealous that its power was being eroded. Sir John Shaw told of an incident at Colchester in which this very clash of interests occurred. After a soldier had seriously wounded a civilian, the Mayor asked permission from a commissioned officer to arrest the man. This was duly given and the soldier taken into custody, but no sooner had this taken place than the man's comrades marched to the 'Sessions Hall with their muskets charged with powder and ball'. They succeeded in breaking into the magistrate's court where they pointed their weapons at the gentlemen of the bench and demanded the immediate release of their colleague. When the Chairman tried to reason with them they 'hallooed and made a noise', forcing the magistrates to adjourn the session and free the prisoner. Secretary Coventry was able to assure Sir John Shaw that several men of the Earl of Ogle's Regiment had since been cashiered for misdemeanour.[16] In the same year there was a serious riot in London when several soldiers tried to rescue one of their number who had been imprisoned for debt, the relief attempt being led by Captain Robert Walton and his sergeant of the 1st Foot Guards. The Privy Council ordered both to be cashiered and then delivered to the civil magistrates.[17]

There were many more instances of co-operation than of dispute between the military and the common law. One hundred and three soldiers of Sir William Lockhart's Regiment mutinied at Ashford in Kent, assaulted their officers, and stole a great deal of money. With assistance from the King's Troop of the Life Guard, six of the worst offenders were apprehended and brought before a justice of the peace who remanded them in custody in Canterbury Gaol. They were then prosecuted according to the 'due process of the law'.[18]

Whereas Charles had contemplated introducing martial law in 1673, the thought did not enter his head in 1678. He allowed his army of 10,000 assembled on Hounslow Heath to be governed by the common law and military law, 'for as yet the army is not so great but that the Kingston Assizes are better than Martial Law'.[19] Soldiers who committed felonies were hanged at Tyburn in the same way as civilians, and, more important, military offences—desertion, mutiny, disobedience—could be adjudged either treason or felony and tried before a common law court. In practice this confused arrangement made some sense. Parliament and the civil authorities made little attempt to interfere with the internal running of the army, being content to allow the king to administer it by royal prerogative without reference to themselves. In return, if a member of the army broke the criminal or civil law, then the majority of officers were quite willing to grant permission for the offender to be tried and punished according to the law of the land.

The judicial organ of the army was the court martial. Technically, the court martial could only be used for the administration of martial law, but in Charles's reign it was used to carry out military law, and all the various Articles of War provided for courts martial and went to some lengths to describe the manner in which they should be conducted. The court martial was a toothless and ineffective body. It dared not execute any sentence on a soldier which extended to loss of life or limb, or even liberty; such actions came under the provisions of the common law and the royal prerogative no longer stretched to overriding the law or running a parallel system. All a court martial could do was to cashier men from the army, in much the same way as a private club or institution may accept and dismiss members within the terms of their own charters. Only on foreign stations, Tangier and Dunkirk, did the court martial have any power.

Records of general and regimental courts martial in England are scant, indicating that there were very few held between 1660 and 1685. A register of 'General Courts Martial, confirmed at home',[20] has been partially destroyed and only a fragment remains. Prior to 1666 there were no courts martial as the first code of military law did not appear until that year, but after that there were only twenty-one general courts martial until 1685. Thus, the court martial was hardly ever used in England and nearly all offences were dealt with by the common law courts where military crimes were translated into treason and felony. The court martial was little more than a gentlemen's debating chamber where officers thrashed out their personal disputes. Five of the cases were over alleged false musters and the most severe punishment given was the cashiering of Lieutenant-Colonel John Pinchbeck in 1673.[21]

A case in 1666 arose over a difference in the company accounts of Sir Charles Wheeler, but all the court did was to appoint two referees to settle the matter. Typical cases were those which involved officers fighting or duelling when on duty. Lieutenant George Lascelles and Ensign Roger Kirkby were suspended from their commands 'and left to his Majesty's mercy', for fighting on the guard, but this had no effect on their careers, both achieving captaincies soon after. Ensign James Hilton was cashiered in 1684 for wounding Captain Henry Rowe, and this was the worst punishment given to an officer by a general court martial in England.

Only three of the twenty-one cases involved other ranks. Corporal Pye of the Royal Horse Guards was cashiered for quarrelling with his cornet. Private Alexander Ellis was accused of using 'mutinous and offensive words', to Captain John Peter of the Coldstream Guards, whilst Private Thomas Hanslope was found guilty of uttering 'mutinous and opprobrious words' against Sir Thomas Daniell. Only one notice of a regimental court martial survives. Privates Albany Headley, Thomas Bowers and Thomas Reaveley of the 1st Foot Guards were tried before a court of that regiment in 1674 for 'heinous misdemeanours'. They were banished into foreign service. Probably there were more regimental courts martial than this.

In general, military law was largely theoretical and the common law covered both civilians and soldiers. False musters and disputes amongst officers were of little concern or interest to anyone outside the army and Parliament was content to let the army run itself in such matters, but as soon as an officer or ranker broke the criminal or civil law then he was automatically transferred before the local magistrates for correction.

Desertion was the main offence with which the common law courts had to deal, and it was also an issue of some dispute amongst lawyers. If a soldier robbed or murdered then there was little doubt that he could be tried for a felony under the common law, but desertion was more awkward. Not recognising the standing army as legal, for never during the reign did Parliament pass a statute mentioning the legality of such a body, it was difficult for the Lords and Commons to take a serious view of desertion. Henry VII had made it a felony under certain circumstances,[22] and this had been further developed by his son.[23] In 1601 the judges confirmed that desertion from the army was punishable under the common law and represented a felony, but this only applied to temporary wartime levies and not to a standing army, which was unknown at that time. This issue was not advanced by Charles II and there was no firm definition of when desertion represented a felony, although in practice it was accepted as such. Thus it was feasible for all military offences to be translated into terms of the common law and tried before civilian courts, and not until the Mutiny Act of 1689 were military law and courts martial recognised as legal entities.[24]

If martial law had ever been introduced in England it would have been based on the codes of the various sets of military law,[25] and the Restoration army had its own legal structure to administer both types of law. The chief legal officer was the Judge Advocate General. Sir Edmund Pierce was appointed to this post in January 1661, a man well qualified having held the same rank in the army of Charles I.[26] His daily pay was 8*s* with an allowance of half a crown for the hire of a clerk.[27] Dr Samuel Barrow succeeded Pierce in 1666 and he remained in office until 1682 when George Clarke, son of the late Secretary at War, bought him out. An excellent example of the king rewarding the son of a former supporter of the Restoration, Clarke received the post in recognition of his father's services. His commission made him 'Advocate General or Judge Martial' of all the troops in England, Wales, and all other dominions, except Scotland, Ireland and Tangier, and other stations where particular Advocates General had been appointed.[28] The Judge Advocate's title is misleading as he was not a judge but the principal administrative officer for military law; he arranged for courts martial to be held, took the depositions and informations of witnesses, ensured that the accused were detained in the proper custody, and conducted the prosecution at the trial.

Each regiment had its own Provost-Marshal (Martial) whose duty it was to apprehend offenders and hold them in custody until the time of the court martial, or until they were handed over to the civil magistrates.[29] The four standing foot regiments had one Marshal each, paid 4*s* a day, whilst the Life Guards and Royal Horse Guards shared one 'Marshal to the Horse', who received 7*s* a day.[30] This gentleman acted as the deputy to the Judge Advocate, and the Marshal of the 1st Foot Guards was the senior Marshal of all the foot.

A provost's position was reasonably lucrative. Any prisoner in his custody had to forfeit the whole of his pay during the first day of his detention, and thereafter three-quarters of each day's wages until he left the Marshal's care. During the expansion of the army in 1678 all the Marshals were organised under the supervision of a Provost-Marshal General.[31]

On his arrest a soldier was taken to the regimental Marshal to be remanded in custody. Within forty-eight hours of his commitment, informations and an indictment had to be laid before the Judge Advocate, but if this time limit was not met then the prisoner was automatically set at liberty and the charges dropped. When in possession of the indictment, the Judge Advocate decided whether the offence was suitable for trial at a court martial, or whether it ought to be handled by the magistrates. If a court martial was thought necessary then the Judge Advocate informed the Secretary at War who proceeded to nominate the regiments which were to forward officers to serve on the court. Should the accused be a subaltern or a ranker then any thirteen commissioned officers could sit with one of them appointed as president. However, if a field or general officer was on trial then no one below the rank of captain could sit in judgment. General courts martial of the army dealt with all officers and any cases which might involve punishments of death or mutilation. Non-commissioned officers and privates whose crimes warranted lesser sentences were tried before regimental courts martial where they were judged by five commissioned officers from their own regiment.

As soon as the court was in session the charges against the

defendant were made known and his answer to them read out. Witnesses were then sworn in by the Judge Advocate and cross-examined by the bench of officers *viva voce*, and any depositions which had previously been sworn before the Judge Advocate were heard. Both the prosecution and the defence were allowed to produce witnesses, and at the end of all the evidence the officers considered their verdict. A majority vote was decisive, although the President had a casting voice in the event of 'an equality of votes'.[32] The sentence had to be in accordance with that specifically mentioned in the Articles of War and was pronounced with due solemnity by the President of the Court. Following this the man's regimental Provost was given a warrant to execute the sentence on a given day at an appointed time.

In England, even if a court passed a sentence inflicting physical punishment, it was unable to carry it out, but in Tangier the courts martial operated under the full rigours of martial law. Punishments were savage, although congruous with those in other countries and not far removed from the criminal code in England, and normally carried out in front of the man's assembled regiment. Death by hanging was the reward for desertion, mutiny, or cowardice, although the Tangier courts martial usually allowed soldiers a more honourable death by firing squad. Theft and insubordination were punishable by flogging, riding the wooden horse, tying neck and heels, or imprisonment. The latter was not a favourite correction as it took men out of action for long periods of time, a serious matter in undermanned Tangier, and it did not have the shock effect of a brutal sentence before the public eye. Tangier, Dunkirk and the Flanders Expedition of 1678 were the only stations on which the full weight of military law was applied to the army. In England, any consideration of military punishment was largely academic.[33]

Throughout England the army lived in garrison or in quarters. There was no set rule as to who went into garrison and who into quarters, but it was normal for the cavalry to be housed in towns and villages whilst the foot lived in the garrisons. A list of how the army was distributed in 1665 showed the Life Guards centred, as always, on Whitehall and Westminster, with the Royal Horse Guards based at Salisbury,

York, Uxbridge, Colesbrooke, High Wycombe, Bromley, Dartford, Aylesbury, Thame and Leyton. Apart from the duty companies of the Foot Guards in London and Westminster, the remainder of the standing infantry regiments were almost exclusively housed in garrisons.[34] When the army was enlarged in 1666, 1672 and 1678, it was impossible to fit all the new units into the often cramped garrisons, and so they were dotted around East Anglia and the home counties.[35] East Anglia was a favourite area for quarters amongst the cavalry, where the 'great' towns of Colchester, Ipswich, Woodbridge, Halesworth, Bungay, Blythborough, Harleston and Beccles provided plentiful stabling for horses.[36]

Another list for the distribution of the forces for 1674 showed much the same arrangement with the Life Guards and the Foot Guards quartered in London, Westminster and Rochester, the Royal Horse Guards divided from Chichester to York, and the Holland and Admiral's regiments split between the various garrisons. In addition there were twenty-nine independent companies in the garrisons.[37]

Even in peacetime, the standing regiments did not remain together as single units in their quarters. A regiment might be spread over the whole of one county, or even all over England. In December 1665 the Admiral's Regiment had two companies stationed at Harwich, another at Landguard Fort, three in Hull, and one each at Plymouth, Deal, Chepstow Castle, Guernsey and Sheerness. Likewise, the Holland Regiment had two of its companies at Windsor Castle, three at Plymouth, two at Berwick-on-Tweed, and three in Carlisle. This system was carried on throughout the reign, so, in England, the army consisted of a number of troops and companies and not of regiments. The regiment existed as an administrative and executive formation only when it went abroad on foreign service, but for all other purposes the company or troop was the operative body. How the regimental staff officers carried on their functions when their commands were spread over impossibly large areas is a matter of conjecture, and we can only conclude that the regimental staffs were all but useless and fulfilled their duties in theory only.

The question of which towns and villages to use for quarters was approached haphazardly until 1686, when Blathwayt made a systematic survey of all the major centres of population in England and Wales which could accommodate men and horses. He and his clerks prepared a volume of 635 manuscript pages, listing all the towns and villages which could house men and horses in public houses.[38]

Very few barracks were built during the reign. Albemarle caused some to be built in Hyde Park during the Great Plague in order to isolate his men from possible infection,[39] but apart from these there were only two barracks in the whole of London: the Savoy, and the quarters of the Life Guards and the duty companies of the Foot Guards in Whitehall. Even in the garrisons soldiers were rarely housed in barracks. Due to the inefficiency of the Ordnance Office and the shortage of money for things military, most of the castles and forts were in bad repair and unfit to accommodate soldiers. The sole alternative was to quarter the garrison companies in the local towns. Whenever assizes or Parliamentary Elections were held in a town, any soldiers quartered there had to leave temporarily. The presence of armed men in such situations might have caused serious rioting, and, at the very least, would have been viewed as an attempt by the king to pervert the course of justice.

The Petition of Right had simply declared that the quartering of soldiers on private individuals was illegal, but it did not rule out the quartering of troops in public houses. Immediately after the Restoration this regulation was strictly obeyed, and in 1661 a Captain Swinhoe had to appear before the House of Lords on a charge of quartering his soldiers upon private citizens in Northumberland. He had to beg forgiveness on his knees before the bar of the House and pay all moneys due to the wronged persons.[40] This adherence to the Petition of Right soon loosened, and before long soldiers were openly quartered on private householders as well as in public houses. By 1672 a further abuse had developed. So odious was the prospect of having to entertain a number of unruly soldiers that the army was able to charge householders *5d* for the privilege of not having troops quartered on them.[41] As early as 1671 the illegal billeting of soldiers on private citizens was regarded as almost normal practice and was tacitly connived at by the king. The parish constable of St Dunstan-in-the-West was taken into custody by one of the king's messengers 'for not yielding due obedience to his Majesty's Orders about quartering soldiers where they had been quartered for several years past'.[42] Sir John Hotham complained to the Commons that the market town of Beverley in Yorkshire had become totally impoverished through soldiers being billeted there on private householders, and one townsman had even been fined for refusing to take in the military.[43] Three days later Sir Thomas Meres added another objection, announcing that the rate for avoiding quarters had just been raised from *5d* to *6d*.[44]

Not only was this type of quartering illegal, but more often than not the householders received no payment for their hospitality. This was unofficial free quarter. William Lyne petitioned the Privy Council in 1663 for reimbursement of £83 0*s* 11*d* owed to him by men of the King's Troop of the Life Guard 'for diet and Horse Meat'. Lyne had tried to recover the debt from Lord Gerard of Brandon, the troop commander, but had met with no success, Gerard refusing to stop his men's pay.[45] It was almost impossible for civilians to regain debts from the army. Redress had to be sought through the Judge Advocate in the first instance, then the commanding officer's permission had to be obtained, and only then could a suit be filed in a common law court. To go this far was expensive, and, even if the case did come before the court there was no surety of conviction and no guarantee that the soldier would even appear. The only real hope of redress rested in petitioning the king or the Privy Council, as did the inhabitants of St Albans in 1673 after Captain Nicoll's company of the Earl of Peterborough's Regiment had marched out of the city owing £44 11*s* 0*d* for quarters.[46]

If matters were bad during the levy for the Third Dutch War they were infinitely worse during the enlargement of the army for the projected French War in 1678. Some soldiers of Sir Charles Wheeler's Regiment of Foot threatened to quarter themselves on householders unless they compounded with them for money. Wheeler was at least able to assure the Commons that the guilty men had been sent before a Justice of the Peace to be dealt with as 'rebels and rogues'. Earlier in 1678, Sir John Hotham had been forced to remind the government of the terms of the Petition of Right: 'There shall be no quartering of soldiers, for continuing them here, any longer than in their passage to the place where they are to go; else 'tis a grievance to the people.'[47]

The Disbanding Act of 1679 paid special attention to the question of illegal quarters and for the first time wrote the illegality of billeting soldiers on private householders into a statute:

And whereas by the Laws and Customs of this Realm the Inhabitants thereof cannot be compelled against their wills to receive soldiers into their houses and to sojourn them there. Be it Declared and Enacted by the Authorities aforesaid That no Officer Military or Civil nor any other person whatever shall from henceforth presume to place, quarter or billet any soldier or soldiers upon any Subject or Inhabitant of this Realm of any Degree, Quality, or Profession whatever without his consent. And that it shall and may be lawful for every such Subject and Inhabitant to refuse to sojourn or quarter any soldier or soldiers notwithstanding any Command, Order, or Billetting whatever.[48]

Once this Act had been passed the authorities displayed more tact and circumspection in quartering the army. Monmouth was instructed by the Privy Council to build some barracks for the duty units of the Guards in and around Westminster so as to avoid the need for quartering altogether. This scheme came to nothing, although some extra places were found in the Savoy and in the Office of Tents and Toils in Clerkenwell. For the rest of the reign the army observed the 1679 Act and no more trouble occurred over quarters until after the succession of James II. From 1679 onwards all Marching Orders contained preambles ordering officers to make certain that their men paid for their quarters *en route* and behaved themselves on the journey. This dispute over quartering provided one concrete instance in which the army was a real grievance and vexation to the people.

V

The Staff and Administration

ENGLAND, Scotland and Ireland each possessed their own establishments, staffs and command structures. Within each country the army was a separate entity, each owing allegiance to Charles II, but otherwise independent. England was the largest of the three standing armies, and without exception the administrative methods practised there were echoed in the other two.

The influence of the army command was limited. The king was the supreme commander-in-chief and in no respect was the army answerable to Parliament, hence the senior officers acted as the monarch's deputies in military affairs and executed his orders. However, their authority only extended over the standing army and troops actually in the pay of the Crown: the six standing regiments, the garrison companies, Tangier and the colonies. The British regiments raised in England and hired out to France in 1673 ceased to be the responsibility of the English martial administration the moment they left the shores of the British Isles. Similarly, the mercenary regiments in foreign pay, principally the Irish in Flanders and France, were nothing to do with the staff at Whitehall. In general, if a regiment was ordered for overseas service it ceased to come under the command of the English establishment and passed into the authority of the hiring power. The expedition to suppress Bacon's Rebellion in 1676, Tobias Bridge's Barbados Regiment of 1667, and the Flanders Corps of 1678 were all under the direction of the English staff as they remained in the pay of the king, there being no temporary transfer of allegiance. Our concern here is with the command of the army in England.

For the first ten years of the reign, the command of the army was clear and well regulated. George Monck, the first Duke of Albemarle, served as Lord General, receiving general orders from the king and relaying detailed instructions to his junior officers. The chain of command was thus very simple: from the Lord General orders went directly to regimental colonels and garrison governors and then to the company and troop commanders. There was no intervening brigade or corps structure of any sort, and, really, the command system was even simpler. When in England the regiments were broken up into quarters so that one unit might be spread over the whole of the country. Clearly, the issue of orders to the colonel and then to the company captains was unnecessary, and in practice orders were frequently sent directly from the Lord General to company level. Regimentation in England was embryonic; the effective sub-division was the troop or company.

There were central staff officers in the headquarters at Whitehall, but their duties were administrative and not connected with field command. The Paymaster-General, Commissary-General of the Musters, Judge Advocate General, and Secretary at War were not commissioned general officers, but bureaucrats and professional administrators whose theoretical duties we shall study shortly.

Although the ultimate commander of the army, Charles was content to leave the day-to-day running of the forces to the politically safe and militarily competent George Monck. It was natural that a command vacuum should have been created on his death in 1670. This was the year of the Secret Treaty of Dover and the prospect of the army being used as a political pawn made it essential to succeed Monck with a truly loyal and devoted servant of the king. No such man appeared and so the command of the army was entrusted to a committee,[1] with the king reserving the personal right to sign all important army documents which previously he had been happy to leave to Monck.[2] This committee turned out to be a Council of Colonels with the Duke of York in the chair,[3] who took into their consideration 'military affairs and the well ordering of the forces . . . unregulated since my Lord General's death'. High sounding words, but the Council did nothing. In any peacetime army, command equals administration, for command only becomes a separate entity during active service. During the early 1670s it was impossible to divide command and administration for they amounted to the same thing. There was little point in having a powerful Council to order one company to march from Chatham to Rochester and a separate staff to see that the order was relayed and carried out. Too cumbersome to deal with either function efficiently, the Council was also racked with dissension and rivalry. The result was for the command and administration to fall into the hands of one man, Arlington, the Principal Secretary of State.

Under the occasionally watchful eye of the king, Arlington ran the army from 1671 to 1674, and after him Sir Joseph Williamson continued as virtual commander-in-chief and head bureaucrat. None of the leading soldiers could challenge the dominance of the politicians. Craven and Oxford had seats on the Privy Council but were removed from the real centres of power, Prince Rupert was old, ignored, and ineffective, whilst the Duke of York was more interested in the navy than the army. So weak was the high command of the army in 1672 that the major commands for the Anglo-Dutch War went to foreigners: Schomberg took over the Zealand Expedition and the Blackheath Army, whilst Blanquefort, a Frenchman and later Earl of Feversham, assumed command of the brigade sent over to fight under Louis XIV. For the Flanders Corps of 1678 all the preparations and planning were organised by Williamson.[4]

The Third Dutch War was managed without a soldier in the government. York was removed from circulation by the Test Act, Craven and Oxford were passed over, and only Monmouth achieved a little fame and recognition and this was largely due to amplified stories of his success at the Siege of Maestricht in 1673. From 1670 till the end of the reign, the army was commanded and administered by politicians and civil servants. Monmouth gained titles during the later 1670s but he was only a paper commander-in-chief. In 1676 he obtained the right to order 'removals of quarters, the reliefs of any of our established troops or companies, and the sending of all convoys needful for our service',[5] but he was not granted Monck's vacant title of Lord General. The best he could do was Captain-General of the Flanders Expedition of 1678, but, even then, he had none of the old soldier's duties or privileges. All Monmouth's orders had to be countersigned by the Secretary at War, imposing a bureaucratic check on his freedom of action, and were only permitted to pass the Sign Manual and not the Signet. Normally, Crown administration passed both, and so this regulation distinguished army concerns from civilian matters. The Secretary of State ran the army for Monmouth.

The emphasis of Charles's policy over the army was civilian control at all costs. An exception was made with Monck as his experience was invaluable and his loyalty to the Crown beyond doubt. Parliament was of the same opinion, although it considered that the civilian control ought to rest with them and not with the king and his ministers. After Monmouth had been commissioned Captain-General for Flanders and had then defeated the Covenanters at Bothwell Bridge, there was a fear that soldiers might come into their own again, but his political disgrace ended that threat. The effect of Monmouth's dismissal was to pour discredit upon the rank of Captain-General and clear the way for absolute civilian domination of the military. This process reached final fruition with a civilian Secretary at War sitting in the Commons running the army for the king whilst being answerable for his actions in Parliament.

An army commanded and run by non-military men and amateurs cannot be a very effective instrument of war, and certainly the performance of the British troops in Flanders in 1678 proved the point. In Tangier, where the army was directly commanded by a professional soldier on the spot, the efficiency and fighting ability of the soldiers increased enormously, whilst the regiments which fought for Louis XIV formed the best fighting units in the English army. The most competent officers were those who had seen action abroad in foreign armies. Those officers and soldiers who stayed permanently in England never fired a shot in anger, did little training, and possessed little idea of military life. It was small wonder that James II insisted on recalling the experienced Anglo-Dutch Brigade before marching to combat Monmouth's Rebellion in 1685. This was the penalty of having an army commanded and administered by civilians, instead of being commanded by professional soldiers and administered by professional staff officers.

Between 1660 and 1685 the office of Secretary at War developed from obscurity to mild importance; from little more than a clerk, the Secretary ended the reign as a very junior minister of state. Sir William Clarke was commissioned into this office on 28 January 1661, but then it was a military appointment paid from the army establishment. This 'honest gentleman, [who] wrote himself almost blind' had been Monck's private secretary in Scotland and so his was an obvious appointment at the Restoration.[6] Unfortunately the popular and likeable man was killed at sea during the Four Days' Battle in 1666. Clarke had been no more than a secretary to Monck with no official powers of his own, and his successor, Mathew Locke, 'another old and trusty servant and secretary of the Duke of Albemarle', assumed an even more minor role until his patron's death. At this time the Secretary at War was frequently referred to as the 'Clerk to the Lord General', or, 'The Secretary of the Forces', and not always by his later title. His pay reflected his status, and on the establishments he ranked below the other staff officers.[7] If the sums of money spent on stationery and office equipment are true indications, then the Secretary had little work to do; £10 *9s 4d* covered the running costs of his office in the Horse Guards for six months in 1674, a time when the country was at war.[8]

After Monck's death, the Secretary rose to a slightly higher position. In recognition of the additional responsibility which fell on his shoulders he was granted an increase in salary and employed two clerks to do his copying.[9] Locke's work was routine and dull. The Secretary of State sent him warrants and orders, which he and his clerks copied, countersigned, and then distributed to the officers concerned.[10] His office served as a general clearing house for army administration; he liaised with the Paymaster-General, and kept the Secretary of State informed of the state of the army, but he had no power. He could do nothing on his own authority and simply took orders from the Secretary of State, the King, and sometimes from the General. Another of his functions was to assist the Judge Advocate General in compiling cases for courts martial: copying depositions, and organising the transport of witnesses and officials to the location of the court. Marching orders, commissions and warrants, were drafted by the Secretary of State and entered in his own Domestic Entry Books; financial questions were handled by the Paymaster-General; arms and equipment were dealt with by the Ordnance Office. The Secretary at War was the equivalent of a minor civil servant making other people's decisions workable.

In practice, Locke and Clarke were not as powerless as the theory supposed. William Clarke was held in high regard by Albemarle and it is probable that much of the day-to-day running of the army was left in his control. Certainly, many petitions were sent directly to him rather than the Lord General, and he was 'always charitable, and of great dispatch'. The intention was that the Secretary at War should look after the civilian duties of the commander-in-chief, but, as we have seen, Albemarle's death and the muddle resulting from it caused both the army command and administration to pass into the realm of the Secretary of State, stripping the Secretary at War of his duties. However, an incident in the Commons suggested that the Secretary of State was content to permit the Secretary at War to run military affairs much as he pleased.

During 1678, Sir Joseph Williamson was censured by the Commons for commissioning catholics in the army. Some remarks passed during the debate illustrate the power and influence of the Secretary at War. Sir Christopher Musgrave testified:

> I have been with him when several orders have been brought. His Chamber Keeper told him, 'they came from the Commissary-at-War'. He said, 'he knew them not, but signs them of course'.[11]

A little later, Sir John Birkenhead enlarged on the procedure for granting army commissions:

> Lord Digby moved the late King, that no commission might be valid that was not signed by the Secretary of State—I have known particularly that they have been first shaped and formed by the Secretary at War, and allowed by the Secretary of State to avoid clashing about it.[12]

When questioned about the matter, Williamson admitted that his having to countersign commissions was,

> a trouble and no advantage to me to sign them. . . . This is the practise, and the constant practise. . . . All dispatched have been under this method. I have found them so, and I continue them so.[13]

Mr Papillon wound up the proceedings by caustically commenting that 'at this rate, Williamson might have commissioned the Pope's Army'.[14]

Whether this signing of commissions without first bothering to read them was due to Williamson not wishing to offend Locke, or overwork, is not clear, but it demonstrates that a forceful personality could make more out of this ineffectual office than the rule officially allowed.

On 18 August 1683, Mathew Locke sold his office to William Blathwayt.[15] This Londoner rose via a legal training to become a civil servant of the first rank. After attending the Middle Temple Blathwayt entered the office of Sir William Temple, ambassador at The Hague, remaining in the diplomatic corps until 1675. He then removed to the Plantation Office, becoming Secretary to the Lords of Trade and Plantations by 1679. During the short Secretaryship of State of Lord Conway, Blathwayt served as his clerk and virtual under-secretary, in much the same way as Williamson had served Arlington. On the fall of Conway he cast around for a vacant position. Already, Locke had made it known that he wished to resign as Secretary at War and was happy to sell his seals to the unemployed Blathwayt.[16]

On assuming office, Blathwayt had little experience in military affairs, although he gained some acquaintance with the colonial forces during his time at the Plantation Office. However, ignorance was no handicap, for over the previous thirteen years no army administrator had known much of his duties and none had been soldiers. With Blathwayt in occupation, the Secretary at War became a vastly more important official. In some ways Blathwayt was the Pepys of the army, and although his main achievements came under James II and William III, the beginnings of his prominence were witnessed in the last two years of Charles's reign.[17]

Exactly why the Secretary suddenly rose in power is not clear. Louvois and the successful model of French military administration provided some incentive, but, more obviously, under James and William a large standing army and continental war became part of the British way of life. The corollary was for the officials connected with the military to gain correspondingly in importance. This was not the case between 1683 and 1685.

In these years, it was Blathwayt's proven skill as an administrator which took duties away from the Secretary of State and transferred them to his own department. Following the dismissal of Williamson in 1679, both Secretaryships of State had passed through the hands of new men, Sunderland and Sidney Godolphin, or old and tired politicians like Leoline Jenkins. There was no Arlington or Williamson to control the government, and so it was an easy task for Blathwayt to poach and build up his own office.

Immediately after his assumption of duties he began to copy warrants, orders, and letters in his own Entry Books; this one action created a separate War Office within the domain of the Secretary of State. A junior ministry had come into being. Blathwayt still had to suffer the indignity of being referred to as a member of the Secretary of State's staff, but, from 1683, the War Office existed. The new Secretary started to countersign all army papers and issue orders on his own authority 'at the King's Command'. This power extended over such mundane items as the movement of forces within England, the quartering, levying and disbanding of troops, and other minor services. This might sound inconsiderable, and indeed the work was not arduous and the Secretary of State retained the ultimate power over military administration, but, effectively, the peacetime administration of the army had passed from his control to Blathwayt. Within two years, Blathwayt's achievement was very great.

His official functions dealt with three major areas; the issuing of Marching Orders, the drawing-up of Military Codes, and the adjudication of regimental seniority.

Before him, Locke and Clarke had ordered the movement of forces in England, although not on their own authority.[18] Before soldiers could begin a long march, quartermasters had to be sent out to arrange accommodation in advance at the various overnight stops, necessitating that the precise route of march be worked out well before the time of departure. Once *en route*, officers had to ensure that 'the soldiers satisfy their landlords for what shall be due unto them, and behave themselves orderly in their march and during their stay at the places aforesaid'. Troops and companies were frequently moved around the country, it being bad practice to allow a unit to remain in one locality too long. If this happened, discipline suffered, soldiers became over-friendly with civilians, and the unit became part of the town and not part of the army. More to the point, the citizens soon grew heartily sick of the presence of badly behaved soldiers.[19] Other than these small and continual movements, there were sometimes large-scale marches to be organised. During the Second and Third Dutch Wars, most of the standing regiments had to be moved to quarters near the east coast and the Channel ports, and in 1683 some major removals had to be performed in order to accommodate the returning garrison of Tangier.

Long journeys, Hull to the Tower of London, Plymouth to Berwick, were made by sea—one company conveniently fitted on board a navy frigate. Troops of horse were shifted more often than foot companies, due to their role as the nation's mobile police force. A route was laid down in precise detail by the Secretary of State before any formation could commence its march. Roger Langley, commanding the new battalion of Monmouth's Foot, was ordered to transfer four of his companies from Edgeworth, near Brentford, to Hull in 1678. His route of march stated the exact distance between each stopping place and the date by which each was to be reached. Soldiers marched for three days and then enjoyed one day's rest; the 128 miles of Langley's journey took sixteen days, an average of eight miles a day.[20] A company was allowed *6d* a day for the hire of a cart to carry its baggage and any sick men. Marches averaged between eight and fifteen miles a day, a considerable distance for men carrying field equipment, and no allowance was made for the season of the year. One writer is of the opinion that the troops marched without their arms in peacetime, all weapons belonging to the garrison where they were to be quartered.[21] Evidence for this is non-existent. Most of the army spent the majority of their time in towns and villages and not in actual garrisons, so such a system could not have operated.

Officers had to seek Blathwayt's permission to go on leave, and he had to liaise between the officers of the Militia and those of the regular army. His second important function was the drafting of Articles of War and codes of military law. All the codes were basically the same differing only in detail according to the special circumstances for which they were intended. The model was the set of 'Martial Laws' used at Dunkirk by the Cromwellian garrison. Some extra clauses were tacked on by the Restoration government to cater for the altered political situation, and it was this combined code which formed the basis for all future codes up to 1685. The Articles dealt with all aspects of discipline: theft, murder, obedience to officers, and the proper observance of religion. Clauses ensured the security of the garrison in a foreign country and attempted to safeguard the civilians from the excesses of the soldiery.[22] Punishments for breaking each clause were included. Most were savage by modern standards, but congruous with similar articles of war in use in seventeenth-century Europe. Espionage, refusing orders, duelling, and 'using menacing or braving words' before a court martial all carried an automatic death penalty. 'Severe punishment' was meted out for nearly all other serious crimes, implying that the court martial had almost total discretion as to what punishment to fit to each offence.

'The Laws and Ordinances of War established for the Better Governing of His Majesty's Forces in the Kingdoms of Suz, Fez, and Morocco'[23] were stricter and more comprehensive than those for Dunkirk. The very first clause forbidding a man to blaspheme 'upon pain of having his tongue bored through with a red hot iron' set the tone for the remainder. These laws had to cover every aspect of military life and all possible crimes and misdemeanours; this resulted in many of the paragraphs being left deliberately vague so that a number of offences could be dealt with under one general head. Officers were included in the provisions, but dismissal from the service was their severest punishment, whilst a common soldier could be executed for drawing his sword without an order. Finally, if a misdemeanour did not come under one of the 130 articles, then, 'All other faults, disorders, and offences not mentioned in these Articles, shall be punished according to the general custom and laws of war'.

Such then were the Articles of War. In Dunkirk, Tangier and Flanders they formed the codes of martial law by which all soldiers had to live when outside England. In England, they formed the military law. Most of the Restoration laws were based on those of Cromwell and the French army. So imbued with the French spirit were Locke and Blathwayt that they reserved a special entry book for recording the more important French military reforms.[24]

Blathwayt, and before him the Secretaries of State, had continually to tactfully deal with matters of regimental precedence and seniority of commissions. These were questions of vital importance to the armies of that time. Officers were frequently of high birth, and often a junior subaltern could be the social superior of a general officer, so some method of overcoming these social discrepancies had to be found in order for command to function efficiently. Career and professional officers relied heavily on the seniority system, for on the date of their commissions hung their pay, rank and prospects. The date of an officer's commission determined his position in the army. The precedence of regiments, whilst closely allied to seniority of commissions, was somewhat more complicated.

One of the fundamental manœuvres of an army was the movement out of column of march into line of battle, and it was customary for an army to march in 'order of battle' so that the station of each regiment in the column corresponded to its position in the battle formation. This avoided much confusion. Always, the place of honour was on the right of the first line and this belonged to the senior regiment. The second most senior took the next place of honour on the left of the first line, the third was second on the right, and the fourth second on the left. The most junior regiments were found near the centre of the line. This precedent was followed in peacetime reviews and parades.

No firm directive on precedence was issued in England until the Second Dutch War. Prior to this the order of regiments had been obvious,[25] but the sudden appearance of many units for the duration of the war complicated the picture. The 1st Foot Guards were declared to be the most senior regiment of foot, 'and the Colonel be always reckoned, and take place, as the first foot colonel'. Next came the Coldstreamers, then the Admiral's, with the Holland Regiment bringing up the rear. After these, all the new regiments took precedence according to the date of their colonel's commission. This also meant that the seniority of an officer was dictated by the date of his own commission and that of his regiment's formation, the two going hand-in-hand.

In the cavalry, a special arrangement took place to assure the absolute mastery of the aristocratic Life Guards. The captains of the three troops ranked as the most senior colonels of horse, lieutenants ranked as the most senior majors, and cornets as the most senior captains. In this manner, a cornet of the Life Guard could command a full captain from the Royal Horse Guards. Naturally, the captain of the King's Troop of the Life Guards was the first colonel of all the horse. However, there was one slight difficulty for the Royal Horse Guards were also a 'royal' regiment and so provision was made for its colonel to take precedence immediately after the three captains of the Life Guards. When additional cavalry regiments were raised they took station after the 'Blues', again according to the date of their colonel's commission.

The question of whether the horse should command the foot, or vice versa, was never satisfactorily answered. General officers were usually appointed to command both in a combined force, but if there was no general officer present then the command fell on the most senior officer of either wing. The regulations stipulated 'that the eldest colonel do on all occasions command', and if there was no colonel then the senior lieutenant-colonel, and so down through the ranks. In garrison the word of the governor was law and even general officers were bound to obey him, although regimental officers retained their authority over their own men within the bounds of the governor's jurisdiction.

These were the guide lines for precedence throughout the reign. Additions were made as conditions demanded, as in 1669 when a directive stated that, 'the Colonel of the Regiment of his Majesty's Foot [1st Foot Guards] shall be looked upon, and obeyed, as a General Officer in the Field . . . to command both Horse and Foot accordingly'.[26] Thereby, John Russell received the privilege of becoming the most senior officer in the army under the Lord General; even the captain of the King's Troop of the Life Guard could not aspire to general rank.

With the new levies for the Third Dutch War, another ladder of precedence was issued by Arlington,[27] but this soon proved inadequate. Difficulties over precedence beset the 'Blackheath Army' and extra regulations had to be introduced to deal with them. When a number of troops of horse marched out together then officers of the same rank commanded according to the seniority of their troops, but if there were a number of troops from different regiments in a 'commanded party' then officers of the same degree commanded according to the dates of their commissions. Greater complexity was created by the expansion of the army in 1678. Regimented companies were declared to be always senior to independent companies 'and shall draw up on the right of a garrison independent company'. However, the company of the garrison governor was senior to any regimented company stationed in that garrison unless some of the Guards were present.[28] Then, to make matters worse, the Royal Dragoons were added to the permanent establishment in 1683 and a new type of unit had to be fitted into the table of precedence. This was achieved in a typically confused fashion. Dragoons counted both as horse and foot and were thus included in the precedence of both, 'according to the nature of the place where they shall be'. If in the field they were regarded as cavalry, but in garrison they were treated as infantry. From this tangle of regulations, the Secretary at War had to sort out quarrels between officers, a task which frequently called on Blathwayt's experience in diplomacy.

Army headquarters were based on Whitehall. The actual staff was minute. Apart from the Secretary at War, the Paymaster-General, and the Commissary-General of the Musters, there was the Judge Advocate General and the Scoutmaster-General. This was an active service office concerned with scouting and the gaining of field intelligence and, although filled throughout the reign, the post was not over-strenuous. The four central officials had their clerks and messengers, but that was all that the army headquarters amounted to.

An Adjutant-General was appointed temporarily in 1673 at the relatively high salary of £1 a day.[29] The rank was borrowed from France and the man who took up the office was himself a Frenchman, Engelbert Renfosse. His exact function was never clearly defined but he appears to have acted as a special staff officer 'without portfolio' to off-load the headquarters during the busy period of the Third Dutch War. He supervised the 'shipping, transportations, landing and marching to their quarters' of 264 soldiers recruited for the Earl of Peterborough's Regiment in France in 1673. In March of the same year, Renfosse repaired to Tilbury and Gravesend to oversee a security operation aimed at preventing officers and men from 'endeavouring to transport themselves into foreign parts without passes'. However, on 3 March 1676, Renfosse was disbanded and his pay granted to Sir Thomas Daniell as a pension following his voluntary retirement from the lieutenant-colonelcy of the 1st Foot Guards. Daniell was thereafter referred to as the Adjutant-General, but it was a sinecure and he undertook no duties.

The English standing army was a miniature copy of the French army of Louis XIV. Louvois's administrative methods were slavishly followed by the Secretaries of State and the Secretary at War, the French system of precedence and seniority was used, and the whole concept of standing 'Household Guards' supplemented by mass levies in time of war was based firmly on the French model. All over Europe France set the military pattern, and with her new army of 1661 England chose to imitate the successful French rather the traditions of her own New Model, which itself had gained the admiration of Europe.

Apart from coming under some pressure in wartime, the staff operated modestly and well; the army was small, little needed attention in a hurry, and the cost of administration was kept as low as possible. Orders from the secretary or general were circulated to the regiments by couriers. Each regiment maintained 'an orderly man' at the Chequer Inn in Charing Cross for the purpose of transmitting orders from London to the regiments. Generally the regiments looked after themselves, receiving only broad directives from the central staff. Provisions, clothing and training were purely regimental concerns, and only pay, musters and quarters necessitated orders and liaison with London. Regimental staff officers were virtually independent of the main headquarters, although nominally chaplains came under the Chaplain-General, quartermasters under the Quartermaster-General, and provosts under the Provost-Marshal General. Each regiment had its own adjutant, or aide-major, another rank religiously borrowed from France, who dealt with the paper work and assisted the field major. A foot regiment had one quartermaster for accommodation and food supply, whilst horse regiments had one quartermaster per troop. It was customary for this officer to double as the provost-marshal. Every regiment had the dubious advantage of a chaplain whose duty it was to read the Common Prayer once a day whenever this was possible, and to preach to the whole regiment on Sundays. A surgeon completed the regimental staff, and, given the condition of seventeenth-century medicine, the work of the last two officers was closely connected.

The most influential figure in the regiment was not a commissioned officer, but a civilian—the regimental agent or clerk to the colonel. He received and distributed the pay to the troops, kept the regimental accounts, and acted as the pivot for all financial dealings. Answerable to no one but the colonel, whose servant he was, his opportunities for swindling the pay were enormous, and the position was much sought after in view of its remuneration. There was no provision for the agent in the establishments, but his salary came from an unofficial deduction of *2d* in the pound from all regimental pay.[30] This office was not new at the Restoration but had existed in the forces of Elizabeth I,[31] where the clerk was noted as truly corrupt, whilst in the New Model the clerk was actually included on the regimental establishment.[32] However, in the puritan army there were few complaints about his conduct.

There was no crowned head of the Restoration army staff. Each department came directly under the Lord General or the Secretary of State. Previously, the commissary-general had always been regarded as the chief of staff, but although this was not the case after 1661, his successor, the commissary-general of the musters, did assume an importance in the headquarters. He was the 'establishments officer' responsible for the strength of the army, supervising its levies and disbandments, as well as organising musters. Even the paymaster-general could not issue money without first receiving a certificate from the commissary-general. Such an eminent official did not actually hold musters himself but commanded a retinue of deputy-commissaries or muster-masters who took musters all over the country.[33]

The muster was the central institution of the seventeenth-century army. It was an occasion to ensure that units were up to strength, that they were correctly armed and equipped, and for the commissary to carry out a general inspection. In addition, the commissaries administered the Oaths of Supremacy and Allegiance, read any relevant proclamations or general orders before the assembled troops, and made sure that furloughs were not extended. In London, the commissary-general kept a register of all commissions; any officer not on the list was ineligible for muster. Every troop or company, for regiments were mustered by sub-unit, was mustered seven times a year until 1675, and thereafter six times. A soldier was paid for each day of that muster, including Sundays, provided that he was on parade and his name entered on the roll. Before a muster took place, the commissary informed the captain of the time and place, and the officers then prepared a list of every man and officer in the company written in alphabetical order.[34] On the arrival of the commissary, this roll, which was in triplicate, was presented to him and he read it over before the troops, each man answering to his own name. If, and when, satisfied that all the names on the list actually corresponded with the men on parade, the commissary and the company officers signed each copy of the roll; one was retained by the captain, one went to the office of the Paymaster-General as a certificate for the issue of pay, and the last copy went to the commissary-general for his records.

Sir Thomas Clarges, the eminent parliamentarian, performed the duties of commissary-general from 1660 to 1679, when he sold his office to the Honourable Henry Howard, the youngest son of the second Earl of Suffolk.[35] The pay was equivalent to that of a middle-ranking office-holder, 10*s* a day until 1666, rising to 17*s* 6*d* in the following year, but the position was not especially remunerative, at least when compared to the profits amassed by the Paymaster-General.

Without regular musters the army could not have been run, yet this institution was a prey to the worst abuses that the contemporary mind could devise. Regulations governing musters came out in 1663, and in revised form in 1683,[36] threatening officers and commissaries with the direst penalties should they try to falsify musters, but it was to no avail. The theory of false musters was disarmingly simple: to maintain a troop or company permanently below its establishment strength but to present a full unit on muster day in order to receive the complete pay. The difference between the real strength of the company and its appearance on the parade represented a straight gain for the officers. Methods of achieving this goal varied. Some captains hired extra men from other formations to fill their ranks for the day, others had their men imitate 'absentees' by answering to two names, whilst the most common trick was to hire civilians off the street, dress them in uniform, and present them at muster. It is impossible to believe that every commissary was sufficiently gullible to believe in these ancient deceptions, and so the successful false muster required the active connivance of the commissary. With a big enough bribe in his pocket, his vision and hearing could become markedly defective. Such conspiracy rendered the toughest rules useless—provided everybody played the game all were safe from detection. Lieutenants, cornets and ensigns, could receive the captaincy of their commander if they informed on his false musters, and a reward of £50 awaited the diligent sergeant or corporal who could expose his officers. These offers were rarely taken up as the practice was regarded as normal and acceptable.

These frauds did not just occur in isolated garrisons, but even in the élite Life Guard. Charles's inspection of them in 1663 revealed a considerable number of 'dead pays', to his evident alarm.[37] There was nothing new in false musters. Serious corruption seems to have dated from the time of Elizabeth I when 'dead pays' and other chicanery were common,[38] although there was little evidence of dishonesty in earlier levies.[39] The 'dead pay' was a sophisticated form of false muster. When a soldier died, a not infrequent occurrence, his name was retained on the muster roll indefinitely, and many captains drew pay for men who had died years before.

The morality of the officers ought not to be judged too harshly. False musters were as much perquisites as the fees taken by government officials. Neither were they a British monopoly for every standing army in Europe suffered from them, and no government found the answer, although the French and Italians came close to success. French companies were mustered every Sunday to ensure that the ranks were complete, with full musters held twice a month to prove the pay certificates. Any soldiers not properly clothed and armed were struck off the rolls and the captain had his own pay stopped until those men were correctly equipped. This made the falsification of musters very expensive and hardly worth the trouble. The Italian method was even more thorough:

> The Muster-Masters enquire the names of the soldiers' parents, the country and place of their birth, and write down the complexions of their faces, and the colours of their hair, and some private mark which the Muster-Master observeth.[40]

Charles II had only himself to blame for the continuance of false musters in his army, for the rot started with the 'official' false musters which he allowed some of the more senior officers. During 1670, John Russell, as Colonel of the 1st Foot Guards, and Lord Craven, Colonel of the Coldstream Guards, were permitted the daily pay of one soldier from each of the companies in their regiments, in addition to their salaries. Accordingly, one man from each company was disbanded and a circular went out to the two colonels, the paymaster-general, and the commissary-general, giving a list of the fictitious names which were to be entered on the muster rolls.[41] Three years later, Charles took another step to encourage corruption in his army. The false musters in the Blackheath Army were so blatant and widespread that he was forced to grant officially ten dead pays in each company, the proceeds from which were to be divided amongst the officers.[42] From here it was but a short step to turning a blind eye to illegal false musters. Legal false musters and the official insertion of dead pays dated from the armies of Elizabeth, only to disappear with the New Model. As in so much after 1660, the new Royalist Army forgot the reforms of the Cromwellian forces and returned to all the bad habits of its royal predecessors.

Only the very worst false musters came before the courts martial. Sir John Robinson, Lieutenant of the Tower of London, committed such frauds on his garrison that he owed them twenty-two months' pay by 1664. He had, of course, received their money but had retained it for himself.[43] Unfortunately, Robinson had in his custody Colonel John Hutchinson who had served in an army where such conduct was not tolerated. When he threatened to expose Robinson, the guilty party paid up fifteen of the twenty-two months due. It took the intervention of an old soldier to secure the basic right of a private soldier to his pay. The men could do nothing to avoid being cheated. If they complained of false musters or arrears of wages they were more likely to be punished for insolence than listened to, and no respectable person took the word of a soldier against that of an officer.

Between 1660 and 1685 only six cases of false musters came before the courts martial. More often than not these only came to light through a subaltern informing on his captain in the hope of gaining his place. Ensign Allen Cotton accused his captain, John Street of the Coldstream Guards, who also happened to be his father-in-law, of holding false musters in 1684. An investigation by the court discovered that Cotton had connived at Street's frauds for over two years before a personal difference between them resulted in Cotton taking his revenge by informing on Street. The captain was cashiered, whilst life was made so uncomfortable for Cotton that he 'left' of his own accord.

Some officers went to immense lengths to falsify their musters, one of the prime exponents being none other than Sir Robert Holmes, the distinguished naval officer and friend of the king. Whilst governor of the Isle of Wight, he was accused by one Joseph Brent of practising false musters in his independent garrison company. The resulting court martial discovered the extent of Holmes's crimes. His steward and gardener were both entered on the rolls of the company but did no duty, nor received any pay, this going directly into Holmes's pocket. The son of the late Keeper of the Isle of Wight Forest found himself mustered, Holmes sending his pay to his widowed mother, and, in addition, Holmes allowed the army to pay his coachman, groom, a brickmaker and a sailor who had been away at sea for four years.[44] Holmes received no punishment.

A more typical case came up in 1674 when Captain James Reade of the 1st Foot Guards was accused by his lieutenant, Edmund Harris, of making continual false musters. Two of Reade's servants had answered to fictitious names at a muster in Rochester, Private James Hamilton was mustered twice after his discharge from the army, many soldiers were instructed to answer to two names, and Reade even managed the incredible feat of burying a soldier and then resurrecting him for the next muster.[45] All told, the king was financially cheated 'and grossly abused to his great disadvantage, when he is made to believe that he hath either more men, or more sufficient men than really and effectively he hath', but he only had himself to blame.

The provision of food and clothing for the forces in England presented the staff with no difficulties. A soldier was clothed out of his Off Reckonings, and his subsistence money was specifically intended to provide food and shelter. Most of a private's life was spent in cheap inns and taverns where food and drink were readily available, if he had the money to pay for them, but he was a target for landlords who did their utmost to cheat the military out of every available penny. Technically, subsistence amounted to *6d* a day for a foot soldier, just enough to keep a man adequately fed, but compared even with the wages of an agricultural labourer the soldier's full pay of *10d* a day was miserable. 'Subsistence Money' was aptly named for it made the soldier probably the lowest-paid man in England. A worker in the fields could earn *1s* a day and an artisan in a town could average *10s*. Food prices for 1664 indicated that a soldier could only have afforded a monotonous and unhealthy diet; beef and mutton cost *3d* a pound, butter *6d*, and a quart of ale *2d*. Little remained for drink or entertainment. If the army went overseas on an expedition in the pay of the British government then the Whitehall staff organised a bread ration for the men, but this still had to be paid for by the soldier out of his subsistence money.[46]

An additional service was provided by the regimental sutler, a civilian contractor hired by the colonel to sell food and drink to the soldiers. When a regiment was spread out in quarters it is difficult to visualise how the sutler functioned, if at all, but when whole formations came together, as on Blackheath in 1673, then the sutler set up a stall in the regimental camp and provided basic foods and cheap liquor for the men. From this privileged position he was able to fix his own prices, and it was a fortunate soldier who was not in debt to this gentleman.

Engineers, gunners, and all matters relating to the artillery and armaments, were the sole responsibility of the Ordnance Office, the army being totally dependent on the master-general for weapons and ammunition, and even for such small items as the repair of pikes and muskets. In every garrison which mounted cannon, the gunners and matrosses came under the command of the Ordnance Office, whilst the garrison soldiers were commanded by the army. One was not bound to follow the orders of the other. These gunners were appointed from a pool of one hundred, trained by the Master Gunner of England, and once on station they had to follow written instructions from the Board of Ordnance.[47] There was little friction between the gunners and the soldiers, for seventeenth-century artillerymen considered themselves infinitely superior to common soldiers. Gunners were the military bourgeoisie. Most of them could read and write, as gunnery was a 'science' and a number of technical manuals had to be read and digested. They deliberately surrounded their profession with a mystique of smoke and gunpowder, jealously guarding their craft after the manner of a medieval guild. Indeed, the artillerymen of the Habsburg army went so far as to call themselves guildsmen and refused to be connected with anything so vulgar as the army. Relations between the army and the artillery were not nearly so strained in England, but contact between the two was, at best, superficial. Tents, bedding, shovels, picks and field equipment came from the Office of Tents and Toils in Clerkenwell. This department was amalgamated with the Ordnance Office in 1685.

In an age of pageantry and splendour, military music assumed some importance. Precisely what was achieved in this direction is impossible to tell as few scores survive, whilst the seventeenth century was hardly the Golden Age of British music, if indeed this country has ever enjoyed one. Most likely the military players transposed folk melodies into march-rhythms. Doubtless the fashionable French had some considerable influence. All foot companies had a side drummer to beat out orders and provide a marching step. The drum was painted in the regimental colours and embossed with the royal crest, or the coat-of-arms of the colonel. Horse regiments had pairs of mounted kettle-drums, and each troop possessed at least two trumpeters to relay orders. The Royal Scots included a bagpiper in the colonel's company from as early as 1662, but in England the fife was the universal wind instrument. One man from every company of the 1st Foot Guards was appointed to learn this simple pipe from a Peter Venhausen,[48] and in 1680 a special fifer was appointed to this regiment, given the pay of a sergeant, and named 'Fife Major'.[49] Drum-majors had been with the 1st Foot Guards and the Royal Scots since 1662,[50] ranking as sergeants on 1*s* 6*d* a day. The hautbois, a forerunner of the modern oboe, gained some popularity during the reign and was much used in military music. Originating from France and the developing musical court of Louis XIV, the hautbois had a strong, clear, penetrating tone, admirably suited to cutting through the noise of marching men and horses.

Part Two

VI

The Garrison of Tangier

Henry Mordaunt, the second Earl of Peterborough, was commissioned captain-general of all the forces in Tangier on 6 September 1661, and with him went a sizeable garrison to occupy the small town in North Africa. Peterborough's own regiment of foot was raised from amongst the disbanded officers and men of the New Model, and numbered 1,000. Another regiment of the same size went directly from Dunkirk to Tangier under the command of Sir Robert Harley, as did two smaller regiments of 500 men each under Colonels John Fitzgerald and Lewis Farrell. A single troop of horse, commanded by Peterborough, accompanied the corps with a train of artillery and the requisite staff officers.

The expedition arrived off Tangier on 29 January 1662,[1] to discover the sailors from Lord Sandwich's squadron already in possession of the new colony. It remained for the governor to take formal possession in the name of Charles II of England. The Portuguese inhabitants were unhappy with their new masters and the majority requested to be shipped back to their home country in Sandwich's ships. This was complied with, leaving the town without a civilian population, apart from the wives and families of the military.

Tangier is twelve miles east of Cape Spartel on the northern coast of Morocco, or Barbary as it was then known, and separated from Iberia by the narrows of the Straits of Gibraltar. Its climate was 'very temperate and less obnoxious to incommodious heats than either Spain or Portugal'.[2] The buildings of the town were in a reasonable condition, and the fortifications adequate, although in need of some repairs. Thus situated on the coastal plain of North Africa, the land about Tangier was extremely fertile, consisting of a 'black soil'. Likewise, the water supply was good with wells inside the town walls and a number of aqueducts, constructed by the Portuguese, which brought water from the surrounding hills. As a trading centre for the Mediterranean, Tangier was ideal. The concept of the capture of Gibraltar in 1705 sprang from the precedent of Tangier, but Tangier needed a mole of considerable size to protect its harbour from the Atlantic weather and the building of this occupied the whole twenty-two years of English occupation and was still unfinished at the evacuation in 1684. The town might have been pleasant enough, but the political state of Barbary gave cause for concern.

The Saadi dynasty, after nearly a century and a half of sovereignty, was coming to an end and the country was splitting into provinces under the control of local chiefs. Fez had invited the rule of Mohammed, one of the race of Filali Shareefs who claimed direct descent from the Prophet and had settled in the fourteenth century in Tafilalt, the date-growing region to the south of the Atlas Mountains. In 1662, Er Rasheed II, one of the Shareefian race whom the English called the 'Great Tafiletta', was fighting for supremacy against his brother, Mohammed, whom he killed in battle in 1664. Later, he seized Marrakesh, and during the eight years of his reign settled the Filalis securely on the throne. Among the supporters of Mohammed against the Great Tafiletta was Abd Allah Ghailan, 'Gayland' or 'Guyland' to the English, who led a group of tribes in northern Barbary. He was a bold and ambitious man who hoped to create a kingdom for himself in Northern Fez as the price of his support for Mohammed. Guyland was the first Moorish leader with whom the English had to deal, but when Peterborough's force landed he was occupied with one of his frequent feuds against the 'Saint of Sallee', ruler of that great den of pirates and corsairs.

Farrell's and Fitzgerald's regiments had served in Charles II's army of exiled royalists in Flanders, but although strongly pro-monarchical they were mostly Irish, except for two companies of Scots which had joined them in Dunkirk, all that remained of the regiment of the Earl of Newburgh.[3] Both these regiments were well below strength when they arrived at Tangier. Their numbers fell steadily throughout 1662, due, as Peterborough thought, to their sloth,[4] but more probably to the unprepared state of the expedition. The Portuguese hardly left a house fit for habitation, and what buildings there were were broken up for firewood.[5] A diet of salt meat caused malnutrition and sickness, whilst the officers spent most of their time bickering and neglecting their duty. Peterborough reported to Sir Henry Bennet:

I have been of late forced to use some severity to the officers of the place . . . [they] began to breed disobedience and neglect of duty, but it has, falling in the Regiment of Harlow [Harley] and among men so bred in the principle of faction and rebellion as the wonder will not be great. Kingwell, his Lieutenant-Colonel, I have sent home, a man so seditious and insolent a native as rendered him incompatible with all government where he may not rule.[6]

Peterborough was an old royalist soldier, but his hand was not firm enough to manage so disparate a population as was in Tangier, so in 1663 he was replaced by Andrew Rutherford, Earl of Teviot, who had previously governed Dunkirk. He had taken no part in the Civil Wars in England but was a soldier of fortune having served with the French Army until 1660. At the Restoration he returned to his native Scotland only to be immediately appointed to Dunkirk to succeed Sir Edward Harley. A mercurial and energetic man, he set about the task of improving Tangier, and his short term of office was the most encouraging during the occupation of the colony. Teviot reorganised the garrison. The four infantry regiments were reduced to two; one English under Teviot himself, and the other Irish under John Fitzgerald,[7] but the benefits which he bestowed upon the soldiery ended in 1664 when Teviot was killed during a disastrous encounter with the Moors. Sir Tobias Bridge stepped in as temporary governor, a man who had the infamous distinction of having been one of Cromwell's major-generals,[8] but he was a very experienced soldier and Charles II was to employ him again to command an expedition to Barbados in 1667.

Following this defeat, the strength of the garrison dropped significantly until each regiment had only about 700 men, and it continued in this condition until 1666 when 300 reinforcements were sent from the British Corps in Portugal. This increased the numbers to 1,800, still 200 short of the official establishment of 2,000. During this emergency Fitzgerald took over from Bridge as the new Lieutenant-Governor. An obscure figure, Fitzgerald is known only to have served with the exiled royalist army in Flanders and later in Dunkirk.

Tangier cost £75,388 *12s 6d* a year in 1662,[9] but by 1666 Charles was growing very short of money. John, Lord Bellasise, who had been posted as governor in the previous year, made proposals for a reduction in the establishment. By cutting the foot to 1,600 there would be a saving of £10,000 per annum, and possibly more if the two regiments were amalgamated into one and the troop of horse reduced by a half. This new establishment was accepted and came into force in January 1667,[10] but in 1668, with the financial situation steadily worsening, the Privy Council authorised a committee to 'consider all the several branches of his Majesty's Revenue, and what proportion of each of them might be conveniently retrenched'.[11] Out of this came another establishment on 15 January 1668, bringing all the 1,600 foot into one regiment, the 'Old Tangier Regiment', and reducing the horse to a mere thirty.[12] This diminished the annual charge to £53,797 *15s 4d*.[13] From the figures given in the abstracts of musters, the strength of the garrison remained static at 1,550 during the period from 1670 to 1672.[14] However, a survey of Tangier taken on 30 December 1676 showed that the number of soldiers was considerably less than in 1672; there were only 1,085 privates, ninety-six non-commissioned officers, and thirty-four troopers.[15]

Fortunately, these years when the garrison was under-strength coincided with periods when the Moorish pressure on Tangier was relaxed, and this was doubly fortunate in that the governors at this time were not men of strong character. Bellasise, an old officer of Charles I, was elderly and achieved little during his term of office. Colonel Henry Norwood, another old royalist, succeeded Bellasise and ruled with good sense and judgment until 1669 when John, Earl of Middleton arrived, a man notorious for his drunkenness and generally dissipated existence. He had been Lord High Commissioner in Scotland from 1660 to 1663, where his high-handed and debauched management of affairs had led to his being dismissed from all his appointments. Middleton is reputed to have ended his life in a particularly congruous fashion; he fell off his horse in a drunken stupor whilst riding at Tangier and died of his injuries. William O'Brien, second Earl of Inchiquin, came to the governorship in 1674, but apart from an exciting youth during which he had been captured by Algerian pirates, he had little to recommend him for the post. His father had been one of the leading royalists in Ireland during the Civil Wars, and it was as a reward for his father's services that Inchiquin received the office at Tangier. Sir Palmes Fairborne, who became deputy-governor under Inchiquin in 1676, thought very little of the Irishman's martial abilities. Fairborne, the most important figure in the last seven years of Tangier's history, was a professional soldier who had learned his trade at the Siege of Candia. He first went to Tangier in 1662 with Peterborough, and there he died in 1680.

During the latter part of 1679, the Moorish pressure on Tangier increased dramatically and a larger garrison was essential for the survival of the colony, regardless of the additional cost. Fairborne had repeatedly requested reinforcements since 1676, especially urging that any troops sent over should be drawn from the standing regiments in England as the men which usually appeared as replacements were either old men or young boys, 'the one never immuned to hardship and the other past helping himself'.[16] Charles Fitzcharles, Earl of Plymouth, a natural son of Charles II, was authorised to raise a foot regiment for Tangier, but the executive command of this formation fell upon the lieutenant-colonel, Percy Kirke, and the major, Charles Trelawney. This regiment arrived at Tangier in December 1680. In addition, 600 men were taken from the 1st Foot Guards and the Coldstream Guards to form a battalion under Brevet-Colonel Edward Sackville, lieutenant-colonel of the Coldstream Guards, whilst another 600 were drawn from the Earl of Dumbarton's Foot to form a second battalion, and 120 newly raised horse completed the party.[17] By the end of 1680 there were 3,010 men in Tangier, further augmented to 3,221 by October 1681. This number had fallen to 2,299 by the evacuation in 1684.

Sackville took over as temporary governor after Fairborne's death in 1680, but he was soon recalled into England to give way to Percy Kirke, the most colourful of all the governors. He was another professional soldier who had learned his craft under Turenne, Luxembourg and de Créqui during the 1670s. After his spell as governor of Tangier he rose to become a lieutenant-general under William III, serving with distinction in Ireland and Flanders. It is through the eyes of Samuel Pepys, a more sober and middle-aged Pepys than we meet in his first diary, and his 'Notes on Tangier' that we see Kirke:

> The Governor [Kirke] is said to have got his wife's sister with child, and that she is gone over to Spain to be brought to bed. And that while he is with his whores at his little bathing house which he has furnished with a jade a-purpose there, his wife, whom he keeps in by awe, sends for her gallants and plays the jade by herself at home.[18]

Pepys held a personal aversion to Kirke so we must not over-emphasise his observations, but his 'Notes' give a glimpse of life in Tangier:

> Nothing but vice in the whole place of all sorts, for swearing, cursing, drinking, and whoring. No going by a door almost but you hear people swearing and damning, and the women as much as the men. Insomuch that Captain Silver, a sober officer of my Lord's, belonging to the Ordnance, did say he was quite ashamed of what he heard himself in their house, worse a thousand times than the worst place that he ever was in, in London.[19]

Objectionable though Kirke's morality was to Pepys, he handled the soldiers with firmness at a time when a weaker man might have reduced the garrison to chaos.

Although the governors and senior officers at Tangier generally had loyalist backgrounds, the same was not true of the junior officers and soldiers. As we have seen, Lieutenant-Colonel Maurice Kingwell, the commander of Harley's Regiment, was sent home by Peterborough for expressing republican views in November 1662, and the first two years of the colony's history witnessed intermittent demonstrations of republican sentiments.[20] This problem was largely solved by the action with the Moors on 4 May 1664. Teviot led out a large party to cut wood, but the Moors intercepted them on Jews Hill and destroyed them to a man. Teviot was killed along with nineteen officers, five reformadoes, and 396 men,[21] but even before that the original troops had been whittled away by disease and the harassment of the Moors. Within the first nine months of English occupation, 605 soldiers were lost through sickness and enemy action,[22] and so, by the time of Teviot's death, one-half of the garrison had died. In a closed community like Tangier, the fate of the officers was that of their men. After the defeat of 1664, little more was heard of political disaffection: the Moors performed the king a considerable service.

Duty in Tangier was most unpopular with the officers. It was far from England, leave difficult to obtain, death never far distant, and for the political animals the service was disastrous, removing them from England for long periods. None of the governors or deputy-governors were heavily involved in English or Irish politics, and very few, if any, of the inferior officers. Tangier attracted the more adventurous man or the professional soldier, who could find no place in English society. Kirke, Charles Trelawney,[23] John Chitam, and Sir Arthur Bassett had all fought for the French, whilst Lewis Farrell had served both Spain and France.[24] Colonel Roger Alsopp had commanded a regiment at Dunkirk. There was another difference between the officer corps in Tangier and that in England—in Tangier there was a shortage of commissioned officers.

Fairborne recommended that ensigns should be abolished from all companies in 1678,[25] as not enough men were available to fill all the ranks, and many of the officers who were at Tangier were not worth their places. A report on several officers of the garrison was compiled by Fairborne in 1677,[26] in which Captain Cuthbert Carr was described as not having done 'three months' duty in a year, and that always at such times when no action appears, and then is still disturbing the peace and quiet of the place, besides his continual endeavours to defraud poor men of their rights'. Captain John Giles was considered to be 'so ill affected to monarchy as having served all along against the King in the late Civil Wars and a person so ill-principalled that he is always cunningly underhand formenting and broaching stories to disturb and incite a discontent in the private soldiers'. Captain Brent Ely 'was so given to laziness that [he] cannot endure the soldiers should do any manner of work least he should be involved in it himself', as well as being prone to republican views, and Captain Scroop was more fit for a hospital than a command. Two Lieutenants, Evan Harris and Richard

Hemmings, were so old that they ought to have been pensioned off, and Ensign Hughs was permanently drunk. In 1677, Tangier was officered by a mixture of old royalists, ex-Cromwellians, Scots, Irish, English, drunkards, and men too old and lazy to do their duty. That such men were able to retain their commands was largely due to the unpopularity of Tangier in England.

Francesco Giavarina, the Venetian Resident in England, wrote to the Doge and Senate in 1661 that when the first expeditionary force under Peterborough was forming, although the drums were beating all over London, very few came forward as they would rather stay at home than go to so different a climate.[27] On the march to Portsmouth for their embarkation there were mass desertions, the men taking their levy money and then running from the colours. Sir Hugh Cholmley considered that the bad diet which had to be endured in Tangier and the sufferings of the soldiers in general 'gave so bad an impression of the place among the Commons of England, that they heard nothing with more detestation than being sent to Tangier, which they usually esteemed no better than an ill prison, from which they could only hope to be freed by the grave'.[28] The rampant epidemics which plagued the town were the chief cause for the public hatred of Tangier, but the seedy nature of the inhabitants must have discouraged people from wishing to live there:

> There wanted . . . neither money nor wine; and this was liberally taken by all sorts as an antidote to drive away sorrow. . . . But what disorders and disreputation did of necessity follow may be concluded from the nature of the Colony, consisting chiefly of soldiers of divers nations that had been long bred in armies of the greatest liberty; of merchants that had been used to the affairs and to the vices of the world, and repaired hither to make up the ruins of their broken fortunes. The rest of the men and the women were but few, and generally as virtuous and as good as those that follow camps. . . . There might be some of sober and orderly living, but certainly of these the number was so small as not to have credit enough to be observed among the crowd of others.[29]

An attempt to send 300 men out of the regiments disbanded in England in 1679, caused the affected troops to mutiny.[30]

There was one section of the military community which found Tangier agreeable and suitable to its needs: the reformado officers. None of the establishments between 1660 and 1685 provided for the reformadoes, and this was also the case in Tangier. They were paid by fictitious musters whereby a set number of false names were entered on the muster roll and the pay drawn on those men granted to the reformadoes. The standard rate of pay for a reformado was *2s 6d* a day,[31] the normal pay of a trooper, or else the pay of four foot soldiers which amounted to *3s*. In 1665 there were fourteen reformadoes in Tangier, increasing to twenty-three two years later to accommodate those officers who lost their places in the garrison reduction of that year.[32] It required the pay of 140 non-effective men, or false musters, to pay the reformadoes in 1667, and in 1670 the garrison included 174 'Reformadoes, Non-Effectives, and Children' who had to be paid from the establishment.[33] With the insufficiency of military places in England to satisfy all the unemployed royalist and Cromwellian officers, the pay of a reformado at Tangier must have been tempting to many of the old soldiers.

With such a reputation in England, it was difficult to find recruits to reinforce the garrison in Tangier. When officers went on leave to England they were often ordered to raise levies by beat of drum and ship them back to Tangier on their return. This was simple as most officers spent far longer on leave in England than they did on duty in Tangier, this being one of the reasons for the acute shortage of officers. Leave passes were officially issued for only six months at a time,[34] but when Kirke was governor over half his officers were on leave and none over-anxious to return.[35] Recruits for the ranks were usually gathered in the West Country so that they were within marching distance of the embarkation ports at Falmouth and Plymouth. However, when Henry Norwood and Palmes Fairborne undertook a recruiting drive in Somerset, Devon and Cornwall during 1665, they found the local tradesmen very unwilling to volunteer. The situation deteriorated so much that it was even suggested that men might be raised under the pretence of serving in the Plymouth garrison, and then once they had arrived ship them off to Tangier. This deceit was not actually employed.[36] In 1672, an Order in Council authorised the use of the press gang; 200 men were thereby raised in the west of England, but they were of very poor quality, 'whereof there was two women that had entered themselves for soldiers in men's apparel . . . some of them are old men and most very poor creatures'.[37]

The only consolation for the pressed men was that they were supposed to serve only for three years and then be discharged, but they were fortunate if they lived that long. In May and July 1672, eighty-two men were discharged through ill health and wounds, and when the reinforcements appeared in 1680 a further 200 of the old garrison were released 'and deem themselves no better than slaves for having been kept there so long'.[38] With the ever-present sickness and almost continual action, there were rarely any surplus troops which could be discharged. For those that stayed life was very hard.

Private men lived on a diet of ship's biscuit, salt beef or pork, dried peas, butter, cheese and oatmeal, with the occasional variety of fresh bread and dried fish.[39] These provisions were sent to Tangier from England by contractors who purchased their rights from the Lords Commissioners for Tangier, but even if the correct amount was shipped there was no guarantee that the stores would actually reach their destination. Victualling vessels could be shipwrecked during the three-week voyage through the stormy Bay of Biscay, or captured by Corsairs, as happened to the *Phoenix* in 1677. Neither was Sir Dennis Gauden, the contractor for victuals during most of the life of English Tangier, in the habit of dispatching generous quantities. Middleton complained to the Lords Commissioners in 1673 that although a shipment had just arrived it was hopelessly insufficient.[40]

Fitzgerald developed some market gardens in the 'dead-ground' covered by the out-forts, but these soon became untenable as the area was overlooked by the Moors, making the cultivation of crops possible only during periods of peace. When the garrison and the Moors were on good terms fresh meat could be bought locally, but this source dried up on a renewal of hostilities. In general, the food supply at Tangier was irregular and inadequate and what little there was happened to be of the kind which produced scurvy and malnutrition and was most unsuitable for men working in a hot climate. There was enough housing for the men, except for the first two or three years when the colony was seriously over-crowded, but the gradual accumulation of casualties eased this difficulty. Bellasise built some barracks in 1665, and the maintenance of shelter was a major concern for all the governors.

Poor food led to disease. Fortunately, the plague which affected the coast of North Africa during the latter half of the seventeenth century, did not chance upon Tangier, a fact largely dependent upon luck and the strict quarantine which was imposed on all ships which entered the harbour.[41] However, there were unspecified epidemics which swept through the garrison. In 1664 a wave of disease affected both the men and the horses, and Norwood reported to Arlington in 1669 that ten men in every company were sick. On the conclusion of a peace with the Moors, the health of the garrison improved dramatically as fresh meat and provisions flowed into the storehouses. A hospital was established as soon as the army arrived in Tangier, but it rapidly gained the reputation of being the worst place to send the sick; it was situated on marshy ground close to the town walls, and more men came out in coffins than they did cured.[42] Four 'Overseers of the Hospital' were appointed in 1675, with instructions to tour the building every Monday in order to make sure that the food, attendance and nursing of each patient amounted to no more than 4*d* a day. This 4*d* was deducted from the sick man's pay, and entrance to the hospital was dependent on a signed form from a military surgeon. The establishment allowed £547 10*s* a year for the running of the hospital, but when pay was often months in arrears soldiers were unable to pay to enter the institution and so the annual allowance had to be used to subsidise the men and often ran out before the end of the year. When an epidemic affected the garrison the money for the hospital was not increased, bringing an additional prejudice against its services. Shortage of funds was the principal cause of the hospital's failure, especially when there were often as many as 400 men in the building at any one time,[43] but contemporary medicine had no answer to tropical disease under any circumstances.

Since the colony was always undermanned, the soldiers had to undertake extra work in a hot climate on a diet which was costive and unhealthy, severely weakening their resistance to illness. There were times in the late 1660s and throughout the next decade, when the effective force fit for duty was well below

1,000 but this number had to man the redoubts and forts, patrol the lines, assist in building the mole, in addition to policing the town and unloading ships in the harbour. Fairborne was forced to place the entire garrison on double duty in 1678 in order to carry out all these chores.[44] Yet, for all this, the soldiers were always in arrears of pay.

A private received *9d* a day but he was given only *3d* of this in actual 'dry money', the remaining *6d* being composed of an equivalent value of provisions.[45] The *3d* was eaten away by deductions for clothing, weapons, contributions to the medical service and the support of lance-corporals and reformadoes. This left very little for the soldier, but, apart from whores and drink, there was not much on which to spend the money. Not only was the pay inadequate, but it was always months, and sometimes years, in arrears.[46] Nearly all the men and officers were in debt to the merchants and tradesmen of Tangier. A list of the men in Captain James Leslie's company showed that they were in debt to the tune of £442 *2s 2½d*, half the total annual pay of the entire company.[47] Cholmley observed:

> the poor soldier, being sometimes six or sometimes nine months without his pay, when he gets a flood of money spends it all in a week and by that intemperance either has suddenly a sickness or by the consequence of it a sickness in a little time, and when there comes to help himself he hath no money because that is spent, or credit because his pay is not till six months afterwards, and few merchants there are in this town can stay so long for their money, and fewer, compassionate enough to supply the necessities of a miserable man. I have been told many have died for want of twelve pence to relieve him.[48]

Until 1668 the garrison was paid at irregular intervals varying from one to five months,[49] but after 1668 it was designed to send out the pay once every three months. The resultant practice was very different from the theory. Pepys, who was both Treasurer and Paymaster for Tangier, was called before the Treasury Board in company with Sir Stephen Fox, the paymaster of the Guards and Garrisons, on 31 August 1668. They both stated that they could no longer afford to pay their respective forces as the allotted funds were anticipated so far into the future that no bankers were prepared to extend them credit.[50] Little was done to assist the two paymasters, for the whole of the king's finances were in a similar predicament. Somehow Pepys and Fox managed to find sufficient loans, but the inevitable corollary was irregularity of payment and delay, aggravated still further after the Stop of the Exchequer in 1672. Shortage of money led to petty theft and the soldiers selling their clothing and equipment to local tradesmen. Uniforms, bedding and weapons were stolen by one soldier from another, and most stole foodstuffs to supplement their meagre diet.

Whatever money the soldiers could discover was spent on the major pastime—drinking to excess. Drunkenness was the scourge of Tangier and the cause of much of the ill-health and poverty amongst the soldiery, but there was little else for a man to do in his leisure hours. A pair of stocks was set up in 1666 which succeeded 'in shaming away much drunkenness from this place',[51] but it was only a temporary expedient and by 1676 Fairborne was forced to alter the guard system in order to lessen the danger of having drunken soldiers on duty:

> Whereas we used to relieve the guards in the afternoon, by which means the soldiers had time to make themselves drunk and so became a shame to the parade and a reproach to the spectators, I have altered that to 7 a clock in the morning, where they are exercised for an hour and then relieve the field guards.[52]

So serious did the problem become that the Mayor of Tangier issued a proclamation in 1679 forbidding licensed or unlicensed purveyors of liquor to entertain any soldier to the extent that he became incapacitated and unfit for duty. Fourteen persons held licences to sell alcohol in 1681, nine of whom were soldiers, but there were a large number of unofficial establishments as well. A report made for the Lords Commissioners in 1682 on the state of the garrison and the colony, gave an impression of the depths to which the soldiers had sunk. After stating that each company needed a cook and a field kitchen, the report continued:

> for want hereof the soldiers sell most of their victuals for drink (which hath killed thousands), having not time or conveniency to dress it. Some are so lazy, others sick and weak, that they eat their meat cold and raw, and so consequently it must needs kill them.[53]

Pepys, when in Tangier in 1683, found officers drunk upon the guard or asleep in their beds when they should have been on duty, whilst Kirke himself, if we are to believe fully the malicious attitude of Pepys, openly sanctioned drunkenness amongst his men:

> And to show how little he makes of drunkenness (though he will beat a fellow for having a dirty face or band) I have seen a fellow reel upon him as he has been walking with me in the street as drunk as a dog, and at this busy time too, when everybody that is not upon the guard, is at work. And he has only laughed at him and cry 'God damn me, the fellow has got a good morning's draught already', and so let him go without one word of reprehension.[54]

By the time of the evacuation in 1684 drunkenness sorely affected the performance of the soldiers. Their routine was to receive their provisions on a Monday and then sell them immediately to the civilians to give themselves money for drink. Many drank away this money within three days and then had to endure the rest of the week without food and, even worse, without drink. Kirke was of the probably correct opinion that brandy had killed more men in Tangier than had the Moors.

Drunkenness on this scale resulted in ill-discipline. The minutes and records of the courts martial at Tangier are very full and have been preserved complete from 1662 to 1674, although after that they are more sparse.[55] During the twelve years in question 531 cases came before the courts martial, the vast majority ending in proof of guilt. Over one-fifth dealt with petty larceny and theft (117 cases), and seventy-one involved the abuse of drink in one form or another. Over a period of twelve years these figures might not appear unduly excessive, but the average strength of the garrison at that time was 1,250. Thus, nearly half the garrison was brought before the court martial, and there was only a very small 'hard core' of regular offenders. The high incidence of petty theft is explained by the faults in the pay system and the poor credit facilities, but the number of cases of drunkenness is surprisingly low when compared with the evidence which indicates that it was a very serious problem. The most reasonable explanation is that the court only heard cases where a man was drunk on duty, or when he caused a breach of the peace. Also the officer corps was never at full strength due to its habit of taking long furloughs in England, whilst the non-commissioned officers appeared as often as the rank and file before the court charged with drunkenness, suggesting that the rate of apprehension was not very high. Finally, the period of really serious drunkenness occurred in the late 1670s, years which are not covered by these particular records. The legal records of the garrison understate the problems caused by drink.

Most crimes were of a military nature; desertion, mutiny, neglect of duty. Despite the brutal punishments handed out by the court martial, the occurrence of these misdemeanours was steady throughout the time covered by the records. Many men found garrison life so disagreeable that they deserted to the Moors, where slavery awaited them, and this as early as 1662 when two soldiers were executed for attempting to desert to the Moors to join their comrades who had made a more successful escape. In the Articles of Peace signed between Bellasise and Guyland on 2 April 1666, a special clause stated that each side should return the deserters and criminals of the other. Some men deserted to avoid the harsh sentences of the court martial. Kirke described this type of desertion as 'too frequent', adding that many soldiers ran away directly after committing an offence for fear of being punished.[56]

Closely allied to desertion was mutiny and disobedience to officers. Mutiny included any crime from refusing an order to a mass revolt. Minor cases of individual mutinies occur throughout the court martial records and were a frequent disturbance to the garrison, but the major revolts happened in the late 1670s when pay was up to two years in arrears and drunkenness and the general boredom of life had a positive effect on the soldiery. Even so, there was never any large mutiny and certainly none which threatened the safety of the colony, a fact reflecting the apathy of the men and the very firm hand with which Fairborne ruled his command. If the men were not required for the guard or patrols they were taken out in parties to undertake manual work on the mole or the fortifications. On 30 May 1676, the soldiers refused to go out to work, but Fairborne forced them at least to march to the defence lines which they were repairing. However, 'when they came to the Lines, little or none would they do.' This small mutiny came about due to mass drunkenness as that day was the King's Birthday and his health had been liberally taken in 'Malaga Wine'. The troops were suffering from hangovers.[57] Fairborne wrote to the Lords Commissioners on 9 November 1678, that discipline would improve greatly if the pay could be sent out regularly. In another incident working parties could only be made to march out after a number of arrests, and even then the more vociferous grumbled that life was 'all work and no pay'.[58] Another latent mutiny was halted by Fairborne shooting the ringleader dead.[59]

In their own, more refined, manner the officers were as badly behaved as their men, although they enjoyed more freedom than the soldiery and only their most serious offences brought them before a court martial. Usually, an officer was corrected by a quiet word from his superior, or was reported to the Secretary of State in England. Two cases involving officers appear in the court martial records: Quartermaster Thomas Winkfield was found not guilty of wounding a corporal, and Captain Cuthbert Carr was accused of possessing a silver watch belonging to Henry Holt. He was instructed to return it. The officers set a bad example to their men, but most of their indiscipline sprang from the clash of religion, politics and nationality, as well as personal feuds and the complex etiquette of the period.[60]

Colonel Norwood and Sir Tobias Bridge are sensible of being much laid aside by the Governor [John Fitzgerald], and, after several quarrels between lesser officers, Major Fairborne and Major White passed angry words at the Governor's table . . . fighting was prevented by Colonel Norwood, and they by him confined. . . . A Council of War was appointed by the Governor to reconcile Major Fairborne and Major White . . . Captain Brain to ask Lieutenant Harris' pardon having caned him in the head on the parade (Harris hath since killed Lieutenant Basset), and I hope that unruly humour hath spent its malice.[61]

Three years later, Fairborne, a very strong character, duelled with Lieutenant-Colonel Edward Fitzgerald after he had supposedly insulted Fitzgerald's lieutenant, whilst Fitzgerald himself had a violent argument with Captain Edward Witham as to whether a horse race should have started from Fort Anne or Fort James. When Middleton arrived to govern the colony in 1669 he was armed with Additional Instructions to reform and punish 'the debauchery and dissoluteness [which] are frequently practised by many officers and soldiers in the garrison'.

After Lieutenant Henry Collier had killed Lieutenant Thomas

Church, he was not tried by a court martial but by the Court of Record,[62] where the jury returned a verdict of manslaughter. Collier was then burned in the hand and continued in his command. Kirke took a serious view of the duelling and bickering amongst his officers, cashiering two ensigns for duelling in 1681. The soldiers copied their officers and fought amongst themselves, but Kirke ordered that any found with a drawn sword or bayonet were to be arrested and sent on fatigues during the governor's pleasure.

Most of the disciplinary troubles at Tangier sprang from the lack of money and the tedium of life. Dice, cards and lying on the sea shore were about the only possible relaxations for men in their off-duty hours. Officers were able to lead a reasonably full and active social life, similar to that which they would have enjoyed in England. Plays were staged by a troupe of Spanish actors in a storehouse at York Castle, and the higher officers held balls and dinner parties. The lower entertainments of bull-baiting and cock-fighting were enjoyed by all. The hinterland abounded in wild game for the hunt—boar, hare, antelope, plover, partridge and curlew. Hawking was popular. Men could fish from the mole in an effort to supplement their diet, but it was unwise to venture into the bay in small boats as Moorish pirates tended to sweep into Tangier harbour and seize whatever vessels were unguarded. A pleasant afternoon could be spent in walking along the sea shore to the ruins of Old Tangier, provided that the tide did not advance too quickly and trap the unwary. Whitehall Fort was the main social centre, 'a place where the ladies, the officers, and the better sort of people do refresh and divert themselves with Wine, Fruits, and a very pretty bowling base'. For those blessed with rank and money life was tolerable, but there was always the threat of a sudden attack by the enemy, the broken ground giving the Moors the chance to come uncomfortably close even to Whitehall. Sir Hugh Cholmley was especially fond of being rowed round Tangier Bay in order to view work upon the mole of which he was the engineer-general for many years, whilst Fairborne took pleasure in riding about the lines during an afternoon in the company of his wife.

Life in Tangier developed a routine all of its own. At six or half past in the morning the drummer of the governor's company (the senior unit of the garrison) beat the reveille, and then the drums of all the other companies took up the roll. At seven or eight the drums beat again to sound the 'Assembly' and every regiment marched to the Parade Ground near York Castle for an hour's drill. On Tuesdays, Wednesdays and Fridays the Town Major, or the adjutant of the governor's regiment, came down to the Parade and detailed troops for the main guard. On the other three days of the week, Sunday being a holiday, the regiments heard prayers and then proceeded to the market-place for a formal garrison parade. Here, any offenders were punished in full view of all the soldiers.[63] After this the guards were sent out and those detailed for manual work gathered their equipment and marched away. Once the guards were settled it was the duty of the field officer of the day, normally a major, to periodically 'go the rounds', checking all the sentry posts and making sure that the password for the day was commonly understood.[64]

England regarded Tangier as a den of popery where a large, pro-catholic army was preparing for future employment in the British Isles. The reality was not so much popery as the cause of the trouble, but a general apathy towards any sort of religion. On Whit Sunday in 1670 Cholmley found only three officers in the garrison church and the total number of the communicants was only thirty-three.[65] There were a large number of catholic officers in the original corps under Peterborough as two of the four regiments were Irish, and Pepys states that in 1662 most of the Tangier officers were papists. Teviot, John Fitzgerald and Bellasise were all catholic governors, and there was no prejudice against catholics within the garrison, the possession of the Roman faith being no bar to promotion. An unofficial religious toleration was practised in Tangier, which was one of the principal grievances which Parliament held against the colony. Not only was it a base of loyal, trained troops, including an unhealthily large proportion of catholics, but it ignored the religious establishment in England, paying scant regard to the Test Acts.

A list of all officers who were of 'the Protestant Faith' and those of 'the Romish Persuasion' during 1667 gave totals of forty protestants and thirty-four catholics.[66] During 1681, officers were offered the Oaths of Allegiance and Supremacy and the Sacrament according to the rites of the Church of England. Only half the garrison officers took the Oaths, the majority of these coming from the reinforcements recently sent out of England. Most of the old garrison officers did not take the Oaths, either in 1681 or before,[67] but this evidence is not definitive as some officers might have taken the Oaths during their frequent visits to England and neither do the lists claim to be complete. However, they serve to show that Parliament's suspicions were based on fact rather than prejudice, for there was still a large catholic population in Tangier in 1681.

As to the religion of the men, we have no real evidence. Most of the Irishmen would have been confirmed catholics, and the old republicans would have held equally strong views in the opposite direction. As many of the recruits and pressed men were drawn from the West Country they probably held dissenting persuasions, but this is only conjecture. However, we can be certain that Tangier supported a variety of faiths in an atmosphere approaching harmony. Portuguese priests, based on the catholic cathedral, administered to the few of their countrymen who remained, whilst the small Jewish community employed their own rabbi and their own synagogue. In 1676 there were eighteen priests and friars but only two protestant ministers,[68] and to one of them, Lancelot Addison, we owe many of the descriptions of life in Tangier.

At the final evacuation in 1684 the troops which returned to England greatly annoyed the Whigs, who viewed the arrival of this corps as another blow against Parliamentary government:

Tis easily to be apprehended that these troops upon their arrival, will be great eyesores, not only to those that own themselves Whigs, but to all that are not thoroughly affected to his Majesty and his Government.[69]

At first, the soldiers must have been both physical and political eyesores, but with better food, regular pay, and the wider variety of life in England, they quickly settled down and we hear of no more outrageous incidents.

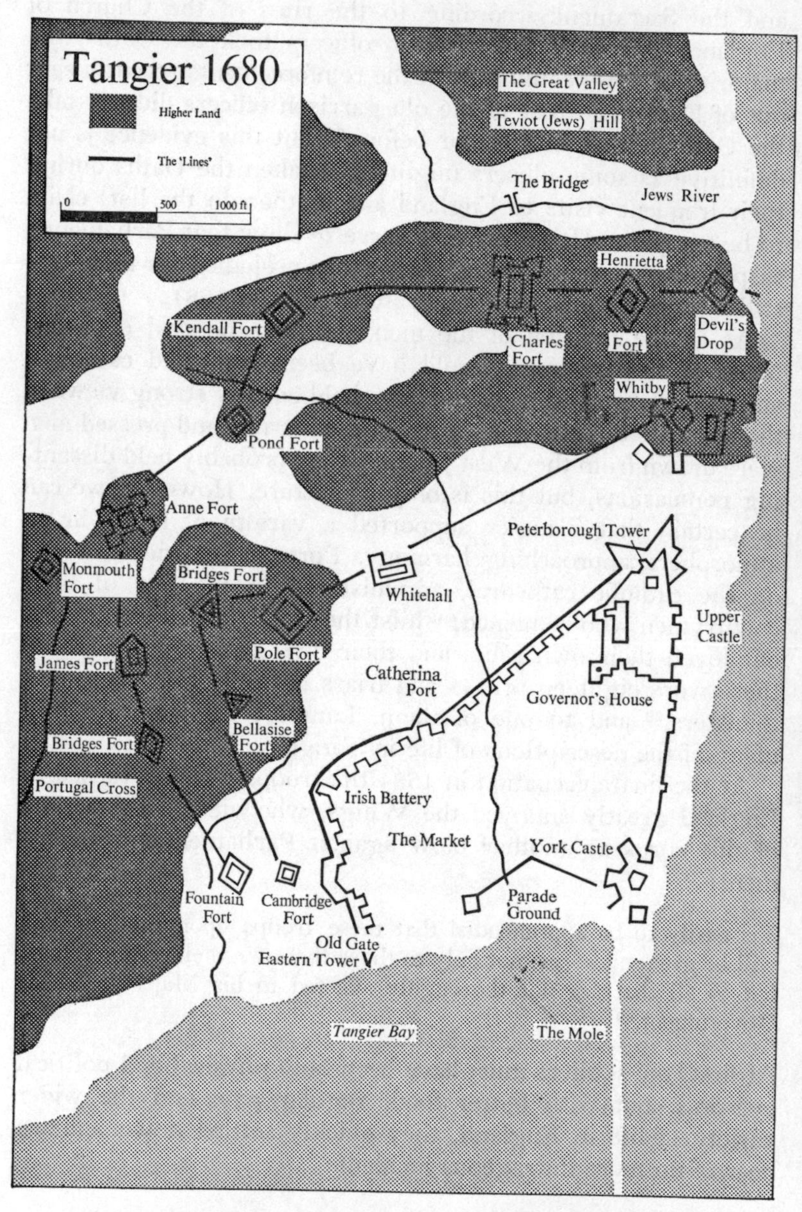

Plan of Tangier, 1662–84 (drawn by Nigel Bradley)

VII

The Fight for Tangier

THE Moors of Barbary were a resourceful enemy. Although they had no organised standing army but fought as a feudal mass, their tactics were so different to anything which the British had encountered before that they were a formidable foe. There were no sub-divisions in the Moorish army; their foot operated as an entire body and their horse as another. The cavalry formed ahead of the infantry and in all set battles the horse opened the action with a general charge,[1] leaving the foot to either exploit their success or cover their withdrawal. Lances and pikes were the main weapons, although they had some muskets, but the proper use of artillery was beyond them. During the Great Siege of Tangier in 1680 the Moorish artillery was ineffectual and caused little damage to the British fortifications. As with the feudal levies in England, an army organised on an *ad hoc* basis could not long remain in the field. Whenever the Moors brought their considerable weight to bear on Tangier they were incapable of sustaining their pressure for very long, and this, added to the fact that the Moors were unable to blockade Tangier by sea, rendered a serious siege impossible. Faced with these difficulties the Moors had to discover alternative methods.

Tangier lay in a hollow on the coast, but the land rose abruptly inland to form an arc of hills overlooking the town. From these observation points the Moors could always see into the town and watch any movements made by the garrison, both inside and outside the city walls. In the possession of this intelligence, they were able to make use of their greatest skill—

surprise attacks and ambushes. Guyland succeeded in drilling his troops to such a peak that two or three thousand men could hide only a quarter of a mile from the town walls to ambush a column of unwary British soldiers. They could keep strict silence for long periods, and their predominant use of cold steel made their sudden attacks doubly effective. The Moors were greatly assisted by the rugged ground near Tangier—innumerable hollows and hillocks covered with a thick, scrubby vegetation and an abundance of ferns and bracken.

At best these ambushes were only an annoyance to the garrison as the superior organisation, discipline and firepower of the British army was more than a match for the Moors in open battle. Any defeat suffered by the garrison was caused by a surprise assault which made it impossible for the British to deploy from marching column into line of battle. The Portuguese had always been able to beat the Moors, and any British reverse was the result of bad generalship, poor intelligence or carelessness. There were no excuses for falling to so primitive an enemy.

However, the fighting performance of the garrison under the Earl of Peterborough from 1662 to 1664 was abysmal. Guyland naturally took great offence at the arrival of the British and their occupation of a town which he considered to be part of his territories. He was unable to bring all his strength against Tangier as he was feuding with the 'Saint of Sallee', but he spared enough troops to taunt the garrison with a number of minor ambushes.[2] Bad health, poor supplies and acute homesickness made the garrison more afraid of the Moors than their operations warranted, although the barbarous nature of their opponents and their reliance on the scimitar had a certain impact on men used to 'civilised' warfare. Peterborough steadily expanded the colony, taking in land around Tangier and then protecting it with fortifications.[3] Guyland protested, but, meeting with no response he marched a large portion of his army to Tangier in April 1663, where he tried to entice the garrison outside the city walls. On 3 May Peterborough succumbed. Major Nathaniel Fiennes was ordered out with 500 men to drive off a party of Moors who were but a short distance from the town. Out they ran 'in a confused manner', with no prior intelligence of the strength or position of the Moors. The result was a disaster. The British pursued the retreating Moors who led them into a prepared trap. Surrounded on three sides, the British were routed and only about a third of the force regained the safety of the town. Fiennes was not among them. This serious setback sapped the confidence of Peterborough and his garrison. No parties were sent out of the town and the gates were permanently shut; the Moors were permitted to steal cattle from under the very noses of the sentries. A change of command was required.

Andrew Rutherford, Earl of Teviot, arrived on 11 May 1663. A professional soldier, he took immediate and energetic action. Teviot realised that the key to a successful defence of Tangier lay in the construction of fortifications which would enable the garrison, and not the Moors, to control the circle of hills overlooking the town. Almost as soon as he arrived, he started building a redoubt, Fort Catherine, 300 yards in advance of the Main Gate, known as Catherina Port. The Moors attacked this work on 9 June 1663 with 500 men, but Captain William Fiennes beat them off after two hours' hard fighting.[4] Four other forts were under construction at the same time, and six days later the Moors launched a fresh offensive against the unfinished Pole Fort, but Teviot had been expecting this and was well prepared. He had the ground near the fort littered with 'Galtraps' and 'Crows' Feet', impeding the advance of the enemy cavalry.[5] British hand grenades finished off the Moorish infantry and the assault failed.

Guyland sued for six months' peace after this defeat. Teviot accepted for he needed all available time to complete his system of fortifications. However, although Guyland and Teviot respected each other, the Moors paid scant regard to the truce. On 3 July the Moors again attacked the new redoubt, but were driven off, losing 100 men.[6] On 16 July came the decisive action.

Instead of the Roman Geese, Teviot employed 'a Guard of Dogs' to discover any Moors hiding within the British 'Lines'. At 2.00 a.m., the canine sentries found a party of enemy horsemen waiting in an ambush. Concentrating the Troop of the Tangier Horse, Teviot charged down upon the Moors. Before either side could become seriously engaged, Teviot fell back as he had spotted an approach by a large body of enemy infantry. Hastily, he ordered his five new forts to be manned and provisioned. A mist had blown in from the sea, and with the aid of a westerly wind the Moors set fire to the grass before Tangier, blinding the garrison artillery. Under the cover of this smoke screen, the Moors advanced to within musket shot of the forts. Then, as if through divine intervention, the wind changed direction blowing the smoke back over the Moors. This was too much and Guyland sent forward a herald to ask for a truce. Teviot consented, and following a banquet and formal ceremonies a peace was signed. Leaving the Lieutenant-Governor, John Fitzgerald, in command, Teviot took six months' leave in Scotland.

In his absence, Fitzgerald continued to build the defence lines around Tangier. The forts and redoubts were positioned between one quarter and one half mile from the city walls, so that the guns on the Upper Castle of Tangier and the artillery along the courtain were able to give supporting fire. In addition, the forts possessed their own lighter artillery, as well as supplies of food and ammunition. These forts differed enormously in size. Fort Charles was the largest and could accommodate a garrison of 300 men, whilst Devil's Drop and Fort Cambridge were little more than crude earthworks with garrisons of ten or twelve men. These fortifications ringed Tangier in a great arc, from coast to coast, occupying the inner line of hills before the town. They were joined to one another by a system of trenches and breastworks, referred to as 'the Lines', often with palisades added along vulnerable sectors. We must not assume that these fortifications were anything wonderful. Images of the angled masterpieces of Vauban and Coehoorn in Flanders and Germany must be dismissed from the mind. The Tangier forts were no more than primitive blockhouses protected by wooden fences and ditches. Only Fort Charles and Fort Anne had flanking bastions, whilst the rest of the forts were mere gun-platforms. English military engineers were not famous for their advanced designs in the seventeenth century and the examples of their work at Tangier reveal the paucity of their imagination. But against an enemy with virtually no artillery and with no conception of how to use what they had, these blockhouses ought to have been sufficient for the defence of Tangier.

In January 1664, Teviot returned to his command only to

find that Fitzgerald had extended the truce by a further two months, but this was the best time of the year for digging as the ground was wet from the winter rains. Furthermore, Charles II had given Teviot instructions not to agree to any peace which did not give him the liberty to continue with his fortifications.[7] Communicating his rejection of the peace to Guyland, Teviot set about building a covering hornwork before the Upper Castle. Guyland replied by marching his whole army up to Tangier; the niggling war of ambushes began again. By his energy and mercurial nature, Teviot infused the garrison with a tremendous enthusiasm, wiping out the legacy of lethargy which Peterborough had left behind. Guyland threw all his troops against the new forts and the lines, but he met with no success and suffered large casualties without inflicting any serious losses on the British. The crisis of the campaign came on 29 February.

Advancing up to the lines, the Moors tried another unsuccessful assault, but, in doing so, Guyland's personal standard was planted on the rampart of the British trenches. Captain Edward Witham led out a party of the Tangier Horse and captured this psychological token, which led to the Moors deserting the field pleading that it was the time of Ramadan.[8] Skirmishing and ambushing continued for another month, but Teviot held the initiative and the morale of his men was far higher than that of the Moors, especially as the fortifications were almost completed.[9]

However, Teviot was running into difficulties. Although he had annexed 800 acres into the hinterland of Tangier, the lands were sandy and furnished little in the way of building materials. Short of building stone and lime, Teviot had to import them from Portugal, which was then allied to England. It would have been easier to have gathered these items from Spain, but she was opposed to the English occupation of Tangier and refused to assist. Indeed, Spain had been suspected of aiding Guyland with weapons and supplies in 1663, although no definite proof of this was ever brought forward.[10] The voyage to and from Portugal was hazardous, for vessels had not only to run the risk of bad weather in the Atlantic, but the Straits of Gibraltar were a favourite haunt of corsairs. Faced with these problems, Teviot looked inland, where, a mile or two in front of the lines, lime and building stone were to be had in plenty.

Whether he was after these requirements or merely out on a foraging expedition is impossible to tell, but on 4 May a composite battalion of 500 men, commanded by the governor, marched towards Jews Hill, two or three miles out of Tangier.[11] Colonel Roger Alsopp gave another explanation of Teviot's manœuvre; the Governor was such an active man that as he was unable to carry out any further work on the fortifications, he took soldiers to cut down the brushwood on the far side of Jews River. The natural cover in this area had long been used by the Moors as a concentration-point, and Teviot wished to deny the Moors this convenience. Also, exactly two years before Nathaniel Fiennes had marched out with his battalion on his ill-fated counter-attack, so there might have been a psychological motive behind Teviot's expedition.[12]

Once over Jews River, Teviot met a force of 3,000 Moors, and these he beat off. It seems that the advance was a calculated risk. Martin Wescombe was certain that Teviot was aware of the presence of a Moorish force around Jews Hill, and the Governor must have known that his approach march would have been observed by Guyland well before he reached Jews River.[13] After repulsing the first assault, Teviot was sufficiently confident to advance further inland, but, like Fiennes, he was moving into a trap. The Moors' first attack had been a decoy luring the British into heavily wooded upland where another 8,000 lay hidden. Unable to assume their stylised order of battle, the British were defeated in clusters of hand-to-hand encounters where pikes and hangers were no match for scimitars. Teviot rallied his battalion on the summit of Jews Hill where they were cut down to a man. Thirty out of the original 500 escaped to Tangier.[14]

Fortunately for the garrison, the Moors did not follow up their success. The war continued in a desultory fashion until 1666, when Bellasise concluded a peace with Guyland.[15] The Moorish chief was under severe pressure himself, and with the bulk of his troops required for a civil war within Barbary he had none to spare to oppose Tangier. Guyland supported Mohammed, the unsuccessful suitor for the throne who had been killed by the 'Great Tafiletta' in 1664. Thereafter Guyland's star was in the descendant, forcing him to fight for his own position and lands. By 1669 Guyland had been driven into exile in Algeria and his provinces taken over by a chieftain appointed by Er Rasheed II, the new King of Barbary. It was with a succession of local leaders supported by the full weight of the Moroccan Kingdom that the Tangier garrison now had to contend.

With the safety of a secure peace, the British embarked on another bout of fortress building. Between 1665 and 1668 £31,230 was spent on strengthening Tangier. The town walls were repaired and bolstered with ravelins and additional ditches along the weaker sections, redoubts were built out from the Upper Castle, and the parapets of the courtain widened and made stronger.[16] Whether all these works were ever completed is open to serious doubt, for the government never spared much money for Tangier and the state of the fortifications in 1678 was bad enough to suggest that no repairs had been carried out on them for years.

Late in June 1669 the Moors reappeared before Tangier. The civil war was over and a new and powerful dynasty settled on the throne; their attention turned to Tangier. From 28 June to 3 July 1669 the Moors managed to lay an ambush within the lines on every day, but were driven out with trifling loss to the garrison on each occasion. How the Moors infiltrated the lines so easily is an interesting point. At this time the garrison was sadly below strength, making it difficult to maintain a proper guard along all the lines. Also the lines were not in a good condition. In any event, the Moors passed through these defences with impunity and withdrew equally easily,[17] for we never read of the Moors being trapped between a garrison sally and the lines. All this suggests that the famed lines were no more than picquet positions around which the Moors infiltrated with facility. This harassing warfare was still going on at the end of July, but casualties on both sides were minute.

Since the days of Teviot the Moors had gained a healthy respect for the British soldiers, in spite of their victories over Fiennes and the unfortunate earl himself. Throughout 1670 and 1671 the ambushes and intermittent fighting continued. During the summer of 1671, 6,000 men of the Great Tafiletta's army lay about Tangier, setting ambushes to cut off parties of haymakers and those who wandered too far from the lines, and again the Moors were able to deliver surprise attacks within the lines themselves. Sir Hugh Cholmley, with his customary directness, went to the heart of the matter:

[The Moors] lodge their ambushes within our very lines, they sometimes killed our men as they passed to discover, which they continually do without any other danger than hazarding a few shots, whilst they leap over the lines and run into the fields of their own country. This insecurity makes all men more shy in passing about the fields, and cannot be prevented but by walling the lines about. I am sure half the money that is said has been spent here in making several insignificant forts, would, if some had been well husbanded, have surrounded our whole lines according to the best way of modern fortifications.[18]

These 'insignificant forts' had been designed and laid out by Teviot, whilst some later additions were the work of Sir Bernard de Gomme, Surveyor-General and Engineer-General of the Ordnance Office in England. He made periodic visits to Tangier to supervise the construction of his designs during the late 1660s and early 1760s. It is upon this man that the inept method of fortification must be blamed. Indeed, so bad were the defences, both in repair and plan, that a commission appointed to inspect them in 1683 estimated that £4,798,561 16*s* 6*d* would have to be spent in order to make Tangier defensible.[19] If a man could 'leap over' the lines then they must have been little more than narrow trenches.

Further ambushes protracted this undeclared war during 1674, but neither side gained any positive advantage. One-eyed William O'Brien, the second Earl of Inchiquin, ruled as Governor in 1675 and during this year the garrison suffered its third serious defeat. On the intelligence of a Moorish Christian, Praytor Hamet, Inchiquin learned of a large herd of cattle within five miles of Tangier and that the Moors close to Tangier had been withdrawn to the Emperor's main army near Fez. To a man with experience of Tangier this information ought to have seemed highly suspicious, but Inchiquin had no knowledge of local conditions and cattle-raiding was in the Irish blood. On the night of 19 September 1675 Major Sir Palmes Fairborne was given the command of 500 men to bring in the cattle. He divided his force into three: a forlorn hope, or vanguard, of 100 under Sir Robert Napier; the main body of 300 under Fairborne himself; and a reserve of 100 under Captain Marmaduke

Boynton. At 9.00 p.m. this force marched out of Catherina Port. Posting himself with the main force on a hill to the west of Fort Anne, Fairborne sent the forlorn ahead to fetch the cattle. Needless to say, there were none. The forlorn ran into a prepared ambush, and as soon as Fairborne heard the firing he decided to beat a hasty retreat to the top of Anne's Lane, where Boynton was waiting with the reserve. Forming a square, Fairborne's soldiers began to march back when they too were assaulted on all sides by a large body of Moors. However, maintaining the difficult square formation on the march, he successfully gained Anne's Lane, but there was no sign of Boynton. Apparently, he had heard the shooting and reported to Inchiquin that it was all over with Fairborne; the governor had ordered him to fall back within the lines. Fairborne reorganised his force and advanced to the hill, hoping to pick up any survivors from the forlorn hope. He remained on the hill for a quarter of an hour, but was then forced to retire in the face of 1,500 Moors. Fairborne's party had ten killed and several wounded, but the forlorn was entirely lost.[20]

This senseless enterprise cost 150 casualties in a garrison which was already seriously depleted. Fairborne wrote in protest to the Lords Commissioners for Tangier, complaining that the governor had acted on poor and unreliable intelligence and that he himself had warned the governor of the 'hazard he was to run by exposing so many men upon the faith of a Moor'.[21] On the morning of the expedition Fairborne had expostulated that the plan was unsound, but Inchiquin would hear none of it, stating that meat was badly needed. The Lords Commissioners took a very dim view of the affair and wrote directly to Inchiquin:

> We wholly disapprove of that affair, both for the design and conduct, the pretence for want of victuals we have already shown to be groundless . . . the sending the forlorn hope so far beyond the main body and the too early withdrawing of Captain Boynton's party, and the not making sure of the Praytor Hamet in all events, are parts of conduct we cannot reconcile with the usage of soldiers in such cases.[22]

Inchiquin never forgave Fairborne for going behind his back, and when he went home for some leave in 1676 he left behind a clique of officers who met at the 'Parson's Green' to drink the governor's health. Conspicuously, Fairborne was not one of those invited. There were signs that Inchiquin tried to stir up the soldiers against Fairborne,[23] so that any mutiny during the governor's absence would be to Fairborne's discredit.

After his display of military incapacity Inchiquin spent most of his time on leave in England, and Fairborne exercised operational command as lieutenant-governor. The problem of the fortifications again came to the fore in 1677. Fairborne had just entrenched the sector between Fort James and Fort Anne, but the Moors took great exception to this; any palisades erected during the daytime were taken down by the Moors at night. Part of the trouble was that Fort Monmouth, which flanked this area, was one of de Gomme's 'insignificant forts', having only six loop-holes. Fairborne decided to build another fort to guard this sector, but in the meantime he employed much resource. By attaching 'fireworks' to the tops of the palisades the soldiers were able to illuminate the entire region, preventing the Moors from approaching. A few mines scattered along the trenches were also of great benefit. There was some fighting at this time, but it was of the normal, feeble nature: on 12 February 1677, one British soldier was wounded in a two-hour fire-fight with the Moors.

The next year witnessed the beginning of the three years' hard fighting when the future of the colony hung in the balance. To face this challenge the fortifications were in their habitual disorder. Inchiquin, on one of his periodic visits, found great defects in the fortifications and even greater defects in the amount of money available for correcting the faults.[24] The forts and lines were in a terrible condition: the perimeter wall of the town was cracked and actually falling down; the towers and cavaliers were crumbling; Teviot's earthworks in front of the Irish Battery had disappeared; and the ravelin and hornwork covering the Upper Castle had eroded away. If the Moors could break through the outer ring of forts and trenches then there was nothing to halt them until they came to the very walls of the town.[25]

At nine o'clock in the evening of 7 January 1678, Fairborne was awakened by 'a continual firing of Charles, Henrietta, Kendall, Pond, and Anne Forts'. The Moors were attacking all along the west front of Tangier. In the confusion of the night fighting, Fairborne was unwilling to risk sending out reinforcements from the garrison, and events proved him to have been wise. Half an hour later Fort Kendall blew up and Henrietta was set on fire. After three hours the Moors withdrew. Taking 200 men up to these forts in the morning, Fairborne found Henrietta to have been burned out, although still serviceable, but Kendall was a total wreck. This damage had been inflicted by the Moors' secret weapon; smoke and stink pots. These were incendiary hand grenades which were lobbed over the walls of the forts (none of the smaller works had roofs) and which once inside gave off clouds of suffocating smoke, rendering the garrison unfit for duty and setting fire to the place. Bad weather prevented the Moors from exploiting their success, and the British spent the remainder of the year in rebuilding the ruined forts, this time with a roof. In the middle of the following year the Moors appeared before Tangier with an army estimated at 15,000, although this is certainly too high a figure.[26] Once more no serious action occurred and the Moors dispersed at the end of the campaigning season.

The Alcaide of Alcazar, the provincial chief of the Moors in North Barbary, was in command of the army which the Emperor sent against Tangier. His objective was to take Fort Charles and make what inroads he could into the defences.[27] He opened his attack on 25 March 1680 with a force of 7,000.[28] On the next day he broke ground and opened his trenches for a formal siege of Forts Charles, Henrietta and Giles.[29] The Alcaide's main camp was on Jews Hill, and he planned to take Forts Charles and Henrietta to clear the right flank of the town's defences. This revealed another weakness in Tangier's fortifications; there was no depth. Once the first line was broken the whole system became untenable.

Both forts were supplied to withstand a siege of five months,[30] but the Moors worked at their trenches with great speed and a skill which surprised the British. Inchiquin sent a reinforcement to Fort Charles, but by 29 March the Moors had dug a trench across the rear of Fort Henrietta cutting it off from the town. They worked at night, and by constructing saps were able to avoid the attentions of the main garrison artillery on the Upper Castle. Inchiquin was struck with total inertia. No sallies were made to divert the Moors from their siege-works, no counterattacks were launched to regain contact with the isolated fort, and even the artillery was ineffective although the range was well under one mile. As well as attacking Henrietta, the Moors dug a mine towards Fort Charles, and immediately Captain John Trelawney the garrison commander started a countermine. With his governor quietly waiting on events, Trelawney acted on his own initiative. On 30 March he succeeded in erecting a battery which overlooked the Moorish trenches, now very close, and hampered their progress for a few days. Trelawney was in a desperate position; his troops were mutinous owing to their hopeless situation and the shortage of wine, and there was no sign of any help from Tangier.

The first assault on Henrietta, now completely cut off from both the town and Fort Charles, was made on 11 April, but Lieutenant John Wilson the fort commander held out. In reply the Moors mined towards his walls. As the siege progressed there occurred one of the little incidents which made the military affairs of Tangier slightly comic. The Alcaide summoned Fort Charles on 29 April that he intended to spring the mine under its ramparts, and he invited Trelawney and his second-in-command, Captain Thomas St John, to inspect it. This they did and, deciding that there was no danger, refused to surrender. Thereupon the Moors exploded the mine, which happened to be some thirty yards short and did no damage at all.

Help arrived at Tangier. The naval squadron of Vice-Admiral Thomas Herbert anchored in Tangier Bay with orders to give the army all possible assistance. The ships also brought back Fairborne with a reinforcement of 250 men. Complimenting Sir Palmes on his safe arrival, the Alcaide announced that it was his intention to reduce the garrison to the size that it had been under the Portuguese; in other words, to remove all the outworks and pin the British into the actual town.

By 11 May Henrietta was in great distress. Three mines were being dug underneath her and she could not resist for much longer. Fairborne offered to surrender the fort if the Alcaide would permit the garrison to march back into the town unmolested, but the Alcaide wanted slaves. Wilson could do no more and on 13 May he and his soldiers surrendered.[31] Throughout the siege Fort Charles had been in contact with the town by means of a speaking trumpet, whilst Henrietta and Charles had been within shouting distance of each other. Irish was spoken to prevent English renegades translating the messages for the Moors, but there were some Irish deserters with the Moorish forces who uncovered the intentions of the garrison. Inchiquin summoned a council of war on 13 May, where it was thought impossible to cut a way through the Moorish lines to reach Fort Charles. Trelawney forced Inchiquin's hand. His men, he reported through the speaking trumpet, were on the verge of mutiny, and he stated that he was going to break out with what remained of his command on the following morning and make his way through to the town. The governor had no choice but to agree to sally out with a large force to meet Trelawney and St John half way and cover their retreat.

The task which faced the men of Fort Charles was formidable. The improved performance of the Moors during 1680 resulted from their being advised in siege warfare by Turks and a number of English deserters, one of whom, Hansett, had been present at the Siege of Maestricht in 1673.[32] The main trench dividing Fort Charles from Tangier was nine feet broad and six feet deep with an abundance of narrow saps and cross works. All of these had to be negotiated in the face of a huge numerical superiority. Trelawney and St John had to keep their men in a tight formation to avoid being beaten in detail. Over such obstacles this was an almost impossible task.

The memorable 14 May commenced with the Moors blowing up Fort Henrietta at dawn. Within the Upper Castle all was ready. At 7.00 a.m., 480 men marched out under the direction of Major Marmaduke Boynton, with Inchiquin and Fairborne standing on the ramparts of Peterborough Tower to observe the action. At Fort Charles the guns were spiked, surplus supplies destroyed, and all the remaining ammunition made into a mine. St John, as youngest captain, commanded the vanguard, with Trelawney bringing up the rear. Leaving the fort at 8.00 a.m., the party safely crossed the first two trenches whilst Boynton advanced to the edge of the main trench and took up a supporting position. All went well until this final trench was reached. Here the party became disorganised as the soldiers struggled through a ditch which was twelve feet deep in places, and the Moors fell upon them. Only forty-four men out of the 200 who had left the fort, made their way up to Boynton's covering position. This force turned about and fought its way back into the town.[33]

Another smaller action had taken place at Devil's Drop, properly known as Fort Giles, by the northern shore. A platoon of twelve men held this work, but the entrenchments around Fort Charles had separated them from the town. On 14 May Admiral Herbert sent some boats to work inshore and rescue this garrison, but they were unable to land due to the close attentions of the Moors and only one of the soldiers could swim. Late in the afternoon this little redoubt surrendered, to complete a day of utter disaster for Tangier.[34]

Faced with a severe shortage of men and broken morale, Inchiquin consented to a truce with the Alcaide on 19 May. In return for a four-month cessation of hostilities, Inchiquin surrendered Pole Fort and Norwood Redoubt, leaving only Forts Cambridge, Fountain and Bridges in the possession of the garrison. In a little over a month of fighting the Alcaide had achieved his aim. The ring of fortresses had proved to be useless when subjected to serious attack, and the Alcaide's assault had illuminated yet another weakness in the design. There was no link between the town and the forts; to contact the outer works, troops had to march for half a mile over open country under observation from the higher ground. One of the main features of the fortifications of Vauban and the Dutch engineers, was that each work within a system was mutually supported, but this sophistication was not found in Tangier. Fairborne directed all money and stores used on the mole to be employed in repairing what fortifications remained in his hands.

The lieutenant-governor negotiated with the Alcaide for a continuation of the truce, but he was thoroughly depressed by the situation. The truce had only been granted on condition that the British built no new defences, leaving Tangier in danger of falling to the next serious attack. Fairborne reported to the king that unless 500 horse and 4,000 foot were immediately sent the colony could not be held and might just as well be evacuated—prophetic words.[35]

The truce expired on 15 September. At once the Alcaide started a desultory artillery bombardment of the town.[36] A council of war held on the same day decided that it would be wise to seize the initiative and take the war to the enemy rather than await the attack of the Moors, for this approach had only resulted in failure in the past.[37] After receiving more reinforcements from England, Fairborne marched out with nearly the entire garrison on 18 September and reoccupied the land around Pole Fort. Major Martin Beckman, the Swede who was Chief Engineer at Tangier, designed and supervised the work of fortification, whilst Fairborne covered with 1,500 men. The operation was remarkably successful and continued until midway through October; on the twenty-fourth Fairborne was mortally wounded.

In many ways 27 October 1680 can be likened to 'Sortie Day' at Gibraltar in 1783, when the final assault on that colony was driven off and the three-year siege lifted. At Tangier a huge sortie took place which removed any further threat from the Moors. Colonel Edward Sackville, commander of one of the reinforcement battalions from England, assumed the governorship on the incapacity of Fairborne and summoned a council of war on 25 October. It resolved to launch a general sally of the entire garrison, about 1,500 men, with assistance from Herbert's Naval Brigade. At 3.00 a.m. on 27 October the garrison marched out, divided into six battalions of foot and seven troops of horse, with the Naval Brigade operating as a separate force. Absolute silence was maintained.

The action opened with Herbert's seamen making a feint attack on some Moorish batteries by the shore of Tangier Bay, whilst a motley collection of cart horses and Tangier militia made another feint on the opposite flank. These two manœuvres had the desired effect; the Moors began to group to their flanks, thus weakening their centre. At a prearranged signal the 150 men in Pole Fort sallied out and attacked the Moorish lines before them, whilst the main force from the town hurried to their support. The infantry went into covering positions as the engineers and pioneers filled the Moorish ditches to make a path for the cavalry. Once this was done the Spanish[38] and English horse charged over and drove the Moors off the field, pursuing them for a mile right into their camp. Fairborne watched the success of the troops which he had so faithfully served, sitting in a chair on the ramparts of the Upper Castle.

He died soon after the news of the victory was brought to him.

It had always been the custom of the Moors to mutilate and decapitate any of the British dead and wounded who were left on a battlefield, but after this action the roles were reversed. The British soldiers committed 'like barbarities', to the shame of their officers who did all that they could to prevent them. Halkett estimated the Moors to have numbered 3,000 before the action, and their casualties he put at 500. This was the only significant victory which the British gained over the Moors during their occupation of Tangier. When the Europeans dictated the terms and fought the Moors in the open field, then the primitive Africans were no match for the training and disciplined firepower of the regular professionals. For too long the British had allowed the Moors to fight in their own fashion and had suffered severely as a result.

Making use of their military advantage the British sued for a lasting peace, and on 29 March 1681 Sackville and the Alcaide signed a treaty which was to give peace for four years. Peace or war, Tangier remained untenable. The old lines and forts were irreparably lost, and those which had been regained needed building anew. Such a reconstruction would have cost £2–3 million, a sum far in excess of the king's annual revenue, and even then it would have required a garrison of 8–10,000 men.[39] The real reason for the evacuation of Tangier was political, but there were a number of practical considerations as well; the colony had failed as a trading station, the mole which was needed to transform it into a naval base was still far from complete in 1683, and the whole establishment cost Charles a sum of money far greater than the rewards he gained from it. Tangier was an expensive liability and showed every prospect of becoming even more so.

Little more could have been asked of the fighting troops. They acquitted themselves bravely and kept good discipline on the battlefield, even if their behaviour when off duty left much to be desired. The same was true of the junior officers. When in action they accomplished all that was demanded of them, and during the actions of 1675 and 1680 they commanded with a diligence and a professionalism that was a credit to the army. Blame for the repeated military failures at Tangier must be laid at the feet of the senior officers.

The governor exercised total operational command and only in very exceptional circumstances was his freedom restricted by the Lords Commissioners in London. They only interfered after the event in 1675 when they had to act on Fairborne's complaint. However, the governors were limited in the amount of money which they could spend, the size of their forces, and the state of supply. A combination of all these factors made offensive postures a rare luxury, but much more could have been done to harass the Moors and carry the war to the enemy, particularly in 1680 when the colony was well reinforced from England and had more than enough men available to relieve the beleaguered forts. Teviot and Fairborne were the most successful commanders, but the former's life was short whilst the latter suffered under the incompetence and timidity of Inchiquin. The overall impression was depressing in that England's regular army was unable to defend a small town against a crude and ill-organised opponent. It was a story of irresolute command, lack of money, badly designed fortifications, but of remarkable gallantry under appalling conditions by the common soldiery.

VII

The Colonies

According to John Brydall, the colonies provided the king with 'a Magazine of Arms and a Military School or Seminary to breed up soldiers', as well as giving employment to an over-crowded England. Brydall's observations were mainly directed at Tangier and Dunkirk, but he did mention Bombay as a base from which all India could be taken.[1]

This ill-begotten establishment fell into England's hands through the Portuguese Marriage Treaty of 1661, along with that other dubious acquisition, Tangier.[2] In November 1662 the government allotted £7,000 a year for the upkeep of Bombay. Sir Abraham Shipman, an old royalist officer, was commissioned as governor, and on 6 April 1661 he embarked on board the fleet of the Earl of Marlborough.[3] With him sailed four companies of foot, each of one hundred men, under the Governor, Colonel John Hungerford, John Shipman and Charles Povey. The expedition was doomed from the very beginning.

The Portuguese governor was out of contact with European politics, and when the English fleet arrived off Bombay he refused to surrender to a nation of heretics. Their strength being inadequate to force Bombay, Shipman settled his party on the island of Anjadiva, near Goa, and set about negotiations for the fall of Bombay. This island was notoriously unhealthy and one-third of the soldiers and nearly all the officers died within two years. Shipman himself perished on 6 April 1664, to be replaced by Sir Gervase Lucas, another zealous cavalier. Lucas did not reach Bombay until 5 November 1666, but in the meantime the

Portuguese had finally given way, allowing the remnants of the British battalion to occupy the colony.[4] They numbered ninety-seven privates and one officer; disease had accounted for the remainder.

Lucas brought with him the first pay which the troops had received since their departure from England and a reinforcement of sixty men. Another twenty unwilling recruits followed in May 1668, but the tales of Bombay which circulated in England did little to assist a recruiting campaign. The shortage of men was made up by the employment of native Indian troops, the 'Decanies'.[5] On 21 May 1667 Lucas succumbed to the climate, to be replaced by Henry Gary, the only Englishman available. This saga of misfortune and negative achievement was too much for a government burdened with debt. Charles II offered Bombay to the East India Company for an annual rental of £10, and all the officers and soldiers in the colony were given the chance of joining the Company with the same rank and pay. Most accepted.[6] From this point, the soldiers passed beyond the concern of the standing army of Charles II and went on to form the basis of the army of the East India Company which blossomed into prominence during the eighteenth and early nineteenth centuries.

Brydall mentioned nothing of North America or the West Indies, but it was in this area of the world that Charles II harboured his meagre colonial schemes. During December 1654 five newly raised regiments of the New Model Army sailed from England under General Robert Venables, with the objective of capturing Hispaniola. The Spanish defenders inflicted a severe defeat on Venables, but rather than return home empty-handed, he alighted on Jamaica and claimed it for England. In 1659 this force was still in occupation, although only 1,500 remained out of the original 5,000, costing £50,000 a year.[7] On the accession of Charles II these forces were disbanded along with the New Model in England, but the Council for Trade and Plantations decided to leave a standing force of 400 foot and 150 horse in Jamaica on half-pay. This design was ultimately abandoned, although the disbanded soldiers remained in Jamaica as planters and settlers. A militia of 2,000 was raised from amongst these old soldiers in 1662, divided into five regiments, a relatively efficient force although it was never put to the test of battle. A part-time militia was insufficient to keep the peace on a large island like Jamaica, especially with the ever-present danger of the slave population. A mobile, regular force was required. In response to this demand, two companies of foot were raised in England during 1677 and shipped out to Jamaica in the following year, with the staggeringly low wastage of only two men on the voyage.

These two companies, consisting of only 200 men, cost £3,327 11*s* 8*d* a year, but no sooner had they arrived on the island than their pay fell into arrears. This was an occupational hazard of serving in the colonies. Pay was conveniently forgotten in London and only issued after continual reminders from the commanders overseas. Unpaid soldiers were both a burden and a danger to a colony, for without money the men had to be granted free quarters and there was always a risk of mutiny and lawlessness. On Jamaica the danger of a mutiny was not high as there was the militia to rectify any situation, and the regular soldiers were kept very busy. They had to apprehend escaped slaves, act as a police force, and serve as marines on board ships which went in pursuit of pirates.[8] These soldiers worked hard and lived dangerously for virtually no pay: the fact that they did not mutiny was little short of remarkable.

Their ordeal ended in 1681. Charles's Treasury, deprived of Parliamentary assistance, resorted to stringent economies and Jamaica's military establishment was one of the victims. On 8 March 1682 the two standing companies and the offices of lieutenant-general and major-general were disbanded. The settlers had to rely on their own militia for defence and internal security.

France, England and the United Provinces were the major powers concerned in the affairs of the West Indies. The French had settled St Christophers (St Kitts) in the Leeward Isles as early as 1627, and from there they had moved to Martinique and Guadeloupe. Colbert centralised all these proprietary concessions under the French West India Company in 1664. Barbados, and after 1655 Jamaica, belonged to England, who lived happily with her French neighbours, uniting against the common enemy of both, the Dutch. The trading superiority of the Dutch caused hostilities to break out in the Caribbean before the actual declaration of the Second Anglo-Dutch War in

Europe in 1665, with De Ruyter sailing to the Leeward Isles, bombarding Barbados and capturing a great deal of English shipping. England retaliated in a typically confused manner. The Governor of Barbados, Francis Lord Willoughby, planned to seize Tobago, but he was pre-empted by the Governor of Jamaica, Sir Thomas Modyford (Muddiford), who took both Tobago and Statia with the help of the buccaneers.[9] Henry Morgan then sacked Panama and Porto Bello, virtually expelling the Dutch as a territorial power in the West Indies, but they continued to hold Curaçao and played havoc with unescorted English vessels.

During Cromwell's time a number of criminals and undesirables had been sent to Barbados, resulting in a minor exodus of the more respectable settlers in search of somewhere else to live. The French islands of St Lucia and St Kitts were the chosen targets, but on the latter the English could only inhabit the southern half of the island as the French were in possession of the northern part. On the outbreak of the Anglo-Dutch War the French tried to negotiate a treaty of neutrality for their section of St Kitts. This was their weak point, a fact of which the English in London and the West Indies were well aware. During 1665 this treaty was observed, but in 1666 France joined in an alliance with the United Provinces against England. Immediately, the French attacked and forced the English off St Kitts, killing Henry Morgan in the process; 8,000 settlers were forced to leave for Jamaica, Virginia and Nevis. Willoughby then prepared an expedition to re-take the island, but his fleet was destroyed by a hurricane and he himself killed. His brother, William, assumed his title and commission as Governor of Barbados, whilst Charles II gathered reinforcements in England for a serious effort to re-take St Kitts.

During February 1667 a new regiment of foot was raised under the command of Sir Tobias Bridge, with six companies totalling 800 men; this was known as the Barbados Regiment.[10] One company was transferred from the Holland Regiment to stiffen this band of raw recruits, which sailed for Barbados on 11 March 1667. Meanwhile the French had taken Statia and Tobago, although Sir John Berry had regained control of the seas for England with his victory over the combined French and Dutch off Nevis. On its arrival on Barbados half of Bridge's regiment was stationed on the island as a defence force and a reserve, whilst Lieutenant-Colonel Sir William Stapleton took the remainder on the expedition under Lord Willoughby to recapture St Kitts.

The fleet sailed from Nevis, all of five miles from St Kitts, on 6 June, but the vessels lost one another in the darkness and the project had to be abandoned.[11] A new plan was devised, and on the next day a forlorn hope of 1,000 men, including a detachment from the Barbados Regiment, landed at dawn near Pelham's River. All surprise was lost and the force was penned on to the beach. A dispute between the English and Irish officers ended with the Irish soldiers taking one course of action and the British another; the Irish tried to work inland up a gully, suffered a few casualties, and then tamely surrendered. Determined not to be branded with this cowardly action, the English contingent held on to the beach-head until Willoughby came inshore and took them off in small boats. Not more than 100 were evacuated out of the original landing party of 1,000.[12] In terms of minor colonial warfare it was a serious and horrible defeat, far greater than any reverse suffered at Tangier. Unknown to the English, the French had garrisoned St Kitts with a veteran regular regiment from Picardy, a regiment of regular cavalry, and some dragoons, in addition to 2,500 planters in arms.[13] Willoughby sailed away, but the Treaty of Breda ended any further hostilities.

Bridge's regiment was left in the West Indies, not because it was needed but because the impoverished Treasury in London could not afford to pay for its disbandment and passage to England. The usual story of no pay and poor conditions followed. When first sent out to Barbados it was agreed that the regiment should be paid out of the 4½ per cent reserved for the king on all sugar sales, but during the war Willoughby had used this money for general expenses and there was none left to pay the troops. Bridge petitioned the king on 27 May 1668 that his men were in need of pay and clothing, but the only help he received was an order to reduce his men's pay to 6*d* and place all his officers on half-pay.[14] For another three years, Bridge and his men remained on Barbados in poverty and misery. They could not be paid from the 4½ per cent on sugar as that fund was pledged for five years in advance to meet war debts. Finally, in

1671, orders were given to disband the Barbados Regiment, permitting those who wished to remain on Barbados to take up grants of land, whilst those who desired to stay in the army were to come over to England and receive new postings. Enough men to form four companies returned to England towards the end of 1671 and were quartered at Gravesend.[15] On 31 March this old regiment was reformed into a regiment of dragoons for service in the Third Dutch War, and was finally disbanded in 1674. Some of the men of the regiment had still not been paid their arrears by 1674,[16] and isolated petitions from unpaid soldiers can be found as late as 1679.

Barbados suffered no more from the attentions of regular soldiers, but relied upon a civilian militia similar to that of Jamaica. Although two-thirds of the Barbados Regiment returned to England, two companies remained in the Leeward Isles as a garrison for St Kitts. Their situation deteriorated after the departure of Tobias Bridge. Sir William Stapleton begged the Lords of Trade and Plantations to pay the arrears of these soldiers, which stood at four years in 1681,[17] as they were 'naked and starving'. To make matters worse, the French soldiers across the frontier in the French portion of St Kitts were well fed and regularly paid. Not until 1682 were steps taken to pay these unfortunates.

On the larger islands in the West Indies which belonged to England all eligible males were organised into militia regiments, the richer planters in the cavalry and the poorer sort in the infantry. Nevis, St Kitts, Montserrat and Antigua all possessed their militia establishments, although the very small and sparsely populated islands, like Anguilla and Statia, were without these organisations.

North of the Caribbean were the English possessions on the mainland of North America. The smallest and most recent acquisition was New York, formerly the Dutch New Amsterdam captured by the British during the Second Dutch War in 1665. Until the Treaty of Breda in 1667, 300 soldiers were maintained in the colony, although when Sir Edmund Andros went out as governor in 1674 the garrison had fallen to one company of 100 soldiers.[18] By 1679 New York cost only £1,000 a year for the maintenance of forts and military buildings. No soldiers remained.

Further south, in Virginia, matters were better organised. The Governor, Sir William Berkeley, was able to turn out a militia of 4,000 when De Ruyter threatened to make a descent on the Virginian coast in 1665, although he was without regular forces.[19] It was thought that volunteers fighting in defence of their own lands would be more competent and zealous than detached soldiers. If only justifying the parsimony of the English government, this attitude had something to commend it.

The fate of Sir Tobias Bridge and his regiment had demonstrated that the English military administration was incapable of supporting a large force overseas, but in 1676 the army staff was granted a second chance to prove itself. Subjected to persistent Indian raids, the men of Charles City County in Virginia banded themselves into a volunteer force under Nathaniel Bacon, a distant relative of James I's Chancellor. Sir William Berkeley ordered them to disband, but they refused and technically became rebels. At this stage, in April and May 1676, Bacon and his supporters overstepped themselves; instead of concentrating on the Indian question they set themselves up as popular agitators campaigning against the unequal Poll Tax and demanding a wider franchise for the election to the General Assembly of the colony. In return, Berkeley represented Bacon as having started the Indian troubles to find an excuse for opposing the lawful government. On 23 June the crisis of the rebellion occurred. Bacon marched on the State House in James City with 500 men 'whose fortunes and inclinations were equally desperate',[20] and forced Berkeley to appoint him 'Commander-in-Chief of all volunteer soldiers to go against the Indians'. Fortunately, Bacon then departed for the frontier giving Berkeley the chance to call out the loyal militia. To all intents and purposes civil war had broken out in Virginia, and not only was the king's authority threatened but the annual revenue of £100,000 which he drew from tobacco was in danger. Charles decided to send over the army.

Five hundred men were transferred from the standing regiments in England to form the basis of a new composite battalion under the command of Captain Herbert Jeffreys of the 1st Foot Guards, made a brevet lieutenant-colonel for the occasion. To these regulars were added 500 volunteers who were so anxious to serve that they had to be kept in the Tower of London until the time of embarkation. One hundred regulars and 100 new recruits formed a company of 200, and the battalion had five of these along with a Train of Artillery.[21] Transportation to Virginia was the responsibility of the navy, and the Naval Commissioners estimated the cost of feeding and shipping the battalion from Longreach to Virginia at £8,068 *6s 0d.*[22] This sum covered three months' bread and cheese for each man, a bed, pillow, rug and blanket, and a quarter of a pint of brandy. Evidently the military intended to undertake some farming in America as they were provided with 300 hoes and 300 sacks. Not until 3 December 1676 did the Virginia Expedition sail out of the Downs and four days later they had passed Falmouth and were out into the winter Atlantic. With them went the gloomy predictions of John Gibbons, one of Williamson's numerous correspondents:

It must be supposed then, many of these sent, men may die (I have known 50 die out of a Virginia Ship wherein were not above 100 and odd persons). Many may arrive sick, And what then may these avail against 1,000 men in Arms habituated and seasoned to the Climate.[23]

The shortest passage which could have been hoped for from the slow transports was between eleven and thirteen weeks, and the ships gradually arrived off the James River from the end of February until mid-April.

All this expense and trouble was for nothing. During the winter Bacon had died and his rebellion had collapsed when deprived of his leadership. By the time that the expedition sailed in under Sir John Berry and Colonel Jeffreys, Berkeley had regained control of his colony and although still harassed by sporadic Indian attacks he had the situation in hand. The only sensible course of action was to send the soldiers home again. In May they were reported to be 'very sickly',[24] and in June the *Duke of York* hove into Deal from Virginia to inform Richard Watts that half the soldiers were already dead.[25]

When Bacon had marched on James City his parting present had been to burn the town. The Ordnance Office omitted to send tents with the battalion, and without the accommodation in the city the troops had to remain on board their crowded transports anchored in the James River. The deaths were enormous from disease, crossing the Atlantic in the depths of winter, and a diet of biscuit, cheese and brandy. Charles II ordered Jeffreys to return to England with his battalion on 13 May 1677, leaving 100 men behind to keep the peace, but it was not until July that the *Unity* passed Falmouth on her way to Virginia with the king's instructions.

On 26 March 1678 the first shipload landed at Gravesend; the muster rolls made appalling reading.[26] However, the figures are misleading as 200 men remained in Virginia as a permanent garrison. On an approximation, the regiment lost 450 men out of its establishment of 1,000, without having fired a shot in anger.

After this the military establishment of Virginia becomes confused. Two of Jeffreys's companies remained in the colony, but in December 1678 Monmouth ordered levy money to be paid for raising another 100 recruits for Virginia.[27] Again, in January 1678 the Duke of York had instructed Pepys to ascertain the names of the ships which were to carry 425 soldiers to Virginia.[28] None of these men were ever sent, for one year later there were only two companies in the colony and the situation was unchanged in 1681. For these two units, the usual history of lack of pay and necessities applied. Arrears of pay reached twelve months in May 1679, and two years later their condition was so desperate that their pay and arrears did not equal the debts which they had incurred. These factors undermined the discipline until the companies became a liability to the Virginian government, the soldiers being more likely to join with the discontented planters than fight against them.

Accordingly, Charles II ordered that the pay of the two companies should cease from Christmas 1681 and that they should be disbanded unless the governor wished to pay them from colonial revenues. Thomas Lord Culpepper, the new governor, immediately raised a storm of protest, saying how valuable the soldiers were in preserving the peace, collecting the customs, and patrolling the frontier, adding that the presence of regular troops in 1676 might well have nipped Bacon's Rebellion in the bud and saved the king a great deal of money. These arguments convinced the Lords of Trade and Plantations, but not the king. Charles remained adamant; if the settlers wanted military protection then they could pay for it, an argument echoed in more serious vein a century later. On 7 June 1682 the two standing companies in Virginia were disbanded, and most of the soldiers remained in the colony.

Restoration colonial policy did not consider the expense of military support worthwhile. Only cases of extreme emergency, such as the French threat to the British position in the Leeward Isles and Bacon's Rebellion, stirred the Lords of Trade and Plantations into direct action. Such expeditions were very costly for Charles's Treasury, but in neither case was the achievement equal to the expenditure. Bridge failed to take St Kitts and Jeffreys arrived too late to assist in Virginia. When the king was pressurised into maintaining standing units in the colonies, their pay and upkeep was pushed to one side; London considered that the colonists should pay for their own protection, whilst they thought it to be a royal responsibility. The poor soldiers fell between the two and received no pay, no clothes, and little or no food. On St Kitts, English soldiers with their pay four years in arrears were actually able to see the French soldiers being paid at the drumhead once a month.

The colonial military administration was ramshackle and ill-organised. The Barbados Regiment was supposed to be paid out of the sugar tax which was anticipated for years into the future, but when this was pointed out to Lord Willoughby and Westminster they both played for time and did nothing. Jeffreys's battalion was made to sail in slow transports across the North Atlantic in the depths of winter, and then discover that they had no shelter as James City had been razed to the ground and the Ordnance Office had forgotten to provide tents. The one redeeming feature of the Virginia Expedition was the liaison between the army and the navy over the embarkation and evacuation, experience which was evident in the Flanders Expedition of 1678. In the midst of all these conflicting interests, and suffering from the inept administration and general bungling, stood the common soldier. Throughout the twenty-five years of colonial service he did not mutiny or rebel, but simply accepted his lot.

IX

Foreign Service

Foreign service or active service overseas was a major concern for the Restoration Army, implying the hire of British forces by foreign states. When such troops left the British Isles they ceased to be part of the British army, but came under the armies of the hiring powers for their pay, food, clothing and equipment. Within this general principle there were differences of detail. The corps which served in Portugal and the United Provinces, the 'Anglo-Dutch Brigade', were composed of new soldiers specially raised for those theatres, whereas the brigade which fought for Louis XIV during the Third Anglo-Dutch War was a semi-official expedition drawn from the British standing army. Other than these special forces there were a number of individual regiments permanently fighting for foreign governments: the Irish 'Wild Geese' fought for Spain, as did a Scottish regiment under Colonel Gage; Lord George Douglas's was a part of the French army, and after 1678 Thomas Dongan and then Justin Macartie commanded a large Irish regiment in France forming the foundation of the later Irish Brigade.

Thus foreign service was of three types; the semi-official expedition composed of newly levied troops to assist a friendly power; the fully official corps drawn from the standing regiments; and the mercenary units which were connected with the British Isles only in so far as they used them as a recruiting base. This was the area in which the professional officers spent most of their time, and the British Isles were a veritable reservoir of mercenaries in the seventeenth century.

Tangier, Bombay, the colonies and the Flanders Army of

1678, were not connected with foreign service, but were British army expeditions commanded and organised from England. We shall now examine three foreign service stations to illustrate the differences outlined above.

One of the first acts of the Restoration government was to secure the Portuguese Marriage Alliance, whereby Charles II received Catherine of Braganza for his queen as well as the colonies of Tangier and Bombay, in return for his alliance against Spain. Since 1640, Portugal had been fighting with Spain for her independence, but little success had been achieved by either side in twenty years. Spain had dissipated her strength against France whilst Portugal was too weak both financially and militarily to profit from this. The English alliance offered a source of hope for the Portuguese as it committed Charles II to send a brigade to assist her. Simultaneously, France offered a small body of troops and within a few months the apparent stalemate of the war was broken.

England was faced with the problem of which troops to send, but this was solved by recruiting amongst the disbanded New Model and the Dunkirk garrison. Passing through England on his way to take up the command of the French forces already in Portugal, Frederick, Duke of Schomberg, the Huguenot general, advised Charles to send 'the military men that had served under Cromwell, whom he thought the best officers he had ever seen: and he was sorry to see, they were dismissed, and that a company of wild young men were those the King relied on'.[1] Schomberg had a vested interest in the quality of troops sent to Portugal, as he assumed command of the British brigade one year later. Charles accepted his advice.

Three thousand men were to go to Portugal: two infantry regiments of 1,000 each, and a cavalry regiment also of 1,000 under the command of the Earl of Inchiquin, an Irish catholic, assisted by Sir John Talbot, an old royalist soldier. All the foot soldiers were taken from the three New Model regiments still not disbanded in Scotland; their officers were given new commissions from the king and then sent overseas.[2] These regiments had been left by Monck to garrison the Highlands, but owing to the shortage of troops and money the Restoration government continued them in service for a year after the general disbandment in England. In May 1662, the two infantry regiments were shipped from Leith for Portugal.[3] The regiment of horse was a composite unit drawn from volunteers and the Dunkirk garrison.[4] By early August 1662 all the British had arrived and were settled into their winter quarters, but they were poorly received by the local population who did not take kindly to heretics, the catholic church issuing a proclamation protecting any Portuguese citizen who might wound or murder an Englishman. It was an inauspicious beginning to say the least.[5]

Conditions rapidly deteriorated. Initially Charles II and the Portuguese government had agreed that the men were to be paid by England for the first three months, but after that responsibility for payment was to pass to Portugal.[6] Native Portuguese troops received only seven or eight months' pay in a year as opposed to the twelve months of the British soldier. With some justification the Portuguese authorities argued that to pay the British at this rate would cause jealousy, and possibly even mutiny, amongst the Portuguese and French soldiery. The question of pay was a serious controversy throughout the brigade's service. The Portuguese refused an increase in the British pay, stating that the wages given to their own soldiers were quite sufficient as Portugal was a cheap country in which to live.[7]

As early as November 1662 the British thought themselves to be in arrears of pay and generally ill-treated; their quarters were poor and the civilians gave them no assistance. Major Lawrence Dempsey tried to make out that the indiscipline and bad behaviour of the British troops had been grossly exaggerated and that the fault lay entirely with the Portuguese.[8] The blame lay with both parties. Most of the British were old Cromwellians who did not take kindly to a nation of catholics, whilst the Portuguese did not welcome the arrival of a brigade of staunch heretics. As we have seen in Tangier, once on active service abroad the discipline of the British soldier was not distinguished.

Within six months the officers began to resign their commissions and return to England, pleading 'want of due pay and regard', to be replaced by less able men.[9] Disease also took its toll. Thomas Maynard, the English Consul in Lisbon, described the soldiers as 'mouldering away', the horse having only 250 effective men remaining, and the foot only 1,400. Lack of pay and clothing had encouraged desertion, and without food and other necessities the soldiers turned to robbery and begging, further antagonising the civilians who retaliated by murdering any soldiers who strayed from their quarters. During 1664 a group of officers sent a list of grievances to Clarendon: their pay was seven months in arrears, their English commissions were about to be replaced by Portuguese, and henceforth they would have to take orders from Portuguese officers whom they regarded, rightly, as incompetent.[10] The separate identity of the British was of vital importance to morale, and any attempt to break up the brigade or to replace British officers with Portuguese was bitterly resented and contested. Their only hope of gaining better conditions lay in keeping together as a unit.

One thousand recruits from Ireland arrived in 1664, mostly without arms, following the usual practice of making up foreign service regiments with expendable Irishmen.[11] Despite this life was still intolerable one year later: pay was months in arrears, and Lieutenant Ashton and a private soldier had been openly murdered in the streets of Lisbon by some Portuguese troopers. To add insult to injury, the offenders were freed without punishment by the Portuguese authorities. As the 1666 campaign approached, Maynard wrote despairingly to Arlington:

> The English soldiers are discontented, being they are about six months in arrears. I do what I can to prevent disgusts betwixt them and the Court. The worst is they are constrained to straggle abroad to get provisions . . . which hath cost the lives of many of them of late, and if they escape the fury of the country people, they fall under the severity of their officers who endeavour to preserve the reputation of civil men.[12]

By November 1666 the cavalry numbered only 300, whilst the two infantry regiments could muster only 700 between them, and a third of those were foreigners who had been drafted into the ranks. A thousand replacements were urgently required. There was no change in 1668. As no recruits had arrived the two foot regiments were amalgamated into one, but even this was under-strength. Pay was seven months behind and the brigade was in a very sorry state. Fortunately the end was close.

Through British mediation Spain and Portugal had been

negotiating for some years, and on 3 February 1668 the Earl of Sandwich secured their signatures to a peace. Portugal was once again an independent state and the British brigade could return to England. At first it was suggested that the troops might go into the Spanish service to fight in Flanders, provided they could be guaranteed adequate pay.[13] Ultimately this scheme was dropped because England was drifting towards a French alliance. The most obvious solution was to send some of the 1,000 men to Tangier, which was seriously undermanned, and embark the remainder for England. After prolonged discussions over the payment of full arrears and the settlement of numerous petty disputes between the soldiers and the civilians, Sir Robert Southwell and the industrious Maynard managed to evacuate the British brigade. On 23 September 1668, 400 infantry arrived in Tangier only to find the Governor, Henry Norwood, deeply incensed at their appearance as provisions were short enough in Tangier without additional mouths to feed.[14] Such was military liaison. The remaining 600 soldiers had sailed for England on 17 September 1668.

Not all the losses of the brigade were caused by irate civilians and disease, for the soldiers did their fair share of fighting. Soon after their arrival the red coats gained the reputation of being the best soldiers in either the Spanish or Portuguese army, and such success as the Portuguese enjoyed was largely due to the resolution and skill of the British contingent. In spite of their objections to the British on other than military grounds, the Portuguese had a high regard for them as soldiers and employed them as the backbone of their field army. It was in 1663 that the brigade was first able to demonstrate its ability in battle.

Don John of Austria invaded Portugal with an army of 16,000 men. The weak Portuguese frontier garrisons withdrew on Evora which they tried to hold as a breakwater, but Don John soon took the city. As well as commanding the British brigade, the Duke of Schomberg was also the unofficial military adviser to the Portuguese high command. He recommended that they march with the field army on Evora and attack the Spaniards under the very walls of that town; for once the bumptious Portuguese commanders overcame their arrogance and accepted the idea. As the Portuguese approached Evora, the Spaniards marched out to meet them and both armies camped on either bank of the river Eudigby in one of those curious stalemates peculiar to linear warfare. A Spanish effort to force the river was repulsed by 150 English musketeers, but Don John then executed a flank march and crossed the Eudigby higher up. The Portuguese marched to head him off, but again Don John out-manœuvred them by driving for Estremos. However, he moved a little too slowly and Schomberg was able to pin his rearguard and then draw the entire Spanish army into battle at Ameixial.[15]

The infantry of both armies occupied high ground on each wing, with a valley separating the two enemies. It was the plan of the Portuguese to attack the Spanish horse as they stood unsupported by any infantry in the valley. The honour of leading the assault was granted to the British foot. They advanced to within 'push of pike' of the Spaniards and then gave their volley. This was too much for the Spanish who retired, leaving their cannon in the hands of the British. Later in the action the British infantry were counter-attacked by Spanish cavalry, but, by adopting a square formation and holding their fire to the last possible moment, the assault was successfully beaten off. The Portuguese gave the British up for lost as they had never seen infantry allow an enemy to approach so close before giving fire. In the valley the English horse regiment could not equal the achievements of the infantry. Their one charge was premature and unsupported by any Portuguese cavalry, resulting in the death of Colonel Michael Dongan (Dungan) and Captain Paulinge. Not until the British foot marched down the hill to the assistance of the cavalry were the Spaniards finally beaten and driven from the field. So ruined was Don John's army that it had to withdraw back into Spain and abandon the campaign.[16] Ameixial was one of the few decisive actions of the war.

This performance by the British brigade did wonders for its reputation with the Portuguese who 'do say themselves that the English did more than men'.[17] Pepys, when shown a report of the battle in the *Lisbon Gazette*, remarked:

> Here I learned that the English Foot are highly esteemed all over the world, but the horse not so much, which yet we count among ourselves the best; but they abroad have had no great knowledge of our horse it seems.[18]

How much of this and later praise of the brigade, issuing from

British officers and Portuguese ministers anxious to please Charles II, was accurate is hard to say, but it probably contained a good deal of truth.

The next year saw the Portuguese confident enough to take the initiative by striking over the frontier in the direction of Badajoz, and, after the fall of this fortress, moving north to besiege Valencia.[19] The siege opened on 16 June, but not until 24 June were the works close enough to the defences to risk an assault. Once again, the two British infantry regiments led the attack with the supposed support of a French regiment on their left and a Portuguese formation on their right. Neither support materialised, and the British were forced to withdraw after two hours' hard fighting, having suffered severe losses.[20] It was a poor consolation, but this engagement again improved the reputation of the brigade, and the Portuguese were of the opinion that the Spaniards were no longer to be feared now that the British were fighting for Portugal.[21]

Another invasion by the Spaniards was launched on 18 May 1665, and by 9 June they had advanced as far as Estremos. On the following day they stormed the town of Villaviliosa but the citadel held out, giving Schomberg and the Marquis de Marialua time to march up with the Portuguese field army and force the invaders to battle close to Estremos.[22] The British foot were stationed on the left wing of the Portuguese army. The Marquis de Caracena, the Spanish commander-in-chief, opened the action with a charge by his Swiss and German cavalry which smashed through the first two lines of the Portuguese left, only to be halted by a resolute stand by the British. Apparently, the Germans could not tolerate the British habit of using their unloaded muskets as heavy clubs. This action by the British was decisive and Caracena withdrew from the field.[23] Lavish praise was heaped on the brigade as they had saved the day when most of the Portuguese officers had been galloping back to Estremos:

The Conde [de Castelmelhor] fair promises that they shall speedily have some monies, and I believe if the Conde knew where to procure it, he would not keep it an hour from them, being, he tells me every day, that never did soldiers deserve to be better paid than the English troops. The Marquis de Marialua told me about a week since, that no prince in the world had so stout men in the field, nor so civil in their garrisons, as the English in the service of this Crown. Their gallant comportment hath induced the King of Portugal to desire recruits from his Majesty to fill up the two foot regiments, which orders the Ambassador carries with him.[24]

Under pressure from Louis XIV, Portugal launched an offensive in October 1665 directed north into Galicia, and Pearson's regiment, the cavalry and two companies of Schomberg's Foot were included in the expedition. It was more of a large-scale raid than a campaign: twenty-four towns were sacked as well as 'a great many gentlemen's houses'. The force entered La Guarda on 12 November with little difficulty and besieged the citadel. Although entrusted to the British, the enterprise had to be abandoned after a brief fight.[25] Several small skirmishes occurred in the years leading up to the peace in 1668 in which the British continued to distinguish themselves, but the serious campaigning was over by the end of 1665.

From the beginning the officers and men in Portugal had been from many different backgrounds. Some were old royalists who had volunteered for service due to the lack of opportunities for employment in England, whilst others were old Parliament soldiers who had come over with the Cromwellian regiments from Scotland.[26] Colonel Guy Molesworth, a former royalist colonel, was sent out as a captain in the cavalry regiment, but in 1663 he was court martialled and 'disgracefully cashiered' after being found guilty of a misdemeanour against Major-General Christopher O'Brien. One of the charges found against him was that 'he daily disheartened the foot soldiery by telling them that they were Cromwell's whelps and rebels, and that they were sent here for murdering the late King and were banished men'.[27] He also defrauded his men of their pay. The brigade was better off without such officers.

Generally, the officers were well behaved, maintaining tight discipline, and they did their best to attend to the needs of their men under very trying circumstances. With the assistance of the conscientious Maynard, frequent deputations went from the brigade to the Portuguese Court in efforts to obtain pay and the demands of the soldiery, mostly to no avail. Many of the officers went on to become professional soldiers on other foreign service stations: for example, Edmund Mayne, Lawrence Dempsey, John Rumsey and Sir John Talbot.

From the outset service in Portugal was unpopular. The

soldiers felt that they were being exiled, and as early as 1662 Sir Thomas Morgan, himself a Parliamentary officer, reported that many of the officers wished to go home. This feeling was prevalent amongst both the royalist and Cromwellian officers; Molesworth had said that he wished the king had sent him to Tyburn rather than to Portugal. Casualties soon reduced the original officer corps, but replacements were easier to find than they were for Tangier. At least the Iberian peninsula offered 'civilised warfare', although it had not quite the glamour of fighting for the French or the Dutch.

On the return of the brigade into England any officers who so wished were permitted to remain in the Portuguese service, but few took advantage of the offer. For those who went back to England there was a serious difficulty. Their arrival coincided with the disbandment of the army after the Second Dutch War, so there were no vacancies on the home establishment. Also Parliament had just forced the Privy Council into purging the army of catholics by requiring all officers to take the Oaths of Supremacy and Allegiance. Many of the Irish officers from Portugal were catholic. Even for the protestant officers from Portugal the outlook was little better; twenty-four were admitted into the Royal Horse Guards, presumably as reformadoes, certainly not as officers,[28] but the rest had to wait until vacancies occurred and then petition for them. John Rumsey and Edward Trelawney petitioned the Privy Council in October 1669, for employment or some sort of relief, and, surprisingly, they were granted £200 a year each.[29] Most did not have to wait long for work: some entered the Barbados Regiment of Sir Tobias Bridge, whilst the expansion of the army for the Third Dutch War and the expedition to France accounted for the remainder.

Foreign service provided the English government with a corps of trained veterans, hardened by active service, and yet maintained at no expense to the Treasury. This gave the king a professional reserve army which could be recalled into England at any time. There were two distinct advantages in the system: Parliament could not complain of a large standing army in England, and it allowed Charles to support an ally without committing the nation to war. In this way, the brigade in Portugal supported his alliance of 1661 but avoided war with

Spain and cost him little money. When the soldiers returned they provided a ready and trained force of men for the Third Dutch War. The Anglo-Dutch Brigade functioned in the same way.

Since 1585 when Elizabeth I had sent 5,000 men under Robert Dudley, Earl of Leicester, to the United Provinces, a British corps had served the Dutch. By 1593 a separate unit of 6,400 Scots was also in Dutch pay,[30] and both the English and Scots were grouped together as the 'Anglo-Dutch Brigade'. Technically the monarch of England had the right to summon these soldiers into his country at any time and this was twice exercised by the Stuarts; Charles II recalled the brigade at the beginning of the Second Dutch War in 1665, and James II used his option in 1685 when he badly needed experienced troops to deal with Monmouth's Rebellion. Some of the older officers of the Restoration army had learned the art of war with the Anglo-Dutch Brigade, whilst many of the officers of the Civil Wars had a background of service in Holland, Aubrey de Vere, Sir William Constable and Sir John Meldrum among them. Much of the early history of the brigade is uncertain and confused. The English regiments might have been disbanded along with much of the Dutch army after the Peace of Munster in 1648, but if this was the case then they were reformed soon afterwards. A similar, temporary disbandment also affected the Scottish regiments.

On the outbreak of the Second Dutch War in 1665 Charles II issued a proclamation ordering the Anglo-Dutch Brigade to return to England. In retaliation the Dutch government tempted the personnel of the English regiments to stay.[31] Most of the officers returned to England, and the Holland Regiment was formed almost exclusively from returning Anglo-Dutch soldiers. A few found places in the Admiral's Regiment, which had been formed in the previous year under Sir William Killigrew. The States General discharged every British officer on 25 February 1665, disbanded the brigade, and then set about remodelling it. The ranks were filled with Dutch soldiers, and so terminated the Anglo-Dutch Brigade. However, a number of officers accepted the inducements of the Dutch and took the oath of allegiance to the United Provinces.[32] This was an acceptable military practice in the seventeenth century, and the officers who chose to continue in the Dutch army had served it for most of their lives and had much to lose by returning to an uncertain future in England or Scotland.

Following the disbandment of the majority of the army in 1674 after the Treaty of Westminster, many professional soldiers were left without employment in England: Sir John Fenwick, Henry Lillingston and Molyneux Disney, for example. John Bernardi crossed over to Holland as a soldier in search of a career, and on landing at the Brill found twelve English captains with 'as many soldiers as such captains could persuade to go over with them to serve the Dutch, King Charles the Second having disbanded them at Blackheath, and other places, but a little while before, when his Majesty concluded the Peace with the Dutch'.[33] Sir Walter Vane, colonel of the Holland Regiment, was already in Flanders with a separate band of English volunteers, and before the end of 1674 all the English in the Dutch service had been grouped into three regiments; two of Englishmen under Henry Lillingston and Molyneux Disney, and the other of Irish under the Viscount Clare. Three Scottish regiments commanded by Henry Graham, Hugh Mackay, and Alexander Colyear (Collier), were already back in service, and these, together with the three new regiments, formed the new Anglo-Dutch Brigade.[34]

Of the four schools for professional soldiers—Tangier, Portugal, France and the United Provinces—the latter two were the most important and from their ranks came many of the officers who were to fight with William III and Marlborough. Prior to 1678 all commissions in the brigade were granted by the Prince of Orange, although the six regiments were officially British, but in that year the two countries signed a Treaty of Mutual Defence in which the position of the brigade was clarified. It became a permanent part of the Dutch establishment, but was allowed to embark for England whenever that country required its temporary services. William of Orange still signed the commissions, although the appointment of officers was usually amicably arranged between the two heads of state.

Their English identity was maintained by the soldiers of the brigade—Fenwick's regiment wore red coats with gosling green facings, adorned with a badge of St George and the Dragon—

but in England, like all other foreign service stations, the brigade was unpopular. Recruits were difficult to discover. As the British battalions marched to Brussels to embark for England in January 1679 the officers of the Anglo-Dutch Brigade hung around the quay-side trying to tempt men to sign-on, as well as searching for any of their own deserters who might attempt to escape back to England.[35] But 'not one single soldier would have their colours upon any terms they could propose', and neither could they find any deserters.

They were impressive soldiers, fighting hard and long at the second Siege of Maestricht in 1676,[36] and again at the Battle of St Denis in 1678, where they formed the core of every Dutch attack suffering heavy casualties. After the Peace of Nymwegen in 1678 the brigade went into garrison at Graves and Brussels, but they overcame the inertia and general seediness of garrison life remarkably well for James II found them to be very soldierly in appearance in 1685. He was so taken by their uniformity of height and size that he began to purge the English army of all soldiers who were either old or of diminutive stature.

Foreign and colonial service were ideal methods of ridding England of some of the disbanded Cromwellian soldiers. Between them Tangier, Bombay and Portugal devoured 6,000 men. Many more of the old soldiers went overseas as mercenaries into the armies of foreign powers, either individually or in small groups. John Hebdon suggested that a number of volunteers might be sent to fight for the Czar of Russia in recognition of the good relations between the two countries. Accordingly the Privy Council raised 3,000 volunteers, but whether these men actually went to Russia is uncertain.[37] In the following year, the Earl of Castlemaine petitioned the king for permission to raise soldiers in England, Ireland and Scotland to the number of five or six thousand to serve any prince or state with whom the king was in 'amity or friendship'. This scheme was approved by the Privy Council, hopeful that it would drain more disbanded soldiers away from England. These levies were all unofficial and represented the traffic in manpower which filled the ranks of the British mercenary regiments fighting on the continent.

This practice of taking men from England to fight, willingly or unwillingly, for foreign armies had been going on for centuries and was recognised and accepted, although it was technically illegal to compel men to go abroad:

> PROVIDED that neither this Act nor any Matter or Thing therein contained shall be deemed construed or taken to extend to the giving or declaring of any Power for the transporting of any Subjects of this Realm or any way compelling them to march out of this Kingdom otherwise than by the Laws of England ought to be done.[38]

Soldiers for Spain or France were periodically recruited in England by special commissaries sent over by the hiring power. Officially, he had to possess a licence from the English government to raise a stated number of men and transport them overseas under agreed conditions. Very few of these licences exist in the Domestic Entry Books of the State Papers, suggesting that foreign recruiting agents operated without them, or that verbal arrangements were made with the authorities. In any event Parliament was largely uninformed of the true state of affairs.

In fact the Commons had grounds for concern. There was a regular business in obtaining men for mercenary service; soldiers were duped or misled into agreements with the French, Dutch or Spanish armies, and whisked on board ship before they knew what was happening. No scruples hindered the recruiting agents, as their commission was based on the heads obtained. A Captain Tarrant, from France, locked his recruits in jails until they were shipped for France in HMS *Roebuck*, whilst a Captain Dally housed his levies in the 'Eagle and Child' before shipping them for France.[39] The government openly connived at these activities—few licences were issued and naval vessels were employed to carry the human cargo to their destinations. So bad had the problem become by 1668 that the Privy Council requested orders to be prepared preventing men from entering foreign service, either privately or under inducement, unless they formed part of an official British expedition. Even in these recognised expeditions the men were 'reduced to great want, and have perished therein', a reflection on the Portuguese brigade, and so the Privy Council appointed a committee to devise general regulations to govern the recruitment of British soldiers for service abroad.

These articles appeared as an Order in Council on 12 February 1668.[40] No soldier was allowed to serve abroad unless he was a member of an official unit which had government blessing, and even before this was permitted the foreign recruiting agent had to enter into prescribed terms with the officers of the party. The king undertook to pay the soldiers as far as their point of embarkation and provided their transportation. Finally, the articles laid down recommended rates of pay and insisted that all officers who signed such articles had to include a clause allowing their troops to return home at the king's bidding. These regulations failed to control the traffic in illegal mercenaries, as the emphasis was the wrong way round. Instead of the recruiting agent having to seek permission from the king, the potential victims had to come to terms with the agent from a position of weakness. However, the gravest fault in the regulations was that there was no provision for their enforcement after the troops had left England. Sir George Hamilton's Irish regiment entered into articles with the French government in 1671, but once in France the terms were ignored; the regiment became part of the French army and had to abide by the laws governing that body.

The Commons became increasingly aware of the real situation and were opposed to any British subjects serving foreign princes, particularly the French. Foreign service provided the king with a trained reserve over which Parliament had no control. After the conclusion of the Second Dutch War Louis XIV sent over commissaries to recruit as many of the disbanded British army as they could; Douglas's regiment, which had come into England for the duration of the war, returned, and Sir George Hamilton assembled a company of English Gens d'Armes. The purge of catholics in 1667 provided a further excuse for dismissed officers and men to seek employment on the other side of the Channel.[41] This composed another contentious issue for Parliament; the soldiers in French service were often Irish, sometimes Scottish, and usually catholic. Whenever possible, Scotsmen and Irishmen were employed on foreign service in preference to superior Englishmen, and recruiting agents were encouraged to operate in these regions remote from England, well away from the close attentions of Parliament.

On 14 October 1667 the Commons debated whether the king

ought to be petitioned not to allow soldiers to serve in France, but this was defeated, the House thinking it had no right to meddle in such affairs. Ten days later they changed their minds and desired Sir William Coventry to address the king in order to restrain the 'exportations', but to no avail.[42] Under the terms of the Secret Treaty of Dover, signed in 1670, and in a private clause contained in the public version of 1672, Charles II undertook to send a force of 6,000 men to fight under the French flag against the Dutch.[43] The corps which went over was a composite muddle of regular units from England, special levies, and the incorporation of mercenary regiments already in France. From 1672 to 1674, when the British dropped out of the war, this brigade was an official British expedition paid and supported from England although it came under French operational command. However, after 1674, most of the brigade remained in France and became a foreign service force paid and maintained entirely at the expense of Louis XIV. Its sole contact with the British Isles was in recruiting. Thus, until the conclusion of the Third Dutch War, Parliament was unable to complain of illegal foreign service in France, but after 1674 they began to take action.

From Scotland and Ireland men were shipped to France against their wills, and this 'crimping' brought forth an order forbidding the levying of men in Scotland without the king's licence. This had no effect at all and the situation was as bad three years later:

> As it being represented to us that a number of men are levied in this Kingdom [Scotland] for the service of France, whereof some are landed there, and more are expected for the same purpose, and that men are clapped up in prisons, and detained there until there be an opportunity to send them away to France.[44]

The administration of the law was in the hands of the justices of the peace, but in a country with high unemployment and universal poverty coins from recruiting agents and bogus promises of high pay and booty were too much for the law.

As soon as Parliament reassembled in April 1675 the Commons addressed the king to recall the British Brigade in France now that England had ended her hostilities with the United Provinces, but Charles politely declined, saying that he had forbidden any more troops to be sent to France but that the men already there could stay. On 10 May the Commons debated this answer in Grand Committee and the House divided equally. Tempers were high and some Members accused the teller of counting one Member twice. Finally the Commons determined to request the king to recall only those soldiers sent over since the end of the Third Dutch War. This presented Charles with the opportunity of honouring his original commitment to Louis under the public Treaty of Dover, and so he issued a proclamation recalling all those who had gone to France since 1674 and forbidding any more to be sent.[45] The Commons discussed this proclamation on 23 May and resolved to bring in a bill to support it, although the opposition to the continuance of any force in France was strong. Sir Winston Churchill stated that he would 'send for his son home, and engage he shall never go there again'.

For two years the matter was dropped and the brigade stayed in France, but by 1677 English opinion had become pro-Dutch and anti-French, enabling the Commons to argue that the British regiments were contributing to the defeat of protestant Holland. The fact that levies were still being made for the Anglo-Dutch Brigade was ignored, and all attention was concentrated on the dreadful state of affairs which permitted recruits to be sent to the British Brigade in France. According to Burnet,[46] the Scottish authorities gave every encouragement to French agents; public gaols were put at their disposal, and even Edinburgh Castle, to house men until embarkation. The whole business 'looked liker a press than a levy'. Burnet blamed all this on his enemy Lauderdale. On 26 May 1677 the Commons gave a successful third reading to a bill 'for recalling his Majesty's subjects out of the service of the French King', and passed it up to the Lords.[47] Only the adjournment of both Houses on that same day prevented the passage of an Act. When Parliament came together again on 28 February 1678 they had a much bigger question to worry about—the projected war with France.

Some of the regiments in France had been recalled in 1674, but the Royal English, Churchill's Battalion, Hamilton's Irish and Monmouth's Horse had remained as mercenary formations. By the end of 1677 Danby was certain that a war with France was imminent. This, and not Parliamentary pressure, caused these four regiments in France to be summoned back to England, much to the annoyance of Louis XIV who regarded the British as useful and competent. Instead of releasing them close to the Channel ports, Louvois, in a fit of spite, ordered the Royal English and Dumbarton's into the depths of Dauphiné and disbanded them there. Without money or transport the soldiers had to make their way to England as best they could,[48] many not arriving until late in 1678. Dumbarton's alone left debts of £3,700 in France, and this was the sad end of six years' hard fighting. None of the British regiments in France fared very well. They were treated as the most junior regiments in the army enjoying few privileges and low precedence, pay was poor and irregular, and the action and service continual.

The Royal English arrived in France in early April 1672, only to find that the French had not provided adequate provisions or quarters. As the regiment only carried three days' food, over 400 men died from starvation and exposure before the formation approached the front.[49] In October eight of its companies were broken up and replaced by a battalion commanded by Bevil Skelton. Roscommon's Irish regiment thought its initial pay to be far too low, and later in 1672 the entire regiment was disbanded and its men used as replacements for other units.[50] Peterborough's, Vaughan's and Lockhart's arrived at Dieppe in November 1673, 'fine troops . . . although in rags and ill armed',[51] and their march to Castelnovo in Normandy was similar to that of the Royal English a year before—no food, poor quarters, and hundreds of men lost. By 1674 all the forces in France were much reduced through hunger, disease, heavy casualties suffered in action, and desertion. In addition, the regiments went through the thick of the campaigning, and it was often difficult to make up losses by recruiting in the British Isles; Charles's orders had some effect.[52]

France, like all other foreign service stations, was highly unpopular in Britain and the only method of gaining recruits was coercion. Sir Henry Jones asked for volunteers out of his own troop of the Royal Horse Guards to serve in his regiment of light horse in France in 1671, but 'because there were but 14, he was enraged, and sur le champ put out one of those that stayed out of the troop'.[53] Monmouth had great difficulty in raising the Royal English regiment, although two regiments which were simultaneously levied for home service rapidly filled their quotas and closed their rolls; no one wanted to go to France. Similarly, the foot regiments of Peterborough, Vaughan and Lockhart had great trouble in finding enough volunteers for France and there was a 'general unwillingness as well in the soldiers as officers to go into the French service'.[54] When Lockhart's regiment embarked for France a large number deserted:

Sir William Lockhart's Regiment is now gone for France, though many of them are run away, and those that are gone having mutinied before they could be got on board; on which occasion an ensign of one of the companies being somewhat brisk and drawing his sword to frighten them into better order, the poor gentleman was immediately knocked on the head and left dead on the place.[55]

Such unpopularity, coupled with government measures, made it very difficult to find replacements. Officers of the Royal English were often sent back to England to try and smuggle volunteers over to France, but it was in the laxer atmosphere of Scotland that they enjoyed most success.[56]

The Duke of Monmouth was commander of the brigade throughout its six years as well as being created a lieutenant-general in the French Army, but his titles were meaningless. The regiments of the brigade were divided between the various theatres of war and never fought together as a corps. Each regiment was a separate entity and its colonel's word was law. Colonel-Lieutenant Robert Scott of the Royal English was all-powerful, holding his own courts martial, appointing and commissioning officers, swindling the pay, and sometimes reporting back to Monmouth, his nominal superior.[57] Scott even possessed the power of life and death over his men and officers, and in 1675 this one regiment had its own Articles of War. The only orders that had to be obeyed from England were the instructions from the king to return. Once on foreign service, the king lost the right to commission the officers, this authority going to the commander-in-chief on the spot. This brigade in France provided an ideal training in European warfare for professional soldiers, for opportunities for active service with the standing army in England were limited.

The Second and Third Dutch Wars were in the main naval, and although the army had to furnish soldiers to fight on board the fleet as marines, there was little land action. Sir Robert Holmes invaded the island of Schelling on 9 August 1666 with 900 soldiers and 800 seamen, and set fire to the town of Brandaris. This conflagration, added to the burning of 160 Dutch merchantmen in the Schelling Road, comprised his famous 'Bonfire',[58] but the soldiers saw no action besides shooting a few civilians and doing a little routine looting. This event was much lauded at the time, but with no opposition Holmes could hardly have failed.

During the next year, the boot was very firmly on the other foot; the Dutch sailed up the Medway and bombarded Chatham. On 9 June 1667 the garrison of Sheerness was worsted when the Dutch landed on the Isle of Sheppey, after they had put up a stiff fight for two hours.[59] The Dutch vessels broke the boom protecting the mouth of the Medway on 12 June and proceeded to burn some ships and capture the *Royal Charles*. Above Rochester and Chatham stood Upnor Castle manned by two regular companies; their fire halted the advance of the Dutch ships handling them 'as warmly . . . as they could desire'. As soon as news of the enemy activity had reached London, Albemarle set out with the six available companies of the 1st Foot Guards, but they achieved very little. This small force was accompanied by an ensemble of adventurous young gentlemen, amateur soldiers and military hangers-on, who thought that their courtly presence might have an adverse effect on the Dutch. All they did was to earn Albemarle's contempt.[60]

Sailing out of the Thames, the Dutch Fleet moved to the 'Rolling Grounds' off Harwich, with their eyes on Landguard Fort, a strongpoint guarding the entrance to the estuary of the rivers Stour and Orwell. Landguard was held by the companies of Captains Henry Farr and Nathaniel Darrell of the Admiral's Regiment, supported by the Suffolk Militia which had gathered about the fort under the supervision of the earl of that county. A landing party came ashore on 2 July under the command of Colonel Thomas Dolman, one of the old Anglo-Dutch Brigade who had remained in Dutch pay after the reformation in 1665, fully equipped with scaling ladders. Under cover of fire from the fleet, the Dutchmen twice assaulted the fort, but the men of the Admiral's held firm and beat off both attacks. The militia stood around and looked, having 'much to do to keep themselves from disorder',[61] and such fighting as there was was left to the regulars. It was a particularly feeble affair; a lot of smoke and noise impressed eye-witnesses, but out of Dolman's force of three or four hundred not more than four were killed and twenty wounded.[62] Casualties in the fort were so slight as to be unreported.

Whatever else may be said of the military in Charles II's time, it was offensively minded. Sixteen seventy-three saw the departure of units to fight with the British Brigade under Louis XIV, as well as the birth of a plan referred to by Williamson as 'Zealand—the Design'. Such a mysterious name deserved something better than the eventual outcome. The French campaign in the Netherlands in 1672 had smashed the Dutch army and by the end of the year it was bottled up in Holland and separated from the victorious French only by a tenuous stretch of flooded polderland. The combination of Turenne and Condé working in joint harness had proved irresistible, and to add to the problems of the United Provinces the warlike Bishop of Munster had entered the war against them campaigning with some success in the east of the country. With her arch-enemy in such a predicament, the English government thought it high time to enter the war in earnest and glean whatever pickings they could from the expected humiliation of the Dutch. Williamson, who as Secretary of State had overall charge of the planning, chose coastal Zealand as his target. His decisions were based on intelligence reports from his contacts on the continent:

> By the enclosed you may see what condition they are in Zealand, and certainly, if the English do but keep a good fleet ready, well manned both of seamen and land soldiers, they cannot miss of getting Zealand, for there is the greatest disheartening again amongst the inhabitants that ever was, and the least success of the French in Holland will make good what I write here to you . . . the sooner you are in readiness the better.[63]

Nothing could be done until the winter weather cleared from the North Sea and the campaigning season opened in the Low Countries, but by then it was too late. Spain joined with the Dutch and forced the French to withdraw from the United

Provinces: instead of the French distracting the Dutch defenders so that the English could make an unopposed landing, the full weight of the Dutch army would now be available to meet the invasion. A compromise landing on Walcheren was considered.

Twelve thousand men gathered on Blackheath for the 'Design', mostly new levies stiffened by a few regular formations. An artillery train was prepared by the Ordnance Office. These twelve regiments of 1,000 men each were supposed to rendezvous at Blackheath by the beginning of June, but only eight had arrived by the end of the month. They provided a lively spectacle for the people of London, employing 'both the tongues and heels of most of the people . . . all persons travel hither to see the new and fine show'.[64] Finally, the army embarked on colliers on 18 July, seven weeks late. Once at sea the prospects were bleak. Before any landing could be attempted, the Dutch fleet had to be defeated and Prince Rupert could not do this whilst having to escort a large number of slow unwieldy transports. The army was put ashore at Great Yarmouth on 25 July whilst the battle fleet sailed off in search of De Ruyter to clear the way for the invasion. Off the Texel on 11 August Rupert suffered a reverse and the 'Design' was cancelled.

Apart from the inept overall strategy, a number of trivial incidents threatened the 'Design'. When the army came ashore to camp at Yarmouth the tents could not be used as the artillery officers had forgotten to supply any tent poles, and, of course, the moment that the men were on dry land drinking became their chief occupation and discipline suffered.[65] The senior officers spent most of their time bickering. Prince Rupert, as commander-in-chief of the expedition, had Schomberg as his lieutenant-general, but this appointment of a Frenchman to command over the heads of Englishmen, although very wise in view of Schomberg's success with the British in Portugal, was universally hated. Buckingham, a man with considerable martial pretensions but no aptitude at all, refused to serve under Schomberg and threatened to resign his own regiment. Even when the fleet was at sea a dispute over flags nearly caused a duel between Rupert and Schomberg, but these were the results and not the causes of a bungled operation, hastily conceived and poorly executed. The success of the 'Design' depended on the French being able to divert the Dutch away from the coast of

Zealand, but once Spain had entered the war this became an impossibility.

These were the only actions fought by the standing army in England. It was a peacetime formation and active service was only experienced in the colonies and on foreign stations. The officers who later manned the armies of William III were trained in France, the Anglo-Dutch Brigade, Tangier and Portugal. The cream of the armies which won glory for Marlborough was taught the art of warfare in mercenary formations under foreign governments.

X

Flanders 1678

BETWEEN 1674 and 1677 England turned from a pro-French to a pro-Dutch attitude. Parliamentary pressure had forced England to withdraw from the war with the Dutch in 1674, and with the coming of the peace the Cabal fell from power taking with them their foreign policy of favouring France. Even Buckingham preached against popery and favoured a variety of protestant patriotism, but it fell to Charles's new chief minister, Danby, to direct the political nation along its new path. For the military this *volte-face* caused some alarm, as by 1677 it was clear that England was heading for a war with France in alliance with the United Provinces; to have fought alongside the best army in Europe had been one thing but to oppose it was quite another. It took some time for Danby to wean the king towards the new alignment, but, late in 1677, William of Orange married Mary Stuart, daughter of the Duke of York. England was committed to the cause of protestant Europe and its fight against Louis XIV, and it appeared that king and Parliament were in agreement over foreign policy, but the mood was not to last. On 31 December 1677, England and the States General signed a treaty by which each undertook to restore a general peace to Europe on the basis of France surrendering Charleroi, Courtrai, Ath, Oudenarde, Condé, Tournai and Valenciennes, in return for her retention of Franche Comté, Cambrai, Aire and St Omer. This settlement was to be enforced, if necessary, and Ostend was granted to England as an advance base for an expeditionary force of 11,000 foot and 1,000 horse to fight alongside the Dutch and Spanish in the Low Countries. This treaty also required the recall of British troops from France.

The States General ratified the agreement on 20 February 1678, and on 2 March a more general alliance was signed at Westminster and ratified by the States General on 28 March. Significantly, England did not ratify this final treaty—Charles satisfied popular demand by detaching himself from France and apparently joining with the Dutch, but he committed himself to nothing. When Parliament reassembled early in 1678 they voted £1 million for a war with France, although the Commons were not entirely convinced by the king's arguments. However, Danby had done his work well; a large number of commissions in the new army had been granted to Members of Parliament to ensure that the subsidies for the army were passed, and to allay the fears of the Commons about an enlarged standing force for 'what hazard could there be from an army commanded by men of estates'.[1]

As the year progressed, the delaying of Charles and the Commons became worse and worse. The king was still trying to obtain French subsidies and avoid a war with his benefactor, whilst the Commons refused to vote any further money bills until their doubts over religion had been settled and they had sufficient assurances that the new army really was intended to fight the French and not to set up a military government in England.[2] Danby and the Duke of York both wrote to William of Orange, persuading him to come to a peace with the French yet pleading that it was impossible for England to declare war on France if there was a chance that her allies might desert her by reaching a separate peace.[3] If William understood this blatant chicanery and double-talk he did not show it, but merely insisted that the promised British forces be sent over.[4] In the long run Charles lost much credit with the Dutch and Spanish:

> I assure you, if the King had spilt the blood of his subjects, and his own too, in the service of these men [the Spanish], it will never be well valued by them, because he did not declare war against France when they would have him do it, and after their way, and had to be advised by them in the prosecution of the war. Most of them cannot be persuaded that the King ever really intended a war against France upon any account of theirs, and his sending over men as he did was only for the designs of the Prince of Orange, and to maintain an army for himself, which the Parliament sees now well.[5]

With Parliament and the king suspecting the motives of one

another, it is little short of remarkable that a military expedition ever left the shores of England. The army sent to Flanders in 1678 was entirely British with its own services and supply. It was not a mercenary force.

Late in 1677, Sir Joseph Williamson began drawing up plans for the projected war with France. The four standing regiments were to be increased to 2,400 men each, and the same process was to be applied to the three infantry regiments shortly expected out of France.[6] The twenty-nine garrison companies were made up to 100 men each and an additional thirteen companies were recruited. A company of grenadiers was added to each foot regiment.[7] Amongst the horse, Williamson intended the Royal Horse Guards to be augmented to eight troops of eighty men, the Life Guards to remain at 600 and to raise twenty independent troops.

At the end of these drafts, Williamson noted that 'we must have a great care of employing papists except in service abroad, not in service at home'. On 19 December 1677 the total number of new soldiers was raised to 30,000 who were to be clothed 'by tradesmen under contract, to be paid upon defalcations out of the King's pay'. Each captain was allowed levy money of £1 per man.[8]

Monmouth's Royal English was formed into two battalions on its return from France, one under Justin Macarty and the other under Roger Langley; Thomas Dongan's veteran Irish were on hand, as well as Dumbarton's Scots. Monmouth's new regiment of horse was virtually the same as the unit which came out of France with almost no alteration in its officers. However, there was a serious shortage of trained officers for the new regiments. Some of the colonelcies and lieutenant-colonelcies were given to eminent civilians to allay the fears of Parliament, but these needed the support of trained under-officers. The professionals from foreign service were employed extensively, both as field officers and company commanders, whilst junior officers of the four standing regiments were granted dual commissions, usually a captaincy, in the new regiments. This was one of the first occasions on which brevets were issued to the British army.[9] In this way the limited supply of useful officers was eked out. We have no real idea of who volunteered for the rank and file. Many might well have served in the regiments of the Third

Dutch War, many were Scottish and Irish. By 1677 there was no longer a pool of disbanded men from the New Model, but poverty, bad harvests and the desire for booty had a strong influence in recruiting soldiers for the armies of the seventeenth century.

By 10 March 1678 most of the new regiments had been recruited to their full strength, showing the ease with which the ranks were filled, and were quartered in the Home Counties. Colonel John Churchill, envoy to the Prince of Orange, was instructed to tell the Dutch that the British army would consist of seventeen battalions of foot, ten squadrons of horse, nine squadrons of dragoons, and an artillery train of twenty guns—a grand total of 17,860 men.[10] The force was expected to be in Ostend and Bruges by the end of May. Churchill was also required to grant seniority to Spanish regiments and officers, as Flanders was their territory, 'but an English commander or officer, in every rank and degree, is to command the Dutch or any other Confederate officer of the same rank, without any regard to the dates of their respective commissions'. This conceit and arrogance mirrored that of the Royal Navy who considered that all foreign vessels ought to lower their colours at the sight of a superior, English ship. The Dutch ignored this pompous demand.

Wagons for the transport of ammunition and provisions were loaned by the Spaniards. Each day the army required 180 bread wagons and 160 ammunition carts.[11] The bread ration was allocated according to rank, the general receiving 100 rations a day and a private only one. In between, different officers took more or less rations according to their station. The same system was applied to forage and horse feed in the cavalry, although this made more sense as the more senior officers maintained large stables of spare horses.[12] For this bread ration the soldier had to pay 1¼*d* a day which was deducted from his subsistence money, leaving the private in Flanders with only 4*d* a day in 'hard money'.[13] Out of this he was at liberty to buy 'butter, cheese, and biscuit' and, 'pork, beef, and peas',[14] when they were available, if he had been paid, and if he could afford them. Supply and rations were the province of the commissary-general, who in Flanders was Sir Palmes Fairborne of Tangier. He travelled the country with a wagon full of weights and measures to prevent cheating.

Apart from the commissary-general and a number of adjutants for each general officer, the staff was small. A quartermaster-general looked after camping sites and accommodation, and a provost-marshal general and judge advocate general oversaw the maintenance of discipline. This was a time when the Secretary at War lived up to his title and actually travelled with the army, although he only served as the personal secretary to the commander-in-chief. Mathew Locke did not go to Flanders, but James Vernon acted as his deputy and kept by Monmouth's side. The other important official was the Treasurer at War. He operated as the direct deputy of the Paymaster General in England. Moneys for the payment of the forces, the contingency fund, and all other financial matters passed through the hands of a Mr Gosfright and Elnathan Lumm, the two deputies. They carried the treasure around with them in a chest, stopped the deductions for clothing and rations, and issued the pay of each regiment to the agents.

The general officers were more numerous. Monmouth was commander-in-chief, and under him one lieutenant-general commanded the horse and another the foot. Three major-generals, two for the foot and one for the horse, came next, and then there were four brigadiers, three for the foot and one for the horse.

Charles II and the Duke of York reviewed the army on Hounslow Heath on 22 June 1678 and found them all to be well clothed and promising men, although the dragoons and horse grenadiers were 'indifferently mounted'.[15] Ostend was the British base, and by 8 March eight companies of the 1st Foot Guards, commanded by Lord Howard of Escrick, were stationed there as an advance guard. Seven companies under John Churchill stood at Bruges, the advance base, along with four from the Coldstream and eight from the Holland Regiment. These troops prepared the towns for the arrival of the bulk of the expedition, storing tents, medical supplies, ammunition and field equipment. Howard built 'as many barracks in the void space of ground hired for that purpose, as it will conveniently contain'.[16] As the battalions from the standing regiments completed arrangements for their reception in Flanders, the new regiments in England closed their rolls and did what training they could. Lord Alington's battalion led the way, embarking at Harwich on 13 May, and on 4 June Sir Lionel Walden's battalion also sailed for Flanders. The majority of the foot crossed over in July landing either at Bruges or Nieuport, except for Edward Villiers's battalion which went directly to Antwerp. The horse sailed in August. By the end of that month the army was stationed in Flanders. The voyage to Ostend and the coast of the Low Countries was short and could easily be accomplished in a day, given a favourable wind, and so the casualties amongst men and horses were negligible and nothing like those experienced on the voyages to Virginia or Tangier.

As soon as the advance party had arrived in Ostend a proclamation was issued forbidding the soldiers to 'use any incivilities or indecencies at the passing of the Sacrament', an important requirement in a catholic country, and announcing that the quarters provided for the soldiery would be paid for regularly every week.[17] This quieted the worst fears of the burghers of Ostend who had viewed the arrival of a large number of protestant soldiers with some alarm. Very shortly they were to be glad of the British presence. The Duke of Luxembourg opened the French campaign in Flanders with a movement towards Ostend and Bruges, and Sir Charles Littleton reported 'alarms all day long with the French troops that appear in sight of the town, the French King lying with a mighty army, they say 60,000, and I believe a little less, within six or seven leagues between this and Ghent'.[18] However, there was little danger that the French would attack the British, as Charles II had not formally declared war, and after a time the French veered away and went in search of the main Dutch and Spanish army under William of Orange. As far as possible Monmouth placed his regular battalions from the standing regiments in Ostend to act as a solid reserve, using the new regiments to man the advance base at Bruges.[19] Apart from preparing to go into the field, the ceremonial aspect of military life played its part, and on 29 May the regiments in Bruges mounted a parade to mark the King's Birthday:

We begun our ceremony about 9 of the clock in the morning and continued till 2 in the afternoon. Every Regiment were drawn in a line according to seniority upon the Ramparts and stood Regimentally; the pikes were interlined with the Muskets, 30 pieces of cannon were fired three times round the town, and betwixt every round was a volley of small shot, and then an English shout. The

Colours playing and the Drums beating, all the town said they had never seen a finer sight in their life.[20]

By the end of July all was ready for the British forces to join the Dutch field army and take an active part in the fighting.

Monmouth left England on 28 July and crossed over to Ostend[21] in order to supervise the transfer of eight battalions of foot from the west coast of Flanders to the Dutch army centred to the south of Brussels. To have marched this force overland would have been too dangerous in view of the vicinity of the French army, and so the battalions were loaded on board 'bilanders', small flat-bottomed sailing boats, to make the journey via the estuary of the River Scheldt to Antwerp and from there by river and canal to Brussels. Monmouth travelled in advance of his troops, reaching Brussels on 3 August. From here he sent orders to the battalions on the bilanders to direct them to their quarters.[22] The next morning Monmouth was escorted to the Dutch and Spanish army which he met near Brain-le-Comte. William of Orange was about to attack the French in their camp situated close to the Abbey of St Denis, near Mons, but the only British troops able to take part were those of the Anglo-Dutch Brigade commanded by the Earl of Ossory. Monmouth did very little in the battle apart from standing around and looking vaguely military, although Vernon wrote in the fashion of a good secretary and professional flatterer that 'my Lord Duke was in person wherever any action or danger was'. Lieutenant-Colonel Douglas led one of the Scottish regiments in a fierce attack on the French camp, and Colonel Henry Bellasise's regiment was also commended for brave actions. The Anglo-Dutch Brigade operated as the spearhead of the Dutch and Spanish army, sustaining heavy casualties.

The Battle of St Denis was the final engagement of the war and it ended inconclusively. A truce followed the action, and indeed some peace preliminaries had been signed before the battle took place. Ever since there has been a debate as to whether William attacked Luxembourg in the knowledge that a peace had actually been arranged, or whether he was genuinely ignorant of the fact.[23] Whatever the case, the British were too late to take part in the war, to the great relief of their government.

Monmouth left William's camp on 8 August and returned to Brussels to give orders for his eight battalions to march from their quarters to the Allied camp. There Sir Samuel Clarke and Sir John Fenwick gave him all the news from Bruges and Ostend, and then Monmouth rode back to the camp at Roeulx. William of Orange decided to inspect the British troops on his way to The Hague and Monmouth duly organised the parade. He expected to find his command at Tubise, but missed them, and it was only on the following day that he discovered that no one had taken any notice of his orders and the battalions were still camped about Brussels. In spite of this, William's inspection passed off to everyone's satisfaction, permitting Monmouth to return to Brussels having left instructions for the force to continue with its march to the Allied camp. However, the battalions were still camped north of Hal on 12 August contrary to Monmouth's orders, but this time he personally led them to the south. On the following day the British joined the Allied army; Monmouth's work was over and he left for England. The Earl of Feversham commanded the troops for the remainder of their stay in Flanders.

Conditions for the soldiers were poor. Ostend and Bruges stood on the polderland of the coast of Flanders, a region notorious for disease, and by late May the effects of the climate were starting to tell on the soldiery. The townsfolk were beginning to tire of the presence of the foreign military and the men had to live in barracks and lie 'only upon straw and never put off their clothes which occasions a great many of them to fall sick, every day more and more'.[24] By July, sickness was rampant and Monmouth introduced a system whereby the major of each battalion had to draw up a monthly 'Scheme', listing the number of fit men in his unit along with the state of their health, arms and clothes. The 'Schemes' were then passed to the garrison commander for counter-signature and so to the commander-in-chief. In this way, Monmouth possessed an up-to-date assessment of the exact strength of his forces.[25]

As the battalions marched through Brussels on their way to join the Allied army, they left behind a 'multitude of sick':

There are betwixt 8 and 900 sick out of the eight battalions which passed by here to the Army, and in the most miserable condition I have ever seen people. I have at length, with great labour and pains, gotten place for them, where they are daily well provided for, and have Doctors and Chirurgeons to see them daily, which is all I am able to do.[26]

George Legge's battalion was so under-strength that it was immediately sent back to its quarters at Malines. Even the officers were not free from the ravages of disease: Colonel Henry Sidney was ill at Antwerp for some time, suffering from the 'country distemper', and Lord Howard of Escrick, commander of the battalion of the 1st Foot Guards, died at Bruges. The preservation of the soldiers from sickness became the major concern of Monmouth and his staff. Bruges was adopted as the base hospital, probably the very worst place which could have been selected, and Sergeant-Surgeon John Knight came over from England to take charge of the arrangements. If and when any of the men recovered, they were returned to Brussels which acted as the medical clearing depot for soldiers going back to their units. All the while increasing numbers of men succumbed to illness and it was suggested that the army ought to move back into its quarters out of the field, but the idea was rejected by Monmouth.

Bruges had ceased to be the only hospital by September, and over 1,000 sick were reported in Brussels and many more in the camp.[27] Henry Sidney's battalion was so reduced by disease that William of Orange gave it permission to retire into Vilvord. Casualties on this scale were an embarrassment to the army for there was no nursing service of any kind and only one surgeon to each regiment. The junior officers did what they could for their men,[28] but Bulstrode, the English Resident in Brussels and the one man in a position to make arrangements for the troops with the Spanish authorities, was only too pleased to transport the sick out of his domain to their garrisons. He was heartily glad to see the back of them, stating that 'of which trouble I am now freed'. How many soldiers died of fever during the late summer and autumn of 1678 is impossible to calculate as no schedules exist. An intelligent guess suggests that as many as two or three thousand must have perished and many more had to be sent home to England seriously ill.

The maintenance of discipline on a foreign station was not an easy task, but it was especially difficult in Flanders where the troops had to be prevented from offending a catholic population.

In Tangier it had not mattered overmuch whether the civilians were adversely affected by the behaviour of the army, but in Flanders it would have had serious political repercussions if the military had offered any affronts to the inhabitants of the garrison towns. On important religious festivals the troops were marched into the country and exercised for the entire day to avoid any possible confrontations,[29] whilst punishments were executed openly in the streets to show the civilian authorities that the army meant business with its trouble-makers. But the keeping of the peace required an effort by the civil authorities as well as by the military. Following some disturbances between soldiers and burghers in Bruges, Sir Charles Littleton complained to Williamson that 'we have to do with one unruly rabble which neither the Governor, nor the Magistrates, can control. . . . I hope this will not happen again'.[30]

The original Articles of War, read on 3 March, were revised on 13 July for the benefit of the troops housed in Nieuport; death was inflicted for drunkenness, fighting, looting churches, affronting the religious, and even for entering churches and convents.[31] Governors of garrisons, general officers and battalion commanders, could hold their own courts martial with the power of life and death, but none of this stopped the number of offences.[32] Desertion, disobedience and theft, all went on much as before, regardless of the severity of martial punishments, but the discipline of the army was better than that experienced in Tangier:

> His Excellency is much pleased with the civil comportment of our officers and soldiers in their several quarters, and particularly with the good order kept in their march, not having had the least complaint of them, but on the contrary . . . the like not having been known in the march of any other troops.[33]

His attempted foreign policy in tatters and with a definite peace signed at Nymwegen, Charles had little option but to withdraw his army from Flanders and disband it in England. From December 1678 the staff had been preparing for the eventual retirement of the forces; debts had to be cleared, soldiers paid to the end of the December muster, and arrangements made for their embarkation. Captain John Wettwang of the Royal Navy was sent to Flanders to hire 'as many ships as shall be found necessary for transporting the 14 battalions now in those countries into England and to make all other provisions suitable to that voyage'.[34] The Bruges garrison was to lead the way followed by the four battalions from the standing regiments. All the sick were to be brought to Ostend and the deputy paymaster was directed to leave money for their care. On 6 January Monmouth ordered Sir Samuel Clarke to embark the six battalions in Ostend, Bruges and Nieuport, as soon as the vessels were ready, and then to march the remaining eight battalions from the field army to the coast. This journey involved crossing French territory, but Charles settled this matter with the French Ambassador in Whitehall, Maréchal d'Humières.

A sensible plan, in London, but in Flanders it was deep winter, the weather was extremely cold, and soon the army was unable to 'stir by land or water, the frost and snow are so great. The River at Antwerp is frozen.'[35] Four days later, Bulstrode enlarged on the situation:

> This is one of the cruellest winters that has been seen or felt in these countries, so that there is scarce any going by water or by land, which puts a stop to the march of the English troops towards their embarkation. It was resolved the other day to go in boats to Flushing and embark there. Now I think it is resolved they shall march towards Ostend and by land, the ministers here being persuaded to it at last.[36]

The delay continued until the end of January when at last it was decided to march overland to Ostend and Bruges and there embark for England, but just as the eight battalions were ready to depart, a rapid thaw set in and held up movement until well into February. On 12 February the soldiers set off, but they soon lost forty men in the snow and were forced to return to Brussels. The only alternative was to ship them from Antwerp. The embarkation commenced at the beginning of March and a fortnight later all the British soldiers had been ferried across to England. Some had been in Flanders for a year, had not seen any action, and had seen their ranks wasted by disease. Finally they had witnessed the futility of trying to march halfway across modern Belgium during one of the worst winters of the century. Their fate in England was disbandment.

Between January and May 1679, all the newly raised regiments were steadily disbanded. The Royal Horse Guards were reduced to eight troops of fifty men each, and the 1st Foot Guards had their twenty-four companies cut down to sixty men apiece. The Coldstreamers were established at twelve companies of sixty, whilst the Duke of York's and the Holland Regiments were permitted only twelve companies of fifty soldiers. Once the garrison companies had been reduced, the standing army was back to its pre-war size, and the officers who had held dual commissions were allowed back into their old ranks, evicting their temporary replacements.[37]

The new soldiers lined up before the Commissioners appointed by the Privy Council to disband the army, certified that all their debts had been paid and all accounts settled, delivered up their arms to the Commissioners of the Ordnance Office, and were then declared to be disbanded: 'The officers and soldiers are immediately to disperse to their own habitations and places of abode and behave themselves in all things as becomes dutiful subjects.'[38] Their sole mementoes of military service were their clothes, belts, swords and some very vivid memories.

In retrospect, the expedition went amazingly well. The staff in England, acting through deputies actually with the army in Flanders, managed to pay, feed and supply a large corps in a war zone on the other side of the North Sea. Though the forces did not go into action, a factor which might well have strained the field administration, the command and staff functioned with relative efficiency. Nothing went badly wrong. Certainly the medical service was found to be wanting in every respect, but medicine was a crude and primitive science in the seventeenth century, and even the sophisticated French army could boast of little better. Considering the shortage of experience in organising such an expedition, the overall design and execution were commendable when the limitations of contemporary transport and communications are taken into account. There were none of the delays and maladministration which characterised the running of Tangier and the Virginian Expedition. The British in Flanders were accepted by the Dutch, French and Spanish as just 'another army'. That was quite a compliment.

XI

Scotland and Ireland

England, Scotland and Ireland each possessed their own standing armies. Each was legally independent although they all owed allegiance to Charles II as their supreme commander, but in practice all three were interdependent and formed part of the same large whole. Soldiers from Scotland and Ireland were raised to serve on the English establishment whenever forces were needed for foreign service: Dumbarton's, Hamilton's, Roscommon's, Lockhart's, the Portuguese Brigade, and Tangier. It was undesirable to have Scots and Irish on peacetime service in England, as Englishmen regarded Scotland and Ireland with the greatest contempt and suspicion. To them, their neighbours were little more than savage barbarians with the added disadvantage that one sort were mostly papists and the others seriously tainted with non-conformity and dissenting opinions. With the standing army already unpopular in England the use of Scots or Irish troops, other than on station abroad, would have courted disaster and risked a public outcry against both the army and the government. However, it was quite in order to waste 'foreign' lives on active service on the continent, and to this extent the armies in both countries were valuable and complementary to the main force in England.

George Monck left a sizeable force in Scotland under Sir Thomas Morgan when he marched into England in 1660, but not until 1662 were the remains of this corps disbanded. As soon as money was available, these regiments were either paid off or sent to Tangier and Portugal, but their replacement was difficult. Scotland was a poor country and unable to support a large standing army, but a big force was not necessary. The Covenanters were always a threat but sufficient temporary troops could be raised to deal with a specific emergency. In fact, the Scottish contingent was so small as hardly to warrant the name 'army'.

A regiment of Foot Guards was raised together with a troop of horse called 'the King's Guard of Horse'. That, with a few independent garrison companies at Edinburgh, Stirling and Dumbarton, was the standing army in Scotland. It numbered 1,200 men. During internal crises, namely when there was an increase in the frequency of conventicles, these troops were augmented by a few temporary regiments, as in 1674 when three troops of horse and a small regiment of foot were added to the establishment to deal with a few covenanters.[1] During the Bothwell Bridge uprising of 1678–9 the Scottish armed forces reached their maximum size, but the grand total of regular troops only came to 2,754.[2]

Such pay as the men received was miserable. Foot guardsmen received but *6d* a day, and ordinary infantrymen only *5d.*[3] Horsemen of the King's Troop took home the princely sum of half-a-crown and other troopers had 1*s* 8*d*. This money was found from the Inland Revenue of Scotland and was paid by the Paymaster of the Scottish forces. There was a separate train of artillery in Scotland, independent of the Ordnance Office in London. John Slezar was appointed Chief Engineer of Scotland and Lieutenant of the Artillery in 1677, and both his pay and the charges of the train were placed on the Scottish establishment.[4] Slezar had very little to command. His field train consisted of 'eight very fine minions', with some brass culverins and demi-culverins in the castles at Edinburgh, Stirling and Dumbarton, and although Charles II allowed him to do what he could to improve the artillery, shortage of money hampered his efforts.

Money was so short for the Scottish army that a circular went round to the garrison governors in 1682 limiting the amount of powder and shot which could be used in formal salutes and training, and the commanders had to keep 'an exact journal' of all guns fired.[5] Scotland's main function was to serve as a reservoir for English foreign commitments, and the army in

Scotland was designed for ceremonial occasions and to keep the peace in the Lowlands. The maintenance of law and order in the Highlands was a lost cause and Scotland's tiny army never ventured into the area.

As in the colonies, a weakness in the standing forces was rectified by a strong and well organised militia. The Scottish Parliament was able to offer the king a militia of 20,000 foot and 2,000 horse 'sufficiently armed and furnished with 40 days' provisions',[6] but in October 1678 Charles chose to select 5,000 foot and 500 horse from the total offered, sacrificing quantity for quality. When this militia came together to oppose the uprising in 1679 they actually marched towards the enemy, something which their English equivalents were not always inclined to do, and gave a good account of themselves. So good was their performance that the new regular levies in England which were being raised to assist the Scottish army were halted and full trust was placed in the militia.

Trouble first occurred in Scotland in 1666. Some 900 Scotsmen had been granted indemnity in 1660 on payment of a special fine, and in 1666 it was thought high time that these were collected. Scotland was known to be out of favour with the anti-Dutch policy of Clarendon's administration, and both factors offered a favourable opportunity of harrying the dissenters and breaking up some minor field conventicles run by the ejected clergy. The favourite ploy of the Scottish authorities was to quarter troops on their victims, forcing them to feed and house the soldiers free of charge until the fine was paid. Sir James Turner, who had fought in the Thirty Years' War and held the lieutenant-colonelcy of the Scottish Foot Guards, was in charge of these operations in south-west Scotland. Many of his officers had been trained in the service of the Russian czars, and this, added to Turner's apprenticeship in the tough school of Germany, led to some very brutal treatment of the Covenanters. James Sharp, Archbishop of St Andrews, was busy forcing episcopacy on to the Scottish Church, a policy which was very poorly received in western Scotland, and this, together with Turner's ill-considered tactics, led to a rebellion.

In November 1666, 200 rebels took Turner prisoner at Dumfries. This aggressive action brought a number of discontented Covenanters over to the cause of the so-called 'Pentland Uprising', and the rebels marched to within two miles of Edinburgh in the hope of gaining some support from the city. The situation now assumed some urgency for it was feared that the Dutch might assist the Covenanters. Thomas Dalziell (Dalyell), another trainee of the Russians, was commissioned Lieutenant-General in Scotland and he immediately set off in pursuit of the rebels with whatever regular forces he could obtain. He followed the Covenanters as closely as he could but was gravely hampered by their habit of destroying all the bridges and ferries in his path. The militia in Westmorland and Northumberland were alerted and Lord Frescheville's troop of the Royal Horse Guards was ordered to join Dalziell. Soon after, two more troops of the 'Blues' and some of the Life Guards were ordered north, but Dalziell, having been 'led a sad march', caught the rebels in the Pentland Hills at Rullion Green. Three charges by the Scottish Life Guards were enough to break the rebels. Casualties were minute on either side,[7] but the rebellion was over, Turner was released, and the Scottish army had succeeded in keeping its own house in order without assistance from England.

Some ten years later the heavy hands of Lauderdale and James Sharp again caused serious trouble in Scotland. An attempt had been made on Sharp's life as early as 1668 by a James Mitchell. Six years later Mitchell was arrested and a death sentence commuted to imprisonment in return for a confession. In spite of this he was brought to trial in 1676 accused of having taken part in the Pentland Uprising and only another threat to Sharp's life prevented a further prosecution. However, Mitchell was again brought to trial in 1678 and this time executed. Vengeance was soon extracted from Sharp who was pulled from his coach and murdered on 3 May 1679.

Against this backcloth, discontent with the administration of Lauderdale had been growing for a number of years. The Pentland Uprising had never been forgotten, but by 1677 the Scottish government had become even more arbitrary and paid even less regard to the processes of the law. Parliament at Westminster raised its voice against Lauderdale, the only survivor of the Cabal, but he had the support of Charles, Danby and the Tory faction. Against this, Shaftesbury and the opposition could do nothing to effect his dismissal. In Scotland Lord Rothes and the

Duke of Hamilton headed the anti-Lauderdale faction, but beneath the centres of power a grass-roots movement was under way. Sir George Rawdon reported to Lord Conway that field conventicles had again started in western Scotland by August 1677, and Lauderdale reacted with severity imposing huge fines on the offenders.[8] In readiness for the expected outburst, Charles ordered Irish troops to concentrate at Belfast and stand by for embarkation to Scotland.[9] The militia of Cumberland and Westmorland was called out and the garrisons of Carlisle and Berwick-on-Tweed were placed on the alert.

Then the inevitable happened. Lauderdale ordered the Highlanders to be quartered on the Covenanters who had refused to pay their fines, 'to the exceeding great terror of the Lowlanders'.[10] As a further insult, the landlords of western Scotland had to enter into bonds with the government for the good conduct of their households and tenants, and when the majority refused Lauderdale intimated to the king that Scotland was in virtual rebellion. Hamilton hurried to London with some of his supporters to complain of this savage treatment, and his intervention was sufficient to have the Highlanders called off but not before they had done untold damage. Conventicles had become 'so frequent in every corner of the Kingdom, that it makes me believe they will either rise in arms shortly or other ways will all go mad, or they now contemn all authority whatsoever'.[11]

Already the Covenanters had defeated a small party of regulars from the Bass Rock, and this was the cue for Monmouth to order Sir Lionel Walden's foot, four troops of horse, and three troops of dragoons north to the borders.[12] These reinforcements were desperately needed in Scotland, as the army was so low in numbers that the government considered it dangerous to venture against the Covenanters. In the meantime the Scottish establishment was increased by one new regiment of foot under the Earl of Mar, three troops of horse, one company of dragoons, and two new formations of Highlanders. In the north of England the regular forces were alert and ready should trouble spread over the Border, providing some useful training for the new regiments. These units were designed to co-operate with and assist the northern militia which was 'not much conversant in military matters'. None of these regiments were to move into Scotland unless it became clear that the Scottish army could not hold its own.

Not until 1679 did matters finally come to a head. The Privy Council met in London on 9 June and took the resolution to raise extra forces to help Lauderdale,[13] 'although most were against it' on account of the expense.[14] Huge costs had been incurred on the Flanders Expedition and now that these forces had just been disbanded a new levy had to be made for Scotland. At least there was no problem in finding volunteers to fill the ranks. It was decided to raise three regiments of horse, three of foot, eleven companies of dragoons, and three troops of horse grenadiers, a total of 5,520 men. Very few of these forces were actually levied. Monmouth's Horse, which had come from France, was re-raised under Colonel Charles Gerard,[15] the Royal Dragoons were continued from 1678,[16] and the three troops of horse grenadiers were kept on foot.[17] Apart from these none of the new formations were raised.

Monmouth was commissioned as 'General of all the Forces in Scotland', but as the troops were being recruited in England the rebellion in Scotland was reaching its climax. Eighty well armed horsemen rode into 'Rungland'[18] on 29 May, proclaimed the Covenant, burned several Acts of Parliament, pinned a proclamation for the Kingdom of Jesus to the church door, and then announced Charles II to be a usurper. May 29 was the anniversary of the Restoration and by statute its observance was the solemn, although odious, duty of all Scotsmen.[19] On the following Sunday a huge conventicle took place on Lundown Hill. Captain John Graham of Claverhouse[20] marched out with one of the new troops of horse and one of the new dragoon units. Fifteen hundred of the Covenanters' cavalry were awaiting them. With the loss of thirty men, Claverhouse fell back towards Glasgow pursued by the rebels. Scotland was in open rebellion.

Glasgow was held by Lord Ross with eight militia companies, but he barricaded the streets and beat out the Covenanters with heavy casualties on both sides. Behind Ross stood the Scottish standing army based on Edinburgh, and as he gradually withdrew towards the capital the rebels became masters of Glasgow. Their leader Robert Hamilton was assisted by the assassins of Archbishop Sharp, Balfour and Baxter, and it was thought that they 'would probably have all the western part at their devotion'. From Glasgow the Covenanters marched for Stirling, whilst Monmouth hurried north to assume command of the king's army in Scotland. As a holding force the militia had fought sturdily and well, ample proof of the effectiveness of its recent 'new modelling', but the Covenanters were estimated at 8,000 outnumbering the total militia of Scotland.

Monmouth reached Edinburgh by 19 June and immediately drew out the Scottish army and marched in pursuit of the rebels. He found them in camp at Bothwell Bridge and Hamilton Heath, nine miles south of Glasgow on the River Clyde. Monmouth set forth from his camp on 21 June with a force which must have numbered 2,000. No order of battle has been discovered and so it is impossible to be precise as to what units were present, but certainly some of the English horse were with the Scottish army. Major Theophilus Oglethorpe's troop of the Royal Dragoons was there with one other, and Lieutenant-Colonel Edmund Mayne's troop of Gerard's Horse.[21]

As the king's army marched towards Bothwell Bridge, Oglethorpe led forward his dragoons as an advance guard and ran into the rebels at dawn on 22 June, drawn up on the west bank of the Clyde about the bridge. Robert Hamilton knew little of military affairs and had placed no pickets beyond his lines, so his first knowledge of Oglethorpe's approach was gained by spotting the lighted matches in the darkness. The dragoons advanced to within pistol shot of the rebels and then waited for Monmouth to approach with the main body. A parley was beaten and Monmouth offered mercy to those who would lay down their arms, but his terms were refused. The Covenanters had blocked the bridge with barricades of stone and timber, and there was no other way of crossing the deep and wide river.

Accordingly Monmouth moved up his artillery and commenced firing on the barricades.[22] Momentarily the royalist gunners were driven from their pieces by a flurry of small shot, but they quickly returned and drove the rebels from their defences with their fire. Oglethorpe crossed the bridge but then moved forward before the bulk of the army had come up to support him. Noticing that the dragoons were isolated, Hamilton counter-attacked and forced them back to the foot of the bridge. Their success did not endure. Once the main body of

Monmouth's command was on the west bank of the Clyde, his cavalry fanned out and scattered the Covenanters on to Hamilton Heath. Here they rallied and made a stand some quarter of a mile from the river, but their horse was routed by cannon fire and then Oglethorpe's dragoons drove their entire army off the field. Many of the rebels were surrounded on Hamilton Heath by Lieutenant-Colonel James Douglas of the Scottish Foot Guards and forced to surrender.[23] Twelve hundred Covenanters were captured, a further 800 were killed in the battle, and another 400 were killed during the pursuit.[24]

At the opening of the action, around 9.00 a.m., the rebels had numbered about 6,000, but by 1.00 p.m. their army had ceased to exist. Claverhouse led the chase after the broken Covenanters with great zeal. On the following day a skirmish took place when 140 of the rebels made a stand on Cumlock Moor, but they were heavily defeated by eighty of the king's horse. Among those killed was one Cameron, a leading preacher with the Covenanters. With him died the rebellion.[25]

Ireland possessed a large army of Cromwellian veterans in 1660, and at the Restoration this force followed the example of the New Model in England and declared in a body for Charles II. Again, as in England, this army was too big for peacetime purposes and it had to be partly disbanded and purged of all the officers and men likely to cause trouble to the monarchy. Anyone in the army who did not take the Oaths of Allegiance and Supremacy was cashiered, and in this manner the army was reduced during 1660.

Charles II's army in Ireland dated from 11 February 1661, and consisted of thirty troops of horse and sixty-six companies of foot, with the officers receiving their commissions for life under the Great Seal. Many of the officers were ex-Cromwellians who had settled their consciences by swearing to the Oaths and had been cleared under the Act of Free Pardon and Indemnity. This gave Ireland a very experienced and professional officer corps, but it was wasted as there was no organised army in the country: none of the troops and companies were regimented, but were quartered all over the countryside as independent units, lacking a corporate identity. A regiment of Irish Foot Guards was raised in England in April 1662 and shipped to Dublin, but the remainder of the army was not arranged into regiments until 1672.[26] The reason for this loose organisation was shortage of money. Regimental staffs and establishments cost more than the pay of a troop or company without field officers, surgeons, and chaplains.[27] In addition to the regular forces there was a ceremonial 'Guard of Battleaxes' of sixty men. Their function was to attend the Lord Lieutenant on all state occasions after the fashion of the English Gentlemen Pensioners.

A troop of Life Guards of Horse was created in 1664, but other than this the Irish establishment did not alter throughout the reign. As in England, the Life Guards were manned by gentleman privates, some of whom had failed to secure commissions in the general rush of 1661 and others who expected to be commissioned in the future. The Irish army was the largest in the British Isles, averaging around 7,500 men. Even larger numbers were raised for active service outside Ireland—in France, on board the English fleet, in Tangier and in Portugal. On the outbreak of the Third Anglo-Dutch War a foot regiment was raised under Lord Le Power and sent into England. This incident was unique as it was unusual to have Irish troops in England, although some English soldiers served temporarily on the Irish establishment from time to time. Following the general disbandment in 1674, twenty-five companies from English regiments were kept on foot and shipped over to Ireland as an addition to the Irish army.[28] This was a cheap method of building up a reliable standing army close to England. Ireland was always seen as a weak point in the English defences against foreign invasion, and even Parliament realised the benefit of retaining a strong army there. Irish regiments served Spain in Flanders; Roscommon's and Hamilton's fought in France in 1672, and in 1678 Colonel Thomas Dongan was licensed to levy a large regiment for the French service.[29]

By 1676, the army in Ireland cost £146,260 19*s* 8*d* a year for six regiments of horse and six of foot.[30] This was a huge expense for a nation as poor as Ireland, resulting in large and continual arrears of pay. Regimentation of the army occurred in 1672, but even then the army consisted of no more than a collection of scattered troops and companies, the new formations existing only in name.[31]

All Irish soldiers, whether serving in Ireland, England or overseas, had to be paid from the Irish Exchequer,[32] which was neither rich, honest, nor efficient. By May 1661 the army was already eight months in arrears of pay, and a mutiny broke out at Carrickfergus five years later when credit was refused the soldiers. Two further factors conspired to make the payment of the Irish soldiery utterly chaotic; the use of agents, or 'clerks', for each troop and company, and the presence of Richard Ranelagh, the 3rd Viscount Ranelagh, as Chancellor of the Irish Exchequer from 1674 to 1681. Regimental agents were bad enough, but when one was attached to each sub-unit the corruption was multiplied at least ten times. A circular order went round from the Lord Lieutenant in 1671,[33] pointing out that

> information hath been made unto us . . . [that] soldiers are not by the Clerks of the several troops and Companies fully satisfied the pay which is payable to them after due defalcations which is so great injury to the soldiers' suffering and a high abuse to his Majesty.

The captains mustered their men and asked them if they had received their full pay over the past year. If they had not, then the only explanation was that it had disappeared into the agent's pocket. Ten years after the Restoration the arrears of pay were so bad that it was impossible for the Irish Treasury to meet them as well as the current pay.

At this stage Ranelagh and a group of partners contracted to farm the Irish revenues on condition that they undertook the payment of the Irish army. Ranelagh's scheme for meeting the arrears was to issue the soldiers with debentures for the amounts owed which could be cashed at the Exchequer for their face value. In effect, with the soldiery desperate for money of some sort, Ranelagh and his friends bought these debentures from them for as little as *6s* in the £ and then cashed them on the Exchequer at their full value. The profit was never less than 100 per cent whilst the unfortunate soldiers lost over half their rightful pay.[34] Ranelagh's farm of the revenue began on 25 December 1675 and he guaranteed to meet the arrears from Christmas 1672. Very little of the debt was paid due to Ranelagh's tactics, and on 31 August 1677 Charles II had to borrow £36,565 *4s 0d* at an interest of 10 per cent from Robert and William Bridges of London in order to pay off the outstanding sum. A new farm of the revenue was granted to Sir James Shean in 1676 to replace Ranelagh, and after this the payment of the army was steadier and more regular. Ranelagh was not punished for his sins, which were outstanding even for the seventeenth century, and when he became Paymaster-General of the English army in 1689 he was quite unreformed and indulged in the most monstrous peculation and corruption.

Life for the soldiers in Ireland was boring and hard. Often on the verge of mutiny from lack of pay and credit, they could be calmed by 'fair words . . . and the discontented silenced',[35] but sometimes they boiled over, as in 1674 when some of the army rebelled against arrears of pay, false musters, and their officers withholding money from them:[36]

We are at present in a great calm everywhere, the soldiery excepted, whose condition is now worse than ever, and in many places (through absolute necessity and want of pay) grown troublesome to the neighbourhood.[37]

There were some internal duties. Ireland was a lawless country and many of the troops of horse took part in expeditions to track down gangs of brigands, patrolling the highways, and convoying consignments of bullion and merchandise. Six troopers of the Irish Horse Guards were convoying £400 *in specie* to Dublin when they were set upon by fourteen robbers, who were only beaten off after a sharp dispute.[38] For the foot there was endless garrison duty, and in 1676, with pay nine months in arrears, company commanders were permitted to let their men take on labouring work so that they could live without army pay. The horse, being 'somewhat in a better condition', were allowed to break ranks and go home so that they could live off their farms and rents in the absence of army pay.[39] By the end of 1676 there was no army in Ireland.

The routine was occasionally interrupted when some companies were marched off to serve on board the English fleet as marines, but here they found conditions worse than in Ireland. When they were disbanded their return to civilian life was disheartening:

The condition of the late disbanded men, both officers and soldiers, is very miserable for they have not had any part of their pay at their dismission: the orders for disbanding them going out so hastily as they were not accompanied with warrants for a quarter's pay as is directed by his Majesty's letter. I find all their creditors fall upon them for their debts and being discharged from the King's service I can no way protect them nor keep off their creditors . . . so as I fear many of them will run away and turn robbers.[40]

Militarily, as well as socially, the army in Ireland left a lot to be desired. Essex reported to Danby in 1676 that 'all things relating to the army in Ireland, the garrison stores and forts there, are in a most miserable condition'.[41] There were only 300 barrels of powder in all of Ireland, only 500 good muskets, and not one company in the entire army was completely armed. Many muskets were out of order and there were a multitude of different calibres, half the pikes were broken, and the few guns and cannon in the garrisons were dismounted. To correct these faults the Master of the Ordnance computed a charge of £50,000, well beyond the capability of the Irish Exchequer. Two years later, with England about to enter into a war against France, Sir George Rawdon was of the opinion 'that never could a Kingdom be worse provided for' than Ireland: no guns mounted, inadequate stores, and the coastline completely without fortifications.[42]

The officers of this miserable army were part-timers. As the reign progressed, the original Cromwellian veterans were gradually replaced so that only ten remained on the active list in 1684. Gentleman officers took their places, often with little military knowledge or experience, who regarded their commands as possessions valuable for status and profit. The majority of the career professionals served overseas: Thomas Dongan, Justin Macartie, John Fitzgerald and Sir George Hamilton. The soldiers saw very little of their officers. The troop or company commander was usually a landlord who spent most of his time either on his estates or in England, and the care of their units was entrusted to subalterns. These officers, the lieutenants and ensigns, connived with the agents to defraud the soldiers of their pay, and occupied themselves with duels and quarrels. There was a dispute amongst the officers of the Irish Foot Guards and the Life Guards as to whether the officers of either regiment should take orders from any general officer of the army, or whether their status put them above such things. Sir Arthur Forbes, the Marshal of Ireland, tried to give orders to both regiments but they insisted that they could only take directions from the Lord Lieutenant.[43] Such discipline from the officers did little to encourage the men to behave decently.

All the army, officers and men, was supposed to be protestant; the catholic soldiers served abroad on foreign service. Every officer and ranker had to produce certificates from a bishop or minister, stating that he had received the Sacrament according to the Church of England twice in every year.[44] If the Muster-Master found anyone without these certificates he was to stop his pay immediately. As the high tide of the Popish Plot swept into late 1678, these precautions were thought to be insufficient to prevent catholics from creeping into the army. A reward of £10 was granted to any commissioned officer, £5 to any trooper, and £2 to an infantryman, who should discover anyone in the army who had been 'perverted to the Romish religion, or heard mass who had formerly taken the oaths of allegiance and supremacy; and the like to the discoverer of any that should afterwards be perverted'. To the English the Irish army was tolerable provided that it was commanded by gentleman planters and was protestant to a man.

Whereas we have desired the building of an Hospital for the maintenance and convenience of such aged and maimed soldiers of our Army in Ireland as are, or shall be, during their continuance in the said army become unserviceable, and the said Hospital is already begun to be erected upon part of our land in our park called the Phoenix Park.[45]

On sixty-four acres of the Phoenix Park in Dublin, Kilmainham Hospital was constructed. Charles charged no rent to the governors of the hospital, but *6d* in the pound was deducted from the pay of every soldier and officer in the Irish army for the maintenance of the inmates. The hospital, with its 'convivial walks and gardens', was one of the better things to come from the Irish military authorities during the seventeenth century, and its establishment and charter was closely followed by the Royal Hospital at Chelsea. However, the hospital only provided for the aged and infirm; for those disbanded without provision there was no assistance of any kind.

Poor though the Irish army was, it was ahead of the English organisation in two respects: Kilmainham Hospital preceded the foundation of the Chelsea institution by two or three years and provided the model, and also garrison troops were housed in barracks, thus avoiding all the controversy and ill-feeling which the question of quarters caused in England.

Part Three

XII

Society, the Army and Parliament

PARLIAMENT in the seventeenth century did not reflect the desires, fears and condition of the mass of the people. The Lords and Commons expressed the views of their own class, and they only came into contact with the 'vulgar' when an issue accidentally affected both sections of society simultaneously. Trade and employment or the power of the common law courts could produce a combined reaction, whilst the fear of Roman Catholicism brought hysteria to both the gentry and their constituents. A similar common hatred was the army.

Politically and socially the standing army in England represented a force which worked for the good of the king, but to the supposed detriment of both the lower and upper classes. To the gentlemen of Parliament the army was one of the central political questions of the age and formed the core of the struggle between king and Parliament for executive supremacy. Non-Parliamentary gentry in the counties saw the standing troops as an attempt to undermine the position of their cherished militia, indirectly threatening their roles in county politics. The ordinary people in the towns and the country loathed the army. In their eyes it stood for everything that was bad and hateful.

Red coats had been adopted in Cromwell's time when the army ruled the country and acted as a coercive influence, but the Restoration army retained this distinguishing feature and, unofficially, its work was not at all different from that of its predecessor. The army acted as a police force and so stood for the 'establishment'; its behaviour before the public was nothing less than disgusting; it caused more trouble by way of riots and disorders than it ever helped to solve; it frequently housed itself on civilians under free quarter; and it attracted some of the worst dregs of society into its ranks. Families were broken up by the press gang, which was used to recruit for the Second and Third Dutch Wars (even though the regulations forbade any householder to enlist in the army) and for Tangier, the colonies, and foreign service. Soldiering in Tangier or the West Indies meant certain death, or at best a very long period away from home, but this was nothing compared to the fate awaiting those unfortunates pressed into foreign armies. The Irish and Scots transported to Flanders and the United Provinces went into permanent exile.

There was a curious and confusing duality in the public reaction to the army. As a whole, a force of gentleman officers and common soldiers, it was disliked and viewed with the highest suspicion from all quarters. Yet the courtiers and gentry were prepared to accept commissions in the English establishment in return for their loyalty to the court, or to make money, and even as a career, in the case of the younger sons without an inheritance. However, the non-military courtiers considered the army to be beneath contempt, and there is an unfounded story of a Suffolk baronet who appeared at a levée in the uniform of the Guards and was publicly laughed at. Apart from the officers who actually belonged to the army and enjoyed its special privileges, the standing forces were the object of dread and ridicule from all sides. An anonymous letter to the king in 1666 roundly condemned the army, calling it 'a scandal to be a Life Guardsman', and continuing 'the Guards will soon be full of tinkers, robbers, and hackney coachmen, for however stout, well born, or loyal a man may be, he will not get in unless he has money to give the officers.'[1] This summarises the trouble with the Restoration army. The soldiers were the worst possible advertisement, whilst the officers were corrupt, cheating both their men and the civilian population. Henry Savile sarcastically remarked upon the new army of 1678:

I suppose your Lordship has heard that all the fine gentlemen who intended to conquer France are disappointed, and that this noble army is out of hand to be disbanded, to the grief I think of none but those who are of it, and of them many have laid out sums which will inconvenience them; so that if suffering be part of the business of a soldier, divers of them have made a notable progress for the time.[2]

To an officer in the army there was little wrong with the standing forces, but to nearly everyone else, the common soldier included, the military could do very little that was right.

Following the disbandment of the Flanders army in 1679, the Earl of Essex came to hear of a scheme whereby Charles planned to form a new company of Guards consisting entirely of half-pay officers. These would then act as a cadre for expanding the army at any time in the future. Essex was successful in pointing out the dangers of this action to his sovereign: it would enhance the fear of government by a standing army, increase the load on an impoverished Treasury, and might well prove damaging to the government's credit-worthiness in the City.[3] Even a disbanded army was viewed with alarm. When the army was broken up in 1679, the *Courant*[4] noted that the released soldiers were likely to prove well behaved and loyal until their money ran out, but then they would become 'like tinder capable of any evil fire'. In both reality and popular myth the army was always a cause of disturbance.

Its connection with catholicism throughout the reign was not coincidence, but a linking-together of the two bogies which threatened Restoration England, one the slightly irrational and hysterical fear of the Counter-Reformation, and the other the fear that an army meant a return to the dismal days of the Interregnum. Both were connected with violent and unstable episodes in England's past, but whereas the dread of popery was totally unfounded, the hatred of the standing army had a wide foundation of genuine grievance.

Desertions were frequent, resulting in bands of armed soldiers roaming over the countryside trying to evade their pursuers. They rapidly turned to robbery, obliging the parish constables to spend much of their time searching for military miscreants. Most of the desertions resulted from soldiers being marched off to embark for foreign service. As early as 1665 levies for overseas quarrelled with their officers and mutinied, and when the regiments embarked for France to serve with the brigade under Louis XIV serious trouble started. The mass levy of 1678 and the expedition to Flanders witnessed a number of desertions, even though the troops were going to fight with an official British army corps and not for a foreign power. To the soldiers, most of whom would not have journeyed outside their own counties or even parishes, such subtle distinctions of allegiance were irrelevant. Two hundred of Lord Morpeth's regiment ran from their colours,[5] many of them stowing away on outward-bound ships in the Thames.[6] Having survived the expedition to Flanders, men of Colonel Edward Villiers's regiment were ordered to re-enlist for Tangier. Flanders had been bad enough, but the prospect of Tangier was infinitely worse; desertion appeared to be the only hope of survival and so an entire company ran from its colours.[7]

Very rarely there were mutinies over pay. Two companies of the Duke of Buckingham's Regiment deserted and marched to London to complain of their officers who were cheating them. One of their captains was 'Swift Nix', the once infamous highwayman, so their objections were probably justified, but a closer look reveals that these men had only just returned from a period of marine service with the fleet, a duty which was almost as unpopular as foreign service. It would have taken little to make such men desert.[8] Besides mutiny and desertion there was much else for the civilians to grumble about.

If the contemporary letters and petitions to the Privy Council are correct, then the army which was supposed to assist in the maintenance of law and order was itself lawless and a public menace. Five companies of Lord George Douglas's Scottish Regiment waiting to embark for France in 1667 'abused shamefully' the inhabitants of Rye,[9] whilst some of their comrades did 'much mischief by the way by killing farmers' poultry, sheep and hogs' at Dover.[10] The garrison of Dover Castle used to arrange foraging expeditions into the surrounding countryside, causing all manner of damage: damming mill ponds, stealing fish and livestock, physically assaulting householders, and driving the civilians to petition the Privy Council for relief.[11] Lieutenant Gilbert Swiney and Sergeant John Hooper of the Earl of Carlisle's Regiment were reported to the Privy Council for disorderly conduct at Saxmundham, in Suffolk. Four soldiers were convicted of causing a riot at Staines, whilst one private gentleman of the Life Guards was so impatient that he shot a barmaid who was slow to bring him brandy. One of the worst failings of the military was excess of drink. This applied to both officers and men. It was not an age noted for sobriety, and as the soldiers aped their officers by duelling, so they copied them in drunkenness:

On Wednesday a drummer of the Duke of Albemarle's at Blackheath being got drunk and for it carried to the Horse, the soldiers got together and declared they saw no reason to punish him for what the officers had never been free from since their coming thither, and then took him from them and rudely treated their officers.[12]

Soldiers were ill-natured towards everyone; they robbed and maltreated civilians, mutinied against their own officers, deserted the king's service, quarrelled amongst themselves, and were sometimes led into trouble by their officers. At Gray's Inn during June 1673 a huge riot started between some bailiffs and a number of young gentlemen from the inn. Casualties amounted to over forty killed and wounded, but instead of moving in a body to break up the affray, some soldiers who were near at hand joined the mob and fought on whatever side they chose 'and did the most hurt'.[13]

The army thought itself above the law. Parliament and the workings of the common law were viewed with contempt by the military; the coachman of Sir John Coventry was severely beaten by a captain of Sir Charles Wheeler's regiment because his master was 'a Parliament-man'.[14] The army did nothing to improve its image before either the public or Parliament. Instead most of its activities contributed towards its position as national scapegoat. The appearance of the soldiers could have done little to enhance its reputation: many of the Guards were old and decrepit and had to hire young men off the streets to do their duty for them. When these ancient soldiers were finally dismissed they became a burden on the country. Pensions for superannuated soldiers were few and far between and until the advent of the Chelsea Hospital in 1684, most of the old soldiers ended their days as beggars or placed themselves on the charity of the parish. It is unlikely that the army made much impact on the country regions, but in the towns which housed garrisons the local populations must have been continually aware of the presence of the military. At a basic and elementary level their experiences echoed the constitutional and political objections to the army which were voiced in the House of Commons, and less frequently by the House of Lords.

Charles's Restoration indirectly resulted from Parliament's deep-seated hatred of the rule of a standing army,[15] so that opposition to any form of regular land force after 1660 was perfectly natural. Parliament's general policy was to entrust the defence of the nation to the militia in time of war, and use this same force to preserve law and order in peacetime. Venner's Uprising rapidly proved the futility of such a design, but Parliament clung doggedly to its ideals throughout the reign and was loath to grant command of a standing army to the king. A regular army could be used by Charles to overawe Parliament and establish the rule of the royal prerogative—the spectre of Colonel Pride frequently visited their chambers. For twenty-five years the Commons tried to balance their own militia against the standing army of the king, a contest which had no result by 1685. No decision was reached until the Revolution Settlement of 1689 when the Mutiny Act recognised the legal existence of a standing army but placed it firmly under the control of Parliament. However, this was in the future and the years of the Restoration saw a continuing struggle between king and Parliament over the issue of the regular army.

The Militia Act of 1661 recognised the king as commander-in-chief of the militia and 'all Forces by Land and Sea and of all Forts and places of strength',[16] but this statute did not mention a standing army and gave the sovereign no power to raise one. He needed no such sanction. Even Parliament admitted the right of the monarch to raise regular levies to defend the country from invasion in time of war, and the Militia Act simply recognised this prerogative power. However, the Act did not permit the maintenance of regular troops in peacetime in the form of regiments: garrison companies locked to specific towns and strong-points had always been accepted as necessary and these were not in dispute. Parliament only objected to the regiments of guards, which had the liberty to move all over the country at any time, threatening their rule. Against a king with an army of 6,000, Parliament had little effective answer apart from the authority of its utterances, and the Lords and Commons were well aware of the weakness of their potential position should Charles decide to govern by means of the army. Three times during his reign the king proved that he could enlarge his peacetime army into a formidable force, but just as Parliament realised what could be achieved by royal determination supported by an army, so the king remembered what Parliament had achieved against his father. An uneasy balance of power descended after 1660 with the army a pawn to both factions. To the king it was the sword of Damocles which hung suspended above Parliament House, and to Parliament it was an issue on which they could always unite their parties and challenge the king. The final power lay with Parliament as Joseph Williamson admitted in 1678:

> I know of nothing that can hinder the King from raising what forces he pleases, if he pays for them himself. My argument is, you are the pay-masters; if the occasions of the forces cease, how can any man think you will pay these men that are not employed to the interest you mean they should.[17]

This was Parliament's automatic safeguard against the army. In peacetime Charles could just afford to pay his six standing regiments from his revenues, but to increase the army in war-time he had to apply to the Lords and Commons for substantial supplies. If Parliament did not wish the army increased then theirs was the power to deny it. On the three occasions of an expansion of the army in England, the raising of the levies was never opposed by Parliament as they recognised the need to secure the country in time of war. Only when rumours of a peace were heard did the Commons commence worrying that the army would not be disbanded at the end of the war but would be kept on foot by the king in order to usurp their authority. In these situations Parliament was as ready to grant supplies to disband and pay off the forces as they had been to raise them.

Objections and serious challenges to the standing army occurred under set circumstances; after the army had been enlarged in time of war and the conclusion of that war was in sight. On these three occasions Parliament feared that the army would not disband on the signing of a peace, but their anxieties were groundless. There was little evidence to suggest that Charles ever planned to rule with an army at the expense of Parliament, but history and the nature of the armed forces gave the Commons cause for suspicion. The peacetime army was small and officered by men of wealth, good family, and position. Such officers did not rely on their army pay—for most of them soldiering was a hobby—and would not oppose their own disbandment. This was reversed in war. In the three major levies most of the commissions went to career soldiers, men who did live off their army pay and whose interests were limited to army rank and advancement. The fears and prejudices of the Commons meant little to these men and there was a danger that they would resist their own disbandment. Disbandment meant unemployment, and it was fortunate that work could always be found in the Anglo-Dutch Brigade, the French army and Tangier. Parliament's sensitivity about the army was not a fantasy. The dreaded situation did not actually arise, but there was a grave danger that it might have happened on three occasions within twenty-five years.

The legal status of the army was never clarified throughout the reign. It was never declared to be illegal, but neither was it admitted to be legal. It was extra-legal, outside the dictates of the law living within the grey region of the Crown prerogative. By mentioning the army in resolutions and debate, Parliament recognised it but never admitted that its existence was legal. It was simply there.

Although the new army was founded in 1661, the early sessions of Parliament took little notice of it. Even so, the debate on the Militia Act of 1661 found Sir Heneage Finch suggesting that the provisions for martial law might make Parliament the 'wards of an army'.[18] Another Militia Act in the following year shed further light on who commanded what in the military world. It now became the 'undoubted right' of the sovereign to have 'the sole and supreme Power, Government, and Command, and Disposition of the Militia and of all Forces by Sea and Land', with the addition that 'Parliament cannot nor ought not to pretend to the same'. It is hard to see how the same Cavalier Parliament of 1667 or 1674 could have passed such a sweeping concession, but the generosity of spirit after the Restoration accounted for a number of actions which Parliament was later to regret. The Militia Act of 1662 gave the king a *carte blanche* in military affairs; he could do very much as he pleased.

Thomas Trenchard was of the opinion that the Commons attacked the Guards and Garrisons in every session of Charles's reign,[19] but that was a gross exaggeration. Certainly there were some grumbles about the general behaviour of the army, but during the first decade of the reign it was not a serious issue. In 1667, Sir Thomas Tomkins moved that the king be petitioned to disband the new-raised forces for the Second Dutch War as soon as a peace was secured.[20] Quietly, and without fuss, the king acceded to the wishes of the Commons and disbanded the additional troops, leaving the six standing regiments and the garrison companies. Parliament's emphasis was upon reducing the army to its pre-war size, and no effort was made to totally remove the regular forces. Perhaps 1667 was the turning-point in relations between the king and Parliament over the army. In that year one of the articles cited against Clarendon was that he had been in favour of a standing army, whilst similar charges were to be made against Arlington in 1674.[21]

Arlington was asked by the Speaker whether he knew of any member of the government who had advised the king to govern by an army at the expense of Parliament, as well as why the army was raised in 1672, and why a number of the senior officers were catholic. Arlington denied all the charges, adding that the catholic officers had been appointed because they were more experienced and skilful than the protestant alternatives. This brought the two national scapegoats, the army and popery, together. From there on it was not just the standing army which was under attack, but the Popish Standing Army, a groundless accusation which gave emotional weight to the appeal of the anti-standing-army faction. Following the principle that all great politicians who came under fire from Parliament were accused of designing to rule England with a standing army, Danby faced this charge in 1678.

Until the traumatic year of 1678, the best that Parliament could manage was to have the army declared a 'grievance'. New levies were raised for the Third Dutch War in 1672 and 1673, but towards the end of the latter year the war lost its intensity and a peace seemed to be close. This was the cue for Parliament to commence its assault on the army. An address had been sent to Charles on 25 March 1673 recognising the need for an army in time of war, but requesting that the soldiers paid for their quarters, were not recruited by the press gang, and would be disbanded as soon as the war ended.[22] Charles's reply was typically vague saying that he would 'take such care, that no man should have reason to complain'. Throughout the summer and autumn of 1673, the politicians grew increasingly alarmed about the 'Blackheath Army': why was it gathering so close to London, why did the soldiers take so long to come into the camp, and was it really designed for active service or as the basis of a large standing army in England? With the value of hindsight we know that the army was intended for the invasion of Zealand, but this was not common knowledge to contemporaries. Plans for the expedition were kept admirably secret, and the delays were caused by waiting for a favourable military situation in the Low Countries. Parliament and the people did not have access to these facts so they automatically suspected the king of using the Dutch War as an excuse for forming an illegal standing army.[23] The eventual embarkation of the army did something to allay these fears, but once the troops landed at Yarmouth the speculation started once more.

During the debate on grievances, Sir Thomas Meres delivered a long harangue on the bad behaviour of the army, hoping that it would soon be disbanded.[24] Divorcing himself from such emotionalism, Secretary Coventry soberly observed that the army had been raised with Parliament's approval as an insurance against an invasion, and that the army could not be a grievance as no one challenged the right of the king to levy forces when he so desired. This was a little too logical for the Commons and Coventry was answered by complaints against catholic officers and the argument that the army had not been raised for the war but that the war was an excuse for raising an army.[25] With only three votes in the negative the standing army became a grievance, and an address to this effect was sent to the king. Parliament's attitude was very inconsistent: a year earlier they had approved of the raising of an army for the war, but by 1673 they viewed the creation which they had approved of with suspicion, doubted the motives for its being levied in the first instance, and forgot that the nation was still very much at war. The lesson of the Dutch in the Medway had soon been forgotten. In 1667 the Commons had supported an increase in the army after the shock of the Dutch campaign, and had forbidden soldiers to go into foreign service owing to the need to strengthen the home defences.[26] Between 1672 and 1673 Parliament committed a *volte-face*. All too anxious to create a monster they soon became scared of their own creation.

Complaints and grumbles about the continuance of the army went on into February 1674, when peace was signed between Spain, the United Provinces and England. Remembering his pledge of March 1673, Charles came to the Commons and announced that he was about to disband the army and reduce it to its pre-war strength. The Commons had been completely out-manœuvred, and Parliament's achievement during the Third Dutch War was nil. They had taken care over the abuses committed by the military on the civilians, for this was the era of free quarter and serious indicipline, but over the question of the legal existence of the army they totally failed. Charles raised his army when he wished and disbanded it according to his promise under no real pressure from Parliament.

Apart from the army in England, Parliament also objected to British soldiers serving abroad either as private individuals or in mercenary regiments. There was such a racket in gaining men for foreign service that the Commons felt itself duty bound to protect the liberty of the subject from this legalised kidnapping. Also foreign service regiments represented potential units of a standing army in England, as they were on alert for an immediate recall by the king. Parliament was well aware that Charles used these regiments as an overseas reserve at no cost to himself, but their fears were exaggerated by many of the officers being professional and catholic. From 1673 to 1678, there were constant requests from Parliament to recall these regiments, ostensibly because the Commons adopted a pro-Dutch policy, but in reality the reason was much simpler. If these units were recalled into England they would have to be disbanded as the king would be unable to maintain additional regiments without supplies from Parliament. Not until 1677 and 1678 were the regiments fighting in France recalled, but then they came back into an England which was raising a new army for a war against France. So, in this sphere of military affairs as well, Parliament failed to achieve its objective.

Short of money and desperately looking to Louis XIV for assistance, Charles was faced in 1677 with a Parliament which looked forward to an alliance with the Dutch against the French. Fear of France and popery caused this turn in Parliamentary policy which had been vehemently anti-Dutch in 1673, but Charles realised that he might be able to twist the situation to his own advantage. On 16 April 1677, Parliament voted a supply of £200,000 for building thirty ships of war. Louis XIV offered only £100,00 a year for Charles to keep Parliament prorogued, and so Charles and Danby had much to gain by retaining their Lords and Commons. Opinion demanded a war with France in defence of the protestant Dutch, but Charles was determined to receive all the money that he could from Parliament without altering his own personal foreign policy. The king desired a balanced neutrality, taking subsidies from France in return for vague promises of support, but maintaining a friendly posture towards the Dutch at the same time.

In 1677 Parliament was enthusiastic for an enlarged army; by 1679 they were desperate to disband it. The Houses assembled on 21 May 1677 and began to debate foreign alliances. Their consensus was that the king ought to have £600,000 voted to him, but this could not be done until they were certain that England was to be involved in a war.[27] At this impertinence, Charles called the Commons to the Banqueting House and informed them that they were meddling in foreign affairs and infringing the king's 'fundamental power of making Peace and War'. Both Houses were promptly adjourned until 28 January 1678. This lengthy adjournment gave Charles the opportunity of working out his new foreign policy away from the prying eyes of the Commons. By the unratified Treaty of Mutual Defence of March 1678, Charles appeared to have detached himself from France and joined with the Dutch. To increase his credibility his niece, Mary, daughter of the Duke of York, was married to William of Orange late in 1677. Privately, Charles continued to negotiate with Louis XIV and was not at all anxious to part with France in favour of the Dutch.

However, by January 1678 Charles had seemingly achieved enough in foreign affairs to convince the Commons of his sincerity. In his speech reopening Parliament on 28 January 1678 he was able to report the Dutch treaty of 1677 and state hopefully that war with France was expected. As a further sop to the Commons, Charles announced that all the troops in French service had returned to England, and then he went on to ask for an army of between 30,000 and 40,000 men and a 'plentiful supply'.[28] After some hesitation the Commons decided to grant the king additional supplies, bearing in mind that the estimated cost of the new army was £240,000.[29] This question of a new army was the stumbling-block of the entire scheme. Charles had realised this and a large number of peers and Members of Parliament were given commissions in the new forces in the hope that these would form a substantial voting block in both Houses which could ease the passage of the necessary legislation. During the debate on supply held on 8 February most of the fears connected with the new army were raised: perhaps the troops would remain in England and never go abroad, the soldiers would be quartered on civilians, and the money voted for the army might never be used for warlike purposes. However, the Commons passed a resolution approving of the new forces provided that they were employed 'for the preservation of the Spanish Netherlands; and lessening the power of France', and that they only remained on foot 'during an actual war with France'.[30] From this time, suspicion of the king's motives began to grow and the Commons became frightened that the army which they permitted to come into being might be used against them.

Many Members were of the opinion that the projected war with France was a sham, and that the offer of a war was intended only to draw money from Parliament to raise an army which would then be used as a coercive force in England. Sir William Coventry was prepared to spend money in hiring German mercenaries to assist the Dutch rather than levy an army in England, whilst others followed the 'Blue Water' school in advocating English naval action to disrupt French trade. Convinced that their previous resolutions tied the Court to spending any moneys raised on a war with France, Parliament decided to gather £1 million for this purpose.[31] The Commons then turned to debating the state of the nation.

Sir Thomas Clarges, the commissary-general of the musters, desired to have all the officers and soldiers in the new army take the Tests, whilst Sir Thomas Littleton, an army officer, considered that there was a 'universal distrust in the war'. The loyal vote of the commissioned officers was not wholly reliable. The Commons called upon the Lords to join with them in a resolution demanding that the king 'enter into an actual war against . . . the French King', but their lordships made 'no haste to join in it'.

After a short adjournment, the Houses reassembled on 29 April and turned their attention to popery. Immediately Colonel Birch linked the new army and the catholic problem, pointing out that few of the new soldiers had taken the Test, and a large number of the troops destined for Flanders were Irish. Sensibly, Sir Christopher Musgrave, himself a regular officer, said:

This will be a great discouragement to those Forces, that go over to hazard their lives to prevent the growth and power of the French King, to have such a character put upon them, as if they would bring in popery.[32]

All the usual complaints about the army were voiced, with William Williams declaring 'drums ought not to beat here, and the red coats to be about Parliament in terrorem populi'. To this Sir Robert Carr, the Chancellor of the Duchy of Lancaster and a former regular officer, smartly retorted that the Commons had agreed to raise the army, had paid for it, and ought to let it go about its business without interference. The Commons continued their condemnation of the army on 7 May, arguing that as no war had been declared on France the contract between the king and his Parliament had been broken. The Commons thought they had been duped into allowing a new standing army under false pretences, and even the departure of a large number of troops to Flanders did nothing to allay their suspicions.[33]

In his speech opening the sixteenth session of the Cavalier Parliament, Charles announced positive moves between France and the United Provinces to reach a peace, adding that he wished to maintain his fleet and army until a peace was definitely concluded.[34] The Commons saw their chance to press for a disbandment of the army and addressed the king to the effect that if he were still to enter into a war with France then he would enjoy their full support, but if it was to be peace then they would proceed 'to the consideration of providing for the speedy disbanding of the Army'.[35] Accordingly, on 30 May, the Commons resolved to disband all the forces raised since 29 September 1677—all the troops levied for Flanders. To pay off and disband these men £200,000 was voted on 4 June 1678. This precipitate action by the Commons jeopardised the king's plans, and he was forced to play for time by explaining that it would be bad etiquette to march out of the war before peace was finally signed, as well as being unwise to disarm before a settlement. But the Commons were adamant. 'Keep up the Army for fear of the King of France, and keep it up for ever,' roared Colonel Birch, and the Commons resolved to disband the forces in England forthwith and those in Flanders by 27 July 1678. Charles's block of votes from commissioned officers was failing to function as most of them were on active service with the army in Flanders. The anti-standing-army faction headed by Clarges, Powle, Birch, Hotham and Vaughan had the freedom of the floor.

On 18 June Charles dropped a bombshell in the Commons. He quietly informed them that he needed an additional £300,000 a year for life. This was received with dismay, for it was feared that such an increase would enable the king to rule without recourse to Parliament. The sum was also sufficient to maintain a large standing army in peacetime. With virtually no debate, the Commons ignored the royal request and refused to discuss it in a Grand Committee. The Disbandment Act was passed on 15 July, providing £619,388 11*s* 9*d* for disbanding all the new forces by 26 August 1678 at the latest. Charles took no notice of the Act. Many of the Commons thought that Danby and the Court faction held such a strong grip on the House that their will would prevail whatever the opposition. Steadily, the less committed members departed for the country.[36] Without the vocal opponents of the army present in force, Charles used the money from the Disbandment Act to keep his troops on foot. This was an illegal act by the sovereign, as he had disregarded a statute of Parliament and had misused public moneys.

At the opening of the eighteenth session of the Cavalier Parliament Charles weakly excused his actions as having been necessary for 'the preservation of our neighbours, and the well securing what was left of Flanders'.[37] Fortunately for Parliament, the £600,000 could not meet the expenses of the army for long, and on 25 November Charles was forced to inform the combined houses that he could not support the charge of the standing army: the soldiers in Flanders were in want of pay and provisions, and they could not be transported to England without extra moneys. By this time the Popish Plot had broken out. The Members who had earlier despaired of opposing Danby hurriedly returned to London, greatly increasing the anti-standing-army faction in the Commons. In the debate on the state of the nation on 27 November the attack was resumed in strength. Henry Powle quickly linked the army with the new popish menace, but his thesis was disputed by Sir John Ernly: 'Set three Colonels aside, that are Papists, and I know no Army more Protestant. I know who is General, and there are very few Popish Officers. Of 25,000 men, there are not two hundred Papists.'[38] William Williams observed that the standing army was now illegal as it contravened the Disbandment Act, so the Commons resolved that all the forces in Flanders should be recalled to England and the whole of the army raised since September 1677 disbanded.

The twin dangers of a standing army and the apparently genuine Popish Plot forced Parliament to search for a new scapegoat responsible for them both. Danby, with his connections with the pro-French party, was the obvious target and was impeached in 1678. So closely connected had the Plot and the army become that Charles was obliged to give way and surrender his forces. Even his loyal officers in the Commons placed political and religious prejudices before their commissions, and with Danby removed the court party in the Commons was deprived of its manager. The Second Disbandment Act received the Royal Assent in May 1679.[39] providing £206,462 17*s* 3*d* to disband all the troops raised since 29 September 1677. This time the Act was complied with and the army was broken up during the spring of 1679.

The ultimate disbandment of the forces which had been raised for Flanders represented a defeat for the king and a qualified victory for the Commons. Charles had proved unable to maintain an enlarged army without financial help from Parliament, for only by raiding the funds of the First Disbandment Act had he managed to keep it in existence for so long. Following the dissolution of the Oxford Parliament in March 1681, Charles discovered sufficient means to govern without a Parliament, but he was not wealthy enough to reinforce his rule with a large standing army. This state of affairs was largely due to the Parliamentary pressure of 1678. Power of the purse had proved decisive. Charles found that he could neither raise nor disband troops without the approval and fiscal blessing of the Lords and

Commons, so in effect the standing army was in the hands of Parliament and theirs to enlarge and decrease as they chose. Over the six standing regiments and the garrison companies the Commons had little control and almost no influence, but these forces were small and largely irrelevant. The Commons seemed almost to approve of them, or at least turned a blind eye to their maintenance: England needed a police force, the fleet had to be manned by marines, the colonies required garrisons, whilst the Popish Plot had shown that the royal person required military protection. By permitting the garrison companies to remain under the Disbandment Act of 1660, Parliament allowed some standing forces, and as the army often quartered in those garrisons they echoed the spirit of the act. In peacetime the Guards and Garrisons were accepted as partially necessary, although they were never popular.

The final intrusion of the military into the politics of the reign of Charles II came at the Oxford Parliament of 21 to 28 March 1681. By summoning Parliament to Oxford, Charles freed his legislators from the influence of the London Trained Bands and armed mobs, whilst the loyalty of the university provided stability amidst the political confusion. The Royal Horse Guards accompanied the king on his journey from London and the royal procession through Oxford to open Parliament was escorted by elements of the 1st Foot Guards. This was far from unusual. Ever since 1669 Charles had opened Parliament in the company of his guards,[40] and although there might have been an 'unusual number'[41] in 1681, the precedent had been set twelve years before. It is impossible to estimate how many soldiers were at Oxford, but there could not have been more than 500, hardly sufficient to coerce the exclusionist members and their armed retainers. The fact that Charles was able to employ his guards during such a critical period demonstrates the acceptability which the six standing regiments had gained with Parliament. Once the Flanders troops had been disbanded and the threat of a Popish standing army had been removed, the armed forces did not enter into the political arena.

Tangier, another base for the standing army, was controlled by the king and not Parliament, although the latter accepted that the colony required adequate defence. Objections to the Tangier garrison were raised periodically and were usually concerned with either the prevalence of popery, or the colony's function as a reserve for the English establishment. During the sieges of 1680, the Commons considered granting supplies to defray the costs of the defence as they feared that the town might fall into French hands. This discussion was still in progress at the time of the final dissolution in 1681, but already Tangier had been called 'a seminary', and described as 'a nursery of Papists'.[42] It was the religion of the army in Tangier which was attacked, not the military itself.

In 1684 Tangier was evacuated, the town and its fortifications demolished, and the garrison brought home and incorporated into the English establishment. Charles's reasons for this action were simple. Tangier was in such a poor state of repair that it was all but indefensible by 1683 and its capture by the Moors just a matter of time. According to the report of the commissioners appointed to investigate the condition of the colony £4,798,561 16*s* 6*d* were needed to 'make Tangier defensible and viable'.[43] Such an outlay was unthinkable, and so Tangier, which had promised so much but achieved so little, was vacated. Bringing the garrison on to the English establishment made little difference to the royal purse as the pay of the three foot regiments was the same in England as it had been overseas. There was in fact a considerable saving, as the staff and administrative officers from Tangier were disbanded and the crown no longer had to meet the expenses of transporting supplies and equipment to North Africa. Had Charles recalled Parliament to assist him in 1683 it is possible that he might have been able to retain Tangier, but given the Commons' known views on the garrison's religious history it is unlikely that they would have moved to save the colony.

With the exception of the return of the Tangier garrison in 1684, there were few permanent additions to the peacetime establishment between 1661 and 1685. At first sight it seems that Parliament's fear that the king might try to govern with an army was unfounded, but a closer look reveals some hidden dangers of which Parliament was well aware. The experience of the New Model was never far from men's minds and some of the activities of the Restoration army aided the gentry in their suspicions. The behaviour of the army in its peacetime garrisons was disgraceful, but infinitely worse when the three levies were raised for war. Military men attributed this to the lack of martial law to govern the bodies of raw recruits, whilst civilians saw it as typical of any army at any time. Camping the army on Blackheath in 1673 as if to overawe London was not a stroke of political subtlety, but seemed designed to inflame Parliament and encourage thoughts of a permanent coercive army. This lesson was not lost on the future James II. Charles's misappropriation of the money from the First Disbandment Act was a crude ploy suggesting to contemporaries that he harboured ambitions of possibly keeping the army on foot, or of maintaining it for as long as possible. Whether Charles ever seriously intended to govern with an army is open to doubt, but he gave the impression that this was his policy on two occasions —1673 and 1678. That the monarch liked armies and was in favour of maintaining a nucleus of regular soldiers was common knowledge, and it is impossible to avoid the conclusion that the perpetual fear of having to go on his 'travels' once more if he did not protect his own position led to a reliance on the military. His father had been usurped from his throne for want of an army and Charles's own childhood had witnessed political success through armed might: it was hardly surprising that Charles placed emphasis upon the retention of his Guards. Parliament feared a standing army for what it could do to their growing authority, whilst the king favoured an army to defend himself from the possible excesses of the Lords and Commons.

The army itself was never a political force. It did not once enter the political arena and refused to give support to any faction: loyalty to the king was its only allegiance. At times, especially in 1673 and 1678, the army appeared to be coming into politics, but it was only the concept of an army and not the army itself which became a pawn in the game between the king and Commons. By continually linking the army and popery, when in fact no clear connection between the two was ever established and could not have been as the army was 95 per cent protestant, Parliament used the army as an emotive weapon with which to attack the king. Even when the Commons spoke of the excesses of the military in taking free quarter and abusing civilians, they were not complaining out of a concern for the people affected, but were building up an image of the army as something evil. Totally ignored were the army's efforts to apprehend highwaymen, preserve law and order, and assist in the sea battles of the Second and Third Dutch Wars. Such details were unimportant to the Commons. They objected to the concept of a standing army, not the actual guards and garrisons: 'Resolved etc, That the continuing of any standing forces in this nation, other than the Militia, is illegal; and a great Grievance and Vexation to the People.'[44] Parliament knew that the militia was useless, riddled with inefficiency through negligence, and scarcely knew how to march let alone fight, but it was their force and not the king's. When Parliament finally gained control over the army by the Mutiny Act of 1689, they did not disband the military but took it firmly under their own wing: the concept of a standing army then became more acceptable.

The common people hated the army because it was so badly behaved. They were the ones who suffered from free quarters, the press gangs, and the non-payment of debts, not the gentry. Recruitment threatened liberty under the law, whilst foreign service could affect anyone from the lower classes. However, for all its faults, this army was the real founder of the British regular army, and not the earlier New Model. The New Model was the first standing army in time of peace, but it was a political instrument and acted as the mainstay of the Commonwealth. Charles's army was modern in that it was the servant of the civil power and not its dictator. Throughout the reign the military was subordinate to the civilian government, establishing a precedent for the following centuries for the British Army.

Appendix A

The Regiments

This table is a guide to the regiments of cavalry, dragoons and infantry which were raised between 1660 and 1685 by Charles II. For details of the officers in each unit refer to C. Dalton, *English Army Lists and Commission Registers, 1661–1714*, London, 1892, vol. 1.

Regiments	*Formed*	*Disbanded*	*Notes*
For service on the English Establishment			
Life Guard*	1661		
Royal Horse Guards*	1661		
1st Foot Guards*	1661		Amalgamated in 1665
Wentworth's Foot Guards*	1660		Amalgamated in 1665
2nd Foot Guards, Coldstream Regt*	1661		
Lord High Admiral's Regt of Foot*	1664		
Holland Regiment of Foot*	1665		
Royal Dragoons*	1679		
1st Foot, the Royal Scots*	1679		Formerly Douglas's
Duchess of York's Foot	1684		Plymouth's from Tangier
Queen's Foot*	1684		Old Tangier Regiment
Earl of Cleveland's Horse†	1662	1667	
Earl of Craven's Foot†	1662	1664	
Sir William Killigrew's Foot†	1662	1664	

Regiments	Formed	Disbanded	Notes
Earl of Chesterfield's Foot†	1667	1667	Hurriedly raised after the Dutch invasion of the Medway in 1667
Lord Townshend's Foot†	1667	1667	
Lord Alington's Foot†	1667	1667	
Earl of Ogle's Foot†	1667	1667	
Marquis of Worcester's Foot†	1667	1667	
Earl of Manchester's Foot†	1667	1667	
Sir Arthur Bassett's Foot†	1667	1667	None were fully formed at the time of their disbandment
Sir Allen Apsley's Foot†	1667	1667	
Sir John Sayer's Foot†	1667	1667	
Sir Walter Vane's Foot†	1667	1667	
Richard Norton's Foot†	1667	1667	
John Lane's Foot†	1667	1667	
Barbados Regiment of Foot†	1671	1672	The returned Barbados Regt of 1667. Expanded into a Dragoon unit for 3rd Dutch War
Barbados Dragoons†	1672	1674	
John Fitzgerald's Foot†	1672	1674	Employed as Marines
Duke of Buckingham's Foot†	1672	1674	
The Marine Regiment†	1672	1674	
Lord Bellasise's Foot†	1673	1674	
Earl of Ogle's Foot†	1673	1674	
Earl of Carlisle's Foot†	1673	1674	
Marquis of Worcester's Foot†	1673	1674	
Earl of Mulgrave's Foot†	1673	1674	
Duke of Albemarle's Foot†	1673	1674	
Duke of York's Horse†	1678	1679	Went over to Flanders in 1678–9
Duke of Monmouth's Horse†	1678	1679	
Earl of Feversham's Dragoons†	1678	1679	
Duke of Monmouth's Foot†	1678	1679	
Sir Charles Wheeler's Foot†	1678	1679	
Lord Alington's Foot†	1678	1679	
George Legge's Foot†	1678	1679	
Sir John Fenwick's Foot†	1678	1679	
Sir Lionel Walden's Foot†	1678	1679	
Lord O'Brien's Foot†	1678	1679	

Regiments	Formed	Disbanded	Notes
Henry Sidney's Foot†	1678	1679	Went over to Flanders in 1678–9
Edward Villiers's Foot†	1678	1679	
Sir Henry Goodricke's Foot†	1678	1679	
Sir Thomas Slingsby's Foot†	1678	1679	
Duke of Albemarle's Horse†	1678	1679	Remained in England during 1678–9
Lord Gerard's Horse†	1678	1679	
Prince Rupert's Dragoons†	1678	1679	
Sir John Talbot's Dragoons†	1678	1679	
Lord James Douglas's Foot†	1678	1679	
Thomas Stradling's Foot†	1678	1679	
For Tangier			
Old Tangier Regiment of Foot*	1661		Queen's Foot in 1684
Sir Robert Harley's Foot*	1661		Incorporated into the Old Tangier Regiment in 1668
The Irish Regiment of Foot*	1661		
Tangier Horse*	1661	1668	
Earl of Plymouth's Foot*	1680		Duchess of York's in 1684
For the Colonies			
Sir Tobias Bridge's Foot†	1667	1671	Barbados Regiment
Bombay Battalion†	1661	1668	
Virginia Battalion†	1676	1678	
For Scotland in 1679			
Earl of Feversham's Dragoons*	1679		Royal Dragoons
Duke of Monmouth's Foot†	1679	1679	
Lord Gerard's Horse†	1679	1679	
For Foreign Service			
Marquis de Schomberg's Horse	1662	1668	Portugal
Henry Pearson's Foot	1662	1668	Portugal
Francis Moore's Foot	1662	1668	Portugal
Lord George Douglas's Foot	1633		Royal Scots after 1679
Monmouth's Foot	1672	1678	France. The Royal English Regiment
Bevil Skelton's Battalion	1672	1677	France

Regiments	*Formed*	*Disbanded*	*Notes*
Sir Henry Jones's Light Horse	1671	1673	France. Same regiment
Monmouth's Horse	1673	1678	France. Same regiment
Sir George Hamilton's Foot	1671	1678	France
Earl of Roscommon's Foot	1671	1672	France
Sir William Lockhart's Foot	1672	1673	France
Lord Vaughan's Foot	1673	1673	France
Earl of Peterborough's Foot	1673	1673	France
Thomas Dongan's Foot	1678		France

* Denotes permanent standing regiment on the English Establishment.
† Temporary wartime levy on the English Establishment.

Nomenclature of regiments

It was normal practice in the seventeenth century to refer to regiments by the names of their colonels, but this was not wholly consistent. Often a unit might be known by a number of different titles; the Royal English Regiment, Monmouth's Foot, Scott's Foot and Macartie's Foot were all names for the same formation.

To avoid confusion the permanent standing regiments have been called after their official titles: Life Guards, Royal Horse Guards, 1st Foot Guards, Coldstream Guards, Holland, Admiral's, Royal Scots, Queen's and Duchess of York's. All other units, whether temporary wartime levies or for foreign service, have been called after their colonels. With this in mind the reader will be able to tell at a glance which type of regiment is being referred to at any place in the text.

Appendix B

Army Lists of the Brigade in Portugal, 1662–8

These lists have been compiled from the sources quoted in Chapter IX. No army lists or muster rolls have survived, and so the names have been gleaned from casualty returns, petitions and letters. The bracketed date after an officer's name indicates the year in which he is mentioned in the source.

The Regiment of Horse

Colonels
Michael Dungan (1662–3)
James Apsley (1663–5)
Marquis de Schomberg (1664–8)

Lieutenant-Colonel
Thomas Hunt (1664)

Captains
William Littleton (1662)
Richard Mill (1662)
Guy Molesworth (1662–3)
— Paulinge (1663)
Theodore Russell (1664–8)
— Rust (1665)
Sir William Salkeld (1662)
Samuel Sharpe (1665)
Edward Trelawney (1664)
Francis Trelawney (1665)

Lieutenants
William Armstrong (1668)
Richard Gwynn (1668)
William Osborne (1668)

Cornets
Hugh Firman (1668)
John Philipps (1668)

Richard Hill (1668)
Edmund Mayne (1668)
— Meakinge (1663)
William Soulon (1668)
— Wharton (1663)

Quarter-Masters
David Dunbar (1668)
John Hersman (1668)
Richard Rogers (1668)
Thomas Smythe (1668)

Henry Pearson's Regiment of Foot

Colonel
Henry Pearson (1662–8)

Lieutenant-Colonel
John Rumsey (1664)

Major
Lawrence Dempsey (1663)

Captains
— Heathfield (1665)
Charles Langley (1665)
— Turner (1665)

Captain-Lieutenant
— Newsome (1665)

Lieutenant
— Stenhouse (1665)

Ensign
— Berry (1665)

Surgeon
Don John Leadger (1665)

Francis Moore's Regiment of Foot

Colonel
Francis Moore (1662–8)

Lieutenant-Colonel
William Sheldon (1665)

Majors
— Netmore (1664)
Francis Moreneur (1665)

Captains
— Love (1665)
Andrew Maynard (1665)
— Sandys (1665)
Francis Stansby (1665)

Lieutenants
John Jones (1665)
— Sandys (1665)
— Sherwood (1665)

Ensigns
— Emerson (1665)
— Watkins (1665)

Foot Officers who served in either Pearson's or Moore's

Captains
— Atkinson (1664)
John Birch (1664)
— Fitzpatrick (1664)
— Goudinge (1664)
Nathaniel Hill (1664)
— Jones (1665)
William Moore (1664)
Gregory Noland (1664)
Henry Travers (1664)
— Turner (1664)

Lieutenants
— Ashton (1665)
— Boone (1665)
— Cusacke (1664)
— Fitzherbert (1664)
— Morgan (1664)
— Mulberry (1664)
— Terry (1664)

Ensigns
— Pettybons (1664)
— Thomson (1664)

General Officers

Brigade Commanders
Murrough O'Brien, 1st Earl of Inchiquin (1662–3)
Frederick, 1st Duke of Schomberg (1663–8)

Major-Generals
Sir Thomas Morgan (1662)
Christopher O'Brien (1663)
Sir John Talbot (1662)

It is impossible to give dates for any of the commissions as officers on foreign service stations were commissioned on the spot by the local commander-in-chief, whose own commission authorised him to appoint officers in the king's name.

Appendix C

The Anglo-Dutch Brigade

The Anglo-Dutch Brigade, 1660–5

Earl of Craven's Foot

Colonel	*Lieutenants*	*Ensigns*
William, Earl of Craven*	Thomas Honeywood	John Philips
Lt Col.		
Sir Walter Vane*		
Major		
Ferdinand Carrey†		
Captains		
Edward Morgan		
James Culpepper		James Palvesyn
William Swaen		
Thomas Dolman Jnr	Edward Lauwer	
Baptist Alcock*		
Peter Watkins		William Carpenter
Quartermaster		
Josias Stevens		
Provost-Marshal		
Thomas Wood		

Thomas Dolman's Foot

Colonel	*Lieutenants*	*Ensigns*
Thomas Dolman†		Wm Phettiplace*

* Returned to England after the reformation of the Brigade in 1665.
† Stayed in Dutch service in 1665.

Lt Col.		
William Cromwell*		James Rouse
Major		
John Roper†	Edward Sprey	William Norwood
Captains		
William Read	George Williamson*	
Maurits La Mair		
Anthony Wilde	Ambrose Maneton	Robert Boulton*
Edward Astley	Robert Moore	
Robert Mordaunt		
Quartermaster		
Petrus Cool		

Sir William Killigrew's Foot

Colonel	*Lieutenants*	*Ensigns*
Sir William Killigrew*	Richard Griffin*	William Miles
Lt Col.		
Humphrey Peyton†		
Major		
Henry Meoles*		Robert Barnes
Captains		
— Temple		
Henry Pomeroy*		
Robert Sanderson	Thomas Sanderson	Thomas Preston*
— Monily		
John Abrahal		

Robert Sidney's Foot

Colonel	*Lieutenants*	*Ensigns*
Robert Sidney*	Robert Wildbore*	John Andrew
Lt Col.		
Sir William Sayers*	Nicholas Gibson	Richard Sawl
Major		
Sir Thomas Ogle*		Roger Manley*
Captains		
Henry Herbert		Philip Phettiplace*

Thomas Sands
Henry Coventry
William Killigrew
John Coper — James Sterling*

Quartermaster
Hans Albert Warnaer

Provost-Marshal
Joseph Fuggers

The Anglo-Dutch Brigade, 1674–85

Colonels

The Irish Regiment
Daniel, Viscount Clare (1675)
Sir John Fenwick (1675–7)
Patrick Westley (1677–82)
Thomas Monck (1682–8)

1st English Regiment
Henry Lillingston (1674–6)
Edward Astley (1676–7)
Henry Bellasise (1677f)

2nd English Regiment
William Molyneux Disney (1674–6)
Roger Warrington (1676)
Thomas Dolman (1676)
William Macdowell (1676–8)
Thomas Butler, Earl of Ossory (1678–80)
Vacant (1680–5)

1st Scottish Regiment
William Drummond (1646–55. Disbanded)

2nd Scottish Regiment
Alexander Colyear (1675)

3rd Scottish Regiment
John Kirkpatrick (1639–72)
Bathold Balfour (1684f)

4th Scottish Regiment
James Erskine (1639–55)

Walter Scott of Balweary (1655–65)
Henry Graham (1673–7)
Hugh Mackay (1677–86)

Officers. Regiments unidentified

Lieutenant-Colonels
— Magdugle (1676)
— Douglas (1678)

Majors
— Archer (1676)
Philip Babbington (1677)

Captains
Sir Thomas Armstrong (1679)
Philip Babbington (1676)
— Barnwell (1676)
John Beaumont (1684)
— Collier (1676)
— Cranalls (1676)
— Crane (1676)
— Douglas (1676)
— Fryer (1676)
— Hales (1676)
Henry Herbert (1674)
— Lee (1676)
Luke Lillingston (1674)
— Mackinney (1676)
— Maculliot (1676)
— Middleton (1676)
— Morgan (1679)
Sir John Morgan (1674)
— Sabines (1676)
— Savage (1676)
Vincent Shadrack (1676–8)
— Smith (1676)
— Stone (1676)
— Sullivan (1676)
— Taylor (1676)
— Walcop (1676)
Ralph Widdrington (1676)
— Wisdom (1676)

Lieutenants
— Bellasise (1676)
— Butler (1676)
— Clynton (1676)
— Coney (1676)
— Cunningham (1676)
— Giles (1676)
— Lloyd (1676)
— Macullicuddy (1676)
— Netherwide (1676)
— Roberts (1676)

Ensigns
— Anslam (1676)
— Clark (1676)
— Ferrar (1676)
— Fisher (1676)
— Neal (1676)
— Smith (1676)

Appendix D

The English Brigade in the French Service, 1672–8

Douglas's/Dumbarton's/The Royal Scots

This Scottish regiment had been in the French service since the first part of the seventeenth century, but had returned to England at the Restoration. With the raising of the English standing army in 1661 it was unnecessary for the regiment to remain in England, and so it returned to France in 1662. It was again recalled into England to fight in the Second Dutch War, but went back to France in 1667. There it continued until 1678 when it was finally summoned home to serve on the English establishment as the First Royal Regiment of Foot, or the Royal Scots.
Twelve companies of 100 men each.

Colonel
Lord George Douglas, created Earl of Dumbarton in 1675

Lieutenant-Colonels
John Rattray (1666)
Alexander Monro (1673)

Major
Alexander Monro (1666)

Captains
Thomas Bannatyne (1666)
Archibald Douglas (1666)
James Douglas (1666)
Lord James Douglas (1666)
James Graham (1671)
Patrick Livingstone (1666)
Patrick Monteith (1666)
John Stuart (1666)
Robert Touris (1666)
Adam Tyrie (1666)

Lieutenants

James Buchanan (1666)
George Comine (1666)
John Douglas I (1666)
John Douglas II (1666)
Joseph Douglas (1666)
William Douglas (1666)
Charles Karney (1666)
Patrick La Lisle (1666)
James Leith (1666)
Tege Regan (1666)
Alexander Strachan (1666)
James Stuart (1666)

Ensigns

Adam Britton (1666)
George Cockburn (1666)
James Douglas (1666)
John Du Four (1666)
Andrew Hamilton (1666)
Kenneth Mackenny (1666)
John Mackrael (1666)
George Rattray (1666)
John Sandelins (1666)
Alexander Scremger (1666)
Patrick Tyne (1666)
Andrew White (1666)

Services

1673–4 Rhine Theatre under Turenne
1674 Battle of Sintzheim
1675 Siege of Dachstein, Siege of Treves
1676 Siege of Philippsburg
1677 Siege of Freiburg

The Royal English Regiment

Sometimes referred to as Monmouth's Foot or the 'Old Battalion of Monmouth's Foot'. It was raised in England in 1672 and sent over to France, where it remained until recalled into England in 1678. Sixteen companies, totalling 2,000 men.

Colonels

Colonel-in-Chief, James, Duke of Monmouth
Colonel-Lieutenant, Robert Scott (1675–6)
Colonel-Lieutenant, Justin Macartie (1676–8)

Lieutenant-Colonels

Sir Samuel Clarke (1672–5) (Captain in 1st Foot Guards)
Roger Langley (1676)

Majors

Henry Stanier (1672–5)
Percy Kirke (1675–8)

Captains

— Baggott (1672)
— Barber (1675)
— Hilyard (1672)
John Hodgson (1677)

— Barker (1675–8)
Henry Boade (1675)
(Captain in the Holland Regiment)
— Burke (1675)
— Butler (1678)
(Major of the Old Battalion in 1678)
— Carr (1675)
— Cassells (1674)
Robert Clifford (1675–8)
Henry Cornwall (1675–6)
(Ensign in Admiral's Regiment)
— Dannan (1672)
— Dorrington (1675–8)
— Downes (1672)
— Foldarvy (1675)
Roger Langley (1675–6)
(Lt Col. of New Battalion, 1678)
— Leake (1672)
— Lee (1674)
— Oglethorpe (1675)
— Owen (1675)
— Purcell (1675)
Robert Ramsay (1675–8)
Richard Savage (1672)
— Sunderland (1675)
— Throgmorton (1672)
Dominic Trant (1675–8)
George Trapps (1675–8)
(Lieutenant in 1st Foot Guards)

Lieutenants
Percy Kirke (1675)
Francis Hawley (1675)

Ensigns
Ullysses Burke (1677)
— Jephson (1677) (Lieutenant in 1678)

Services
1673 Siege of Maestricht
1674 Rhine Theatre under Turenne, Battle of Sintzheim, Battle of Entzheim
1675 Battle of Altenheim
1676 Siege of Philippsburg

Skelton's/2nd Battalion of the Royal English

This battalion was drawn entirely from the standing regiments in England. It went over to France in 1672 to replace the eight companies of the Royal English which had been disbanded. Once across the Channel, Skelton's was retained as a separate unit and acted as the 2nd Battalion of the Royal English. In 1673 this battalion was granted seniority over the original battalion as it was composed of guardsmen. This created great jealousy between the two formations.

The companies of Skelton, Daniell and Sackville were recalled to England in April 1674. John Churchill assumed command of the remaining five companies and amalgamated them with the Earl of Peterborough's Regiment to form a new regiment which continued in France until 1677.

Eight companies of 100 men each.

Lieutenant-Colonels
Bevil Skelton (1672–4) (Captain in 1st Foot Guards)
John Churchill (1674–7) (Captain in Admiral's Regiment)

Major
Sir Thomas Daniell (Captain in 1st Foot Guards)

Captains
— Ashburnham (Captain in Lord Le Power's Regiment)
John Churchill
John Howard (Captain in Holland Regiment)
John Piggott (Captain in Buckingham's Regiment)
Edward Sackville (Captain in 1st Foot Guards)
Charles Trelawney (1674)
John Trelawney (Captain in Fitzgerald's Regiment)

Services
1674 Rhine Theatre under Turenne, Battle of Entzheim
1675 Battle of Altenheim
1676 Siege of Philippsburg

The Life Guards

On 10 February 1673 a composite troop of cavalry was taken from the three troops of the Life Guard and sent to France under the command of Louis de Duras, Marquis de Blanquefort. This special troop remained in France until 1674, although Duras stayed in France to command the British Brigade after that date.

Captain
Lord Duras (Captain of the Duke of York's Troop)

Lieutenant
Sir Richard Dutton (Lt of the Duke of York's Troop)

Cornets
Sir Henry Fitzjames (Captain of a foot company)
Sir William Throckmorton (Captain in Barbados Dragoons)

Corporals
Ferdinand Stanhope (Duke of York's Troop)
Edward Watson (Queen's Troop)
Samuel Wood (King's Troop)

Trumpeters
Nicholas Chaproon (Queen's Troop)

John Joy (Duke of York's Troop)
Wilfred Morrice (King's Troop)
John Simpson (Duke of York's Troop)

Kettle-Drummer
John Morgridge (Drum-major of the 1st Foot Guards)

Gentleman Privates
Zachariah Bourgeois
— Barrow
Arthur Campbell
John Chitham
— Craddock
Daniel Dufour
— Elliott
— Greene
Henry Griffith
— Hemsworth
William Jones
John Lamb
Henry Maning
John Marlin
Michael Merriman
— Moulton
— Neres
William Oglethorpe
— Pope
— Pursell
— Segar
— Throckmorton
— Tuberville

Services
1673 Siege of Maestricht

Sir Henry Jones's Light Horse/Monmouth's Horse

A company of English Gens d'Armes was raised for the French service by Sir George Hamilton in 1667 from the catholic officers who had been dismissed from the English establishment following the purge of 15 September 1667. Sir Henry Jones, a captain in the Royal Horse Guards, was lieutenant of this company, with Lord Morpeth as cornet. In 1671 Jones replaced Hamilton as commander when the company was expanded to a full-sized regiment.
Total of 505 men.

Colonels
Sir Henry Jones (1672–3. Killed at Maestricht)
Duke of Monmouth (1673–8)

Lieutenant-Colonels
Sir John Lanier (1674)
Ferdinando Littleton (1673–4)
Edmund Mayne (1678)

Major
— Bray (1674)

Captains

John Coy (1678)
— Grimes (1674)
— Hill (1675)
— Hurst (1675)
Charles Kirke (1674)
Thomas Langston (1675)
William Littleton (1672–4)
— Macarty (1675)
Edmund Mayne (1673)
Charles Nedby (1677–8)
Theophilus Oglethorpe (1673)

Captain-Lieutenant

Dominic Sheldon (1674)

Lieutenant

Charles Nedby (1676)

Cornets

Sir William Colster (1675)
Edward Jacobs (1676) (Lieutenant in 1678)
Dominic Sheldon (1674)

Services

1673 Siege of Maestricht
1674 Rhine Theatre under Turenne, Battle of Entzheim, Battle of Waldheim
1676 Siege of Philippsburg

The Irish Regiment/Hamilton's/Dongan's

Sir George Hamilton raised this regiment in Ireland during 1671 especially for France. It was disbanded in France in 1678, returned to Ireland, and was then reformed under Thomas Dongan in the same year. Under Justin Macartie it returned to France as a mercenary regiment in 1679.
Fifteen companies of 100 men each.

Colonels

Sir George Hamilton (1672–6. Killed at Saverne)
Thomas Dongan (1676–8)

Lieutenant-Colonel

Richard Hamilton (1676) (Brother of Sir George)

Services

1673–4 Rhine Theatre under Turenne, Battle of Sintzheim, Battle of Entzheim
1675 Battle of Altenheim
1676 Siege of Philippsburg, action at Saverne

Roscommon's Irish Regiment

This Irish regiment was raised for the French service in 1671 by Wentworth Dillon, Earl of Roscommon, but it enjoyed a very short life. In 1672 it was disbanded in Lorraine by the French and the soldiers drafted into Hamilton's Regiment.
Twelve companies of 100 men each.

Colonel
Wentworth Dillon, Earl of Roscommon

Lieutenant-Colonel
Thomas Howard (Captain in the 1st Foot Guards)

Lieutenant
Bryan Reyley (1672)

Sir William Lockhart's Scottish Regiment

Lockhart's went over to France in 1673 and was used to recruit the Old Battalion of the Royal English. See Dalton, *Army Lists*, vol. 1, p. 121.

John, Lord Vaughan's

Vaughan's was sent to France in 1673 and was again used to fill the ranks of the Old Battalion of the Royal English. See Dalton, *Army Lists*, vol. 1, p. 137.

Earl of Peterborough's

This regiment went to France in 1673 and was amalgamated with the remnants of Skelton's Battalion to form Churchill's Foot. See Dalton, *Army Lists*, vol. 1, p. 135.

Appendix E

The New Regiments of 1678

The following new regiments were added to the six standing units for the duration of the projected war with France during 1678–9.

The Horse

Colonel	*Lieutenant-Colonel*	*Major*
Duke of Albemarle	Sir Thomas Armstrong[1]	Richard Bings[2]
Earl of Peterborough	Sir Jonathan Trelawney	Theodorus Russell
Duke of Monmouth[3]	Sir John Lanier†	Edmund Mayne[4]†
Charles, Lord Gerard	Charles Gerard	Sir John Hanmer

1 Officer in King's Troop of the Life Guard.
2 Quartermaster of the King's Troop of the Life Guard.
3 This regiment was Monmouth's Horse from France.
4 Fought with the brigade in Portugal and in France.

The Dragoons

Colonel	*Lieutenant-Colonel*	*Major*
Earl of Feversham[1]*	Percy Kirke†	Theophilus Oglethorpe†
Prince Rupert	Ralph Hebron	—
Sir John Talbot[2]*	Charles Orby[3]	Geoffrey Arnot

1 Formerly Louis de Duras, Marquis de Blanquefort. Captain of the Duke of York's Troop of the Life Guard. Turenne's nephew.
2 A lieutenant-colonel in 1676, MP.
3 Guidon of the Queen's Troop of thc Life Guard.

* An officer with a commission in the Guards and Garrisons in England.
† A professional soldier returned from a foreign service station.

The Foot

Colonel	*Lieutenant-Colonel*	*Major*
Monmouth[1]	Justin Macartie†	— Butler†
Monmouth[2]	Roger Langley†	Thomas Coale[3]
Thomas Dongan[4]†	Lawrence Dempsey[5]†	Charles Macarty†
Edward Villiers[6]	John Berkeley[7]	Henry Collier[8]*
Sir Charles Wheeler[9]*	John Huitson[10]*	Trevor Wheeler
Lord Alington[11]	Thomas Tollemache[12]*	Francis Radcliffe
George Legge[13]	James Halsall[14]	George Houston*
Sir John Fenwick[15]†	John Sunderland[16]†	Robert Carr[17]
Lord James Douglas[18]†	Robert Touris[19]†	Patrick Lalis[20]†
Sir Lionel Walden[21]	Thomas Coningsby[22]	John Hope[23]
Lord Morpeth MP.	James Graham[24]	Alexander Cannan[25]†
Lord O'Brien MP.	Thomas Salisbury	Sidney Fotherbury
Henry Sidney[26]*	Edward Sackville[27]*	Knyvet Hastings[28]
Sir Henry Goodrick	John Rumsey[29]†	William Lesley
Sir Thomas Slingsby MP.	Charles Godfrey[30]	William Broxholme*
Thomas Stradling[31]	John Carr	Humphrey Wyndham

1 The Old Battalion of the Royal English Regiment.
2 The New Battalion of the Royal English Regiment.
3 Captain in the 1st Foot Guards.
4 Previously Sir George Hamilton's Irish Regiment in France.
5 Fought in Portugal as the major of Pearson's Foot.
6 Royalist colonel in 1644.
7 Officer of the 1st Foot Guards.
8 Officer of the 1st Foot Guards.
9 Royalist colonel in 1645, MP.
10 Officer of the Coldstream Guards.
11 Colonel in 1667, MP.
12 Sometimes 'Talmash'. Captain in the Coldstream Guards.
13 Later Baron Dartmouth. Colonel in 1673 and Governor of Portsmouth, MP.
14 Scout-Master-General of England.
15 Colonel of an English regiment in the Anglo-Dutch Brigade, MP.
16 Former captain in the Royal English Regiment in France.
17 Ensign in the 1st Foot Guards.
18 Captain in Dumbarton's Regiment. Brother of the Earl of Dumbarton.
19 Captain in Dumbarton's Regiment.
20 Lieutenant in Dumbarton's Regiment.
21 Royalist lieutenant-colonel in 1645. Colonel in 1673, MP.
22 Captain in 1673.
23 Ensign in the Coldstream Guards.
24 Captain in the Coldstream Guards.
25 Officer in the Anglo-Dutch Brigade.
26 Captain in the Holland Regiment.

27 Captain in the 1st Foot Guards, and captain in Skelton's Battalion in France.
28 Lieutenant in the 1st Foot Guards.
29 Lieutenant-colonel of Pearson's Foot in Portugal. Lieutenant-colonel in England in 1667.
30 Officer of the 1st Foot Guards.
31 Captain in the 1st Foot Guards.

Appendix F

The Codes of Military Law and the Major Regulations relating to the Army, issued by the Crown between 1661 and 1685

England

17 March 1663, 'Military Orders and Articles made by his Majesty', SP 29/69, ff. 81 and 81a.

9 April 1666, 'Military Orders and Articles of War composed and corrected by the Duke of Albemarle, Captain-General of his Majesty's Armies', SP 29/153, f. 56f.

1673, 'Articles and Rules for the Better Government of his Majesty's Forces by Land during this Present War', SP 30/Case F.

15 August 1674, Special Regulations dealing with drunkenness and indiscipline in the garrison of Windsor Castle, *CSPD, 1673–5*, pp. 334–5.

3 December 1674, Order reducing the annual number of musters from seven to six, WO 26/2, p. 417.

17 May 1676, Special Regulations concerning drunkenness in the garrison of Windsor Castle, SP 44/44, p. 29.

23 February 1680, Revised muster regulations, WO 26/5, pp. 293–5.

1 September 1684, Regulations concerning officers' dress, WO 5/1, pp. 88–9.

Tangier

1661, 'Laws and Ordinances of War established for the Better Governing his Majesty's Forces in the Kingdoms of Suz, Fez, and Morocco, under the command of his Excellency the Earl of Peterborough', CO 279/1, ff. 99–110.

APPENDIX F

Dunkirk

1660, 'Additional Martial Laws for his Majesty's Garrison of Dunkirk', SP 78/115, ff. 147–8.

2 May 1662, 'The 26 Additional Articles concerning the garrison in Dunkirk', SP 29/54, ff. 9 & 9i.

Foreign Service

12 February 1668, 'Rules for making Capitulations for such officers and soldiers, his Majesty's Subjects, as shall be entertained in the service of any foreign prince or state', PC 2/60, p. 180. Add. MSS no. 38694, f. 7.

1675, Special Regulations to be observed by the Royal English Regiment of Foot in the French Service, SP 44/41, p. 32.

Appendix G

Annual Cost of the Army

The following table represents an estimation of the annual cost of the standing army in England, Tangier, and Dunkirk, in key years between 1660 and 1685. The figures include the pay of officers and men, pensions and half-pay, and the contingencies. This was all that the government had to meet, as the troops paid for their own food, clothing and accommodation, whilst weapons, equipment and ammunition were provided by the Board of Ordnance under a separate establishment.

Date	*England*			*Tangier*			*Dunkirk*	*Total*		
	£	*s*	*d*	£	*s*	*d*	£	£	*s*	*d*
1661[1]	122,407	15	10	75,388	12	6	60,000	257,796	8	4
1668[2]	188,581	0	0	31,999	10	0		220,580	10	0
1673[3]	419,975	12	5	31,999	10	0		451,975	2	5
1678[4]	334,366	7	7	42,388	12	3		376,754	19	10
1684[5]	283,775	6	10					283,775	6	10

1 SP 29/29, f. 47; SP 71/13, f. 109; PRO: E 351/344, Declared Accounts for Dunkirk, December 1660 to July 1661; E 351/345, Declared Accounts for Dunkirk, July 1661 to November 1662.

2 WO 24/2, Establishment 1668; BM, Sloane MSS, no. 3509, ff. 230–1.

3 WO 24/3, Establishment 1673; Add. MSS, no. 38694, f. 1.

4 PRO. AO 1/51/28, Audit Office, Declared Accounts for the Army; *HMC*, Dartmouth MSS, vol. 5, pp. 28–9.

5 WO 24/7, Establishment 1684; Add. MSS, no. 38694, f. 1; AO 1/53/38, Declared Accounts for the Army.

Appendix H

Rates of Pay

Throughout the period the pay of both officers and soldiers remained constant, apart from a slight adjustment in the wages of a private foot soldier in 1672. The amounts given in the tables below represent the full daily pay, before any deductions were made. Off Reckonings were subtracted from this sum and the balance paid as Subsistence Money.

The Cavalry

The Life Guards

Captain of the King's Troop	£1 10*s* 0*d*
Captain of the Queen's Troop	£1 0*s* 0*d*
Captain of Duke of York's Troop	£1 0*s* 0*d*
Lieutenant	15*s* 0*d*
Cornet of King's Troop	14*s* 0*d*
Cornet of the other two Troops	13*s* 0*d*
Quartermaster	9*s* 0*d*
Chaplain	6*s* 8*d*
Corporal of the King's Troop	7*s* 0*d*
Corporal of the other two Troops	6*s* 0*d*
Trumpeter	5*s* 0*d*
Gentleman Private	4*s* 0*d*

All other Regiments of Horse

Colonel as Colonel*	12*s* 0*d*
Lt Colonel as Lt Colonel*	5*s* 6*d*
Captain	14*s* 0*d* (10*s* 0*d* pay+2 horses at 2*s* 0*d* each)
Lieutenant	10*s* 0*d* (6*s* 0*d* pay+2 horses at 2*s* 0*d* each)
Cornet	9*s* 0*d* (5*s* 0*d* pay+2 horses at 2*s* 0*d* each)

* Colonels, lieutenant-colonels, and majors were captains of companies as well as field officers. They received pay for both functions.

Quartermaster	*6s 0d* (*4s 0d* pay +1 horse at *2s 0d*)
Corporal	*3s 0d*
Trumpeter	*2s 8d*
Private Trooper	*2s 6d*

The Off Reckonings for the horse amounted to *6d* per man per day, leaving 'Subsistence' of *3s 6d* for the Life Guard and *2s 0d* for all other troopers. From this money the soldier had to care for both himself and his horse.

The Dragoons

Colonel as Colonel	*15s 0d* (*12s 0d* pay+3 horses at *1s 0d* each)
Lt Colonel as Lt Colonel	*9s 0d* (*7s 0d* pay+2 horses at *1s 0d* each)
Major as Major	*6s 0d* (*5s 0d* pay+1 horse at *1s 0d*)
Captain	*11s 0d* (*8s 0d* pay+3 horses at *1s 0d* each)
Lieutenant	*6s 0d* (*4s 0d* pay+2 horses at *1s 0d* each)
Cornet	*5s 0d* (*3s 0d* pay+2 horses at *1s 0d* each)
Sergeant	*2s 6d* (*1s 6d* pay+1 horse at *1s 0d*)
Corporal	*2s 0d* (*1s 0d* pay+1 horse at *1s 0d*)
Drummer	*2s 0d* (*1s 0d* pay+1 horse at *1s 0d*)
Private Soldier	*1s 4d* (*8d* pay+1 horse at *8d*)

The Off Reckonings of the dragoons amounted to *2s 6d* per week, about $4\frac{1}{2}$*d* a day. Dragoons rode poor-quality mounts, rated at half the value of the cavalry horses.

The Foot

Colonel as Colonel	*12s 0d*
Lt Colonel as Lt Colonel	*7s 0d*
Major as Major	*5s 0d*
Captain	*8s 0d*
Lieutenant	*4s 0d*
Ensign	*3s 0d*
Chaplain	*6s 8d*
Adjutant	*4s 0d*
Surgeon	*4s 0d* (+*2s 6d* for a horse to carry his chest)
Quartermaster/Provost	*4s 0d* (performed by the same officer)
Sergeant	*1s 6d*
Corporal	*1s 0d*
Drummer	*1s 0d*
Private Soldier	*10d* for all guardsmen not in garrison or stationed in London, and for all infantrymen up to 1672

Private Soldier—*cont.*	8*d* for all soldiers in garrison or stationed outside London after 1672. All wartime levies were paid 8*d* a day.

Whether on 8*d* or 10*d*, the private infantryman suffered Off Reckonings of 2*d* a day. This left Subsistence Money of either 6*d* or 8*d*.

Deductions from Full Pay applied only to private soldiers and non-commissioned officers. All commissioned ranks received their Full Pay.

Appendix I

Principal Office Holders connected with the Army

The Secretaries of State

Sir William Morrice, 26 May 1660	Sir Edward Nicholas, 1 June 1660 Sir Henry Bennet, 2 October 1662
Sir John Trevor, 22 September 1668 Henry Coventry, 8 July 1672	
Southern Department	*Northern Department*
Sir Joseph Williamson, 11 September 1674 Earl of Sunderland, 10 February 1679	Henry Coventry, 11 September 1674
Sir Leoline Jenkins, 26 April 1680 Viscount Conway, 2 February 1681 Earl of Sunderland, 28 January 1683	Earl of Sunderland, 26 April 1680 Sir Leoline Jenkins, 2 February 1681
Sidney Godolphin, 14 April 1684	Earl of Sunderland, 14 April 1684

Lord General

George Monck, Duke of Albemarle, 3 August 1660 to 2 January 1670

Captain-General

James Scott, Duke of Monmouth, January 1670 to 12 September 1679

APPENDIX I

Secretary at War

Sir William Clarke, 28 January 1661 to 4 June 1666
Mathew Locke, 20 June 1666 to 18 August 1683
William Blathwayt, 18 August 1683 to 1704

Paymaster-General

Sir Stephen Fox, 1 March 1661 to 19 January 1676
Sir Henry Puckering, 19 January 1676 to 1679
Sir Stephen Fox, 1679 to 17 November 1679
Charles Fox and Nicholas Johnson, 17 November 1679 to 21 April 1682
Charles Fox, 21 April 1682

Commissary-General of the Musters

Sir Thomas Clarges, 16 February 1660 to 1679
Hon. Henry Howard, 1679

Judge Advocate General

Sir Edmond Pierce D.C.L., January 1661 to 1666
Dr Samuel Barrow, 1666 to February 1682
George Clarke, 10 February 1682 to 1705

Adjutant-General

Englebert Renfosse, 1673 to 28 February 1676
Sir Thomas Daniell, 1 March 1676 to *c.* 1682.

Scout-Master General

Colonel James Halsall, 14 March 1664 to 1685

Colonels of the six Standing Regiments

The Life Guard

King's Troop	*Duke of York's Troop*	*Duke of Albemarle's Troop**
Lord Gerard of Brandon, 18 February 1661 Duke of Monmouth,	Sir Charles Berkeley, 26 January 1661 Earl of Feversham,	Sir Philip Howard, 18 February 1661 to 1686

* Became the Queen's Troop after 1670.

16 September 1668 | 29 June 1667 to 1688
2nd Duke of Albemarle,
29 October 1679 to 1685

Royal Horse Guards
Earl of Oxford, 16 February 1661 to 1703

1st Foot Guards
John Russell, 23 November 1660
Duke of Grafton, 14 December 1681 to 1690

2nd Foot Guards, the Coldstream Regiment
George Monck, Duke of Albemarle, 18 February 1661
Earl of Craven, 3 January 1670 to 1689

Lord High Admiral's Regiment/Duke of York's Maritime Regiment of Foot
Sir William Killigrew, 3 November 1664
Sir Chichester Wray, 1665 to January 1668
Sir Charles Littleton, 15 February 1668 to 1689

Holland Regiment of Foot
Robert Sidney, 21 June 1665
Sir Walter Vane, 12 August 1668
Earl of Mulgrave, 13 December 1673
Earl of Chesterfield, 6 November 1682
Earl of Mulgrave, 26 January 1684 to 1685

Colonels of Regiments added to the English Establishment after 1665

Royal Regiment of Dragoons
Earl of Feversham, 19 February 1678
Lord Churchill, 19 November 1683 to 1688

Royal (Scots) Regiment of Foot
Vacant, 1684–5

Queen's Regiment of Foot
Percy Kirke, 19 April 1682 to 1688

Duchess of York's Regiment of Foot
Charles Trelawney, 23 April 1682 to 1688

Notes

Introduction

1 F. W. Hamilton, *The Origin and History of the First or Grenadier Guards*, London, 1874, vol. 1, pp. 14–15.

2 See C. H. Firth, 'Royalist and Cromwellian Armies in Flanders, 1657–62', *TRHS*, 1903, vol. 17, pp. 67–75; A. Lytton Sells, ed., *The Memoirs of James II, his Campaigns as Duke of York, 1652–1660*, London, 1962, p. 223.

3 SP 29/20, f. 11.

Part One

Chapter I The New Royalist Army

1 Hamilton, *Grenadier Guards*, vol. 1, p. 37; J. Davis, *The History of the Second Queen's Royal Regiment*, London, 1887, vol. 1, p. 2.

2 G. Davies, *The Early History of the Coldstream Guards*, Oxford, 1924, p. 110.

3 A. Bryant, *King Charles II*, London, 1934, p. 69.

4 *CJ*, vol. 8, pp. 5–6.

5 PRO, E 351/344, Declared Accounts for Dunkirk.

6 *CJ*, vol. 8, pp. 142–3.

7 12 Charles II, c. 9.

8 12 Charles II, c. 15.

9 Monck was created 1st Duke of Albemarle in July 1660.

10 12 Charles II, c. 16.

11 *CJ*, vol. 8, pp. 176–7.

12 SP 29/16, f. 76; SP 45/2, p. 25, 'A Proclamation for speeding

the Payment of the arrears of the seventy thousand pounds for three months' assessments due and payable the First of August, last past', 26 September 1660.

13 Edmund Ludlow, *The Memoirs of Edmund Ludlow*, ed. C. H. Firth, Oxford, 1894, vol. 2, pp. 325–6.

14 Gilbert Burnet, *History of His Own Time*, Oxford, 1823, vol. 1, p. 274.

15 Pepys, *Diary*, 9 November 1663.

16 *Calendar of Treasury Books, 1660–67*, vol. 1, p. 79.

17 SP 44/2, pp. 15, 297. To correct this slackening of discipline new Articles of War were introduced for Dunkirk in May 1662 (SP 29/54, f. 9i). These were additions to those already existing, which dated back to the Cromwellian garrison (SP 29/54, f. 9), although some extra articles were included at the Restoration to ensure the transfer of allegiance (SP 78/115, ff. 147–8).

18 The Duke of York's Troop of the Life Guard was sent from England to Dunkirk in 1660. It amalgamated with the royalist horse from Flanders and returned to England in 1661 to become the 2nd Troop of the Life Guard on the English Establishment.

19 SP 29/54, f. 9i.

20 SP 29/20, f. 11.

21 Ludlow, *Memoirs*, vol. 2, pp. 325–6.

22 Burnet, *History of His Own Time*, vol. 1, p. 273.

23 *Ibid.*

24 Pepys, *Diary*, 9 November 1663.

25 Ludlow, *Memoirs*, vol. 2, p. 329n.

26 D. Ogg, *England in the Reign of Charles II*, Oxford, 1967, pp. 559–60.

27 *LJ*, vol. 9, p. 237, 29 December 1660.

28 *Lords Proceedings*, vol. 1, pp. 40–1.

29 *CSPV*, *1659–61*, p. 231.

30 Hamilton, *Grenadier Guards*, vol. 1, p. 43.

31 SP 29/28, f. 42, Sir John Finch to Lord Conway.

32 *Mercurius Publicus*, no. 7, 14 to 21 February 1661.

33 R. Cannon, *Historical Record of the Life Guards*, London, 1835, p. 2.

34 J. W. Fortescue, *A History of the British Army*, London, 1910–1930, vol. 1, p. 292.

35 Hamilton, *Grenadier Guards*, vol. 1, pp. 43–4.

36 SP 29/29, ff. 45–7.

37 Dalton, *Army Lists*, vol. 1, pp. 10–16.

38 SP 29/52, f. 145, Pamphlet by John Brydall on the advantage of Dunkirk, Bombay, and Tangier, to England, 1662.

39 E. M. G. Routh, *Tangier: England's Lost Atlantic Outpost, 1661–1684*, London, 1912, p. 308.

40 WO 24/1, ff. 4–5; SP 71/13, f. 109.

41 SP 103/57, f. 57 *et passim*, Treaty Papers with Portugal, PRO.

42 *CSPD, 1660–1* and *CSPD, 1661–2, passim.*

43 *A List of the Officers claiming to the Sixty Thousand Pounds etc, granted by his Sacred Majesty for the Relief of his Truly-Loyal and Indigent Party*, London, 1663. This list must be approached with caution as it is not wholly reliable. Officers managed to have their names put on the list when they were not entitled to its provisions, whilst the preamble admits of mistakes which it blames on the printer. The necessity for the production of the list was because 'many certificates have been unduly introduced, whereby not only every man's share will be lessened, through the Multitude of Pretenders: but without Strict and Accurate Inspection, a great part of the Moneys will fall into the wrong hands'. To prevent further frauds the list quoted each eligible officer under his regiment, quality and county.

The money was raised by a Poll Bill and had to be claimed by likely candidates. They petitioned the commissioners appointed to administer the Act and upon their decision rested the success or failure of the claim. If an old officer was thought entitled to a share of the money then his amount was calculated in relation to the arrears which were due to him from the time of his service in the Civil Wars (*CSPD, 1663–4*, p. 76). In spite of all these precautions the Act suffered severe abuse. An undated petition from twelve royalist officers complained that, 'due to the false pretenders and abuses of management', they had received only forty days' pay which they thought a poor reward for twenty years' travel and loyal service (*CSPD, 1661–2*, p. 620). The inadequacy of the Act was proved by other means having to be devised to relieve the indigents. A plate lottery was held in 1663 especially for their benefit (*CSPD, 1663–4*, p. 31).

44 There were 168 commissioned officers in the four standing regiments in 1661 with a further 134 attached to the garrisons.

45 *CSPV, 1661–4*, pp. 63–4.

46 *Ibid.*, pp. 187–8; *CSPD, 1661–2*, p. 475; Dalton, *Army Lists*, vol. 1, pp. 23–4.

47 *CSPD, 1663–4*, p. 352.

Chapter II Officers and Men

1 J. Rosse to Joseph Williamson, 21 June 1673, *Williamson's Letters*, vol. 1, p. 58.
2 Add. MSS, no. 10,115, f. 80.
3 WO 26/6, pp. 9–12.
4 PC 2/64, p. 28.
5 WO 26/5, p. 258.
6 SP 30/Case 'F', 'Articles of War, 1673'.
7 WO 26/2, pp. 373–4.
8 *CSPC, 1677–80*, nos. 1000 and 1002.
9 Figures taken from the signatures on depositions sworn before the Judge Advocate of Tangier. BM, Sloane MSS, nos. 1952, 1961, 3498, 3514.
10 Edward Chamberlayne, *Angliae Notitia: or the Present State of England*, London, 1679, part 1, p. 191.
11 H. Brackenbury, *The Nearest Guard*, London, 1892, p. 123.
12 *CSPV, 1661–4*, p. 18.
13 PC 2/59, p. 369, 12 April 1667.
14 *CSPD, 1667–8*, pp. 53–5.
15 SP 29/249, f. 80, 13 November 1668.
16 SP 44/29, pp. 21–30.
17 About 6,000 in 1667–8.
18 *LJ*, vol. 12, p. 547, 7 March 1672.
19 Grey, *Debates*, vol. 2, p. 91; *LJ*, vol. 12, p. 549.
20 *CSPV, 1673–5*, p. 37.
21 *CSPD, 1673*, pp. 42–3.
22 *Ibid.*, pp. 291–2, 24 May 1673.
23 WO 26/4, p. 429.
24 *CSPD, 1678*, p. 508.
25 John Miller, 'Catholic Officers in the Later Stuart Army', *EHR*, 1973, vol. 88, pp. 35–53.
26 John Miller, *Popery and Politics in England, 1660–1688*, Cambridge, 1973, p. 11.
27 *London Gazette*, no. 1517.
28 PC 2/62, p. 21, 20 October 1669.
29 C. E. Lart, 'The Huguenot Regiments', *Proceedings of the Huguenot Society of London*, 1909–11, vol. 11, p. 479.
30 Aubrey de Vere, 20th and last Earl of Oxford (1627–1703).
31 Later the Royal Scots, or Dumbarton's Regiment of Foot.
32 See Appendix E.
33 SP 44/52, pp. 63–75, 'Monmouth's Journal, 1678'.
34 The biographies of Mayne and Lillingston are based on

unpublished material held by the History of Parliament Trust.

35 For these figures and much other information connected with regular officers who were MPs, see the unpublished biographies and other papers for 1660 to 1688 of the History of Parliament Trust. At the time of writing, the Trust has still to investigate seventy-three MPs but none of these appear to have been army officers.

36 BM, Lansdowne MSS, no. 805, ff. 83–9, 'A Biographical and highly Sarcastical List'.

37 'A Seasonable Argument', in Cobbett, *Parliamentary History*, vol. 4, pp. xxii–iv.

38 Nearly all the officers of the Coldstream Guards came under the patronage of Albemarle until 1670. Other notable Restoration officers who enjoyed Monck's patronage were: Sir Thomas Gower, Richard Ingoldsby (one of the few regicides to find rehabilitation), Ralph Knight, Jeremiah Tolhurst, John Rumsey, Sir Thomas Clarges, Sir William Clarke, Sir Samuel Clarke, Sir Thomas Morgan and his son Sir John Morgan.

39 *Williamson's Letters*, vol. 1, p. 117.

40 *Ibid.*, pp. 27–8, 9 June 1673.

41 WO 26/5, pp. 293–5, 'For the better regulating of the Musters of our Guards, Forces, and Garrisons', 1680.

42 Sidney, *Diary*, vol. 1, p. 192, 20 November 1679.

43 SP 44/69, p. 28, 16 April 1683.

44 SP 29/54, f. 10.

45 *Essex Papers*, vol. 1, pp. 75, 208.

46 Henry Ball to Williamson, 26 June 1673, *Williamson's Letters*, vol. 1, p. 67.

47 *Williamson's Letters*, vol. 2, p. 20.

48 *London Gazette*, no. 703.

49 *Hatton Correspondence*, vol. 1, pp. 127, 128, 134, May 1676.

50 *Ibid.*, p. 131.

51 *CSPV, 1661–4*, p. 236.

52 *HMC*, Dartmouth MSS, vol. 5, p. 75.

53 *HMC*, Bath MSS, vol. 2, p. 166. Howard was captain of the Queen's Troop of the Life Guard in 1678.

54 SP 29/230, f. 86, 'Table of Fees for commissions as they stand proportioned to the officers' monthly pay', 1667.

Lieutenant of Horse	£5
Cornet of Horse	£3
Lieutenant of Foot	£4
Ensign of Foot	£2

55 SP 44/69, p. 105.

56 Clode, *Military Forces*, vol. 1, pp. 69–70.

57 Hamilton, *Grenadier Guards*, vol. 1, p. 250.
58 Browning, *Memoirs of Sir John Reresby*, p. 226ff.

Chapter III Military Life in England

1 *Calendar of Treasury Books, 1660–67*, p. 523, 14 May 1663.
2 SP 29/47, f. 79, 'The Account of what money is assigned upon the Poll Bill for the Payment of the New Raised Forces and of what money is received on that assignment and what money is paid to the Forces', 1661.
3 See Appendix G.
4 *CSPV, 1664–6*, p. 6.
5 John Sackfield, *Memoirs of the Life of Sir Stephen Fox Kt, from his First Entrance upon the Stage of Action under the Lord Piercy, till his Decease*, London, 1717, pp. 17–19.
6 Lemuel Kingdon (*c.* 1654–86). Only son of Captain Richard Kingdon, a Parliamentary soldier, who made his peace at the Restoration. Lemuel was patronised by Monmouth. He was MP for Hull in the first Exclusion Parliament and for Newtown, Isle of Wight, in 1680. He appears to have gone bankrupt in 1680, being evicted from his house.
7 *CSPD, 1682*, p. 177.
8 BM, Lansdowne MSS, no. 805, f. 88.
9 Evelyn, *Diary*, 6 September 1680.
10 See Appendix H.
11 *Calendar of Treasury Books, 1660–67*, p. 686.
12 *Calendar of Treasury Books, 1667–8*, p. 147.
13 SP 44/26, pp. 34–5.
14 Littleton to Lord Hatton, *Hatton Correspondence*, vol. 1, p. 214.
15 SP 44/48, p. 87.
16 SP 44/58, p. 15, 13 May 1679.
17 PC 2/70, pp. 77, 96, 119; SP 44/69, pp. 99–100.
18 *Calendar of Treasury Books, 1660–67*, p. 502.
19 *CSPD, 1667*, p. 528.
20 SP 44/26, pp. 34–5.
21 *Calendar of Treasury Books, 1669–72*, part 1, p. xxx.
22 SP 29/414, f. 172, 'The Deplorable Case of the Poor Sufferers, by that Army disbanded by the Four Commissioners in the Year 1679', 1680.
23 Firth, *Cromwell's Army*, pp. 204–5.
24 WO 33/19, f. 145, 'Memorandum on half-pay, Pensions, etc.'
25 35 Elizabeth, c. 4.
26 *CJ*, vol. 8, p. 213. Ely House, on the south bank of the Thames,

did not long remain as an army barracks. By 1670 it was used neither as lodging nor hospital. From this date London could house soldiers only in the Savoy and Whitehall.

27 WO 24/5, Establishment 1680; WO 24/6, Establishment 1683.

28 WO 26/2, p. 44.

29 PC 2/64, pp. 147, 216.

30 PC 2/61, p. 220.

31 WO 26/2, p. 68.

32 This was not a new deduction but an adjustment of the old 'poundage' which had been granted to Fox in 1668. After 1684 the Paymaster no longer received this perquisite, but the 1*s* in the £ was still taken from army pay by the Commissioners of the Treasury. One-third (4*d*) was used to meet the Exchequer Fees, and the other two-thirds (8*d*) went towards 'the erecting, building, and maintaining our Royal Hospital at Chelsea' (WO 24/7, part 1, f. 13).

33 SP 44/69, p. 105.

34 *CSPD, 1683–4*, pp. 111–12.

35 *CSPD, 1684–5*, p. 58, 14 June 1684.

36 WO 71/121, Court Martial Proceedings, 1668–97, 'Gibbs contra Lt. Col. Pinchbeck', 13 November 1673.

37 WO 26/4, pp. 56–7.

38 Cost of uniforms:

The Foot	£2 13*s* 0*d*	per man.
The Dragoons	£6 10*s* 0*d*	per man.
The Horse	£9 0*s* 0*d*	per man.

39 *CSPD, 1672–3*, p. 225.

40 Nathan Brooks, *A General and Complete List Military of Every Commission Officer of Horse and Foot now commanding in his Majesty's Land Forces of England*, London, 1684 (BM, Add. MSS, no. 10,123, ff. 29–40); Chamberlayne, *Angliae Notitia*, part 1, pp. 191–2; Count Lorenzo Magolotti, *The Travels of Cosmo the Third, Grand Duke of Tuscany, through England during the Reign of King Charles the Second, 1669*, London, 1821, pp. 305–7.

41 Magolotti, *Cosmo's Travels*, p. 123; H. R. Knight, *Historical Records of the Buffs*, London, 1905, vol. 1, p. 141.

42 R. Cannon, *Historical Record of the First or Royal Regiment of Foot*, London, 1847, pp. 68–9.

43 L. I. Cowper, *The King's Own, the Story of a Royal Regiment*, Oxford, 1939, vol. 1, p. 464.

44 WO 71/121, Sheet 1.

45 Further evidence to support the idea that at least some of the regiments wore grey coats as undress uniform comes from *London Gazette*, 27 to 31 January 1687, and 16 to 20 September 1686.

46 Evelyn, *Diary*, 29 June 1678.

47 WO 26/5, p. 61. Each cravat cost 3*s* 6*d*.

48 WO 5/1, pp. 88–9.

49 SP 29–34, f. 127, April 1661.

50 SP 44/59, pp. 86–7.

51 *CSPD, 1678*, p. 125; *CSPD, 1675–6*, p. 293.

52 *CSPD, 1660–1*, p. 486. Matchlocks cost 16*s* 6*d* each, collars of bandoliers 2*s* 0*d* each, and pikes 4*s* 6*d* each.

53 WO 26/2, p. 406.

54 WO 26/1, pp. 98–9.

55 SP 30/Case F, 'Articles and Rules for the Better Government of His Majesty's Forces by Land during this Present war', 1673.

56 WO 26/5, p. 90, 15 November 1678. The bounty paid was only £8 8*s* 0*d*.

57 R. Cannon, *Historical Record of the Life Guards*, London, 1835, pp. 36–7; WO 26/4, p. 319.

58 L. Edye, *The Historical Records of the Royal Marines*, London, 1893, vol. 1, p. 16.

59 SP 44/59, p. 79.

60 SP 44/69, pp. 50, 87; *CSPD, 1684–5*, pp. 141–2. Colonel Charles Trelawney's regiment, the Duchess of York's, was rearmed with some flintlocks and a majority of matchlocks.

61 Sir James Turner, *Pallas Armata: Military Essays of the Ancient Greek, Roman, and Modern Art of War*, London, 1683. Written between 1670 and 1671.

62 *A Treatise of the Art of War*, London, 1677.

63 K. M. Lynch, *Roger Boyle, First Earl of Orrery*, Knoxville, 1965, p. 195.

64 Hamilton, *Grenadier Guards*, vol. 1, p. 192.

65 SP 44/41, p. 41.

66 SP 57–5 (PRO), pp. 330–72. The originals of these Scottish Warrant Books are housed in the Scottish Public Record Office in Edinburgh. Microfilm copies are in the PRO, London, under reference PRO 27.

67 Sir Charles Littleton to Lord Hatton, November 1672, *Hatton Correspondence*, vol. 1, p. 99.

68 Robert Yard to Joseph Williamson, 7 July 1673, *Williamson's Letters*, vol. 1, p. 91.

69 PC 2/68, p. 33, 14 May 1679.

70 SP 29/411, f. 142, 'The humble proposals of Solomon de Fobert Esq. concerning a Royal Academy for Military Exercises here in London'.

71 Magolotti, *Cosmo's Travels*, p. 310.

72 Chamberlayne, *Angliae Notitia*, 1679, part 1, p. 175.
73 Brackenbury, *Nearest Guard*, p. 127.
74 Evelyn, *Diary*, 27 November 1662.
75 *Ibid.*, 4 July 1663.
76 WO 26/4, pp. 278 and 334–6.
77 Add. MSS, no. 10,123, ff. 29–40.
78 Sir Reginald Blomfield, *Sebastien le Prestre de Vauban, 1633–1707*, London, 1938, p. 72.
79 Evelyn, *Diary*, 21 August 1674.
80 SP 29/290, f. 32, 23 May 1671.
81 WO 33/19, f. 338, 'Memorandum on the Removal of Her Majesty's Troops from Towns or Cities during Assizes or Elections held therein', 1868.
82 Narcissus Luttrell, *A Brief Historical Relation of State Affairs*, Oxford, 1857, vol. 1, p. 264.
83 WO 26/1, p. 93; WO 26/3, p. 164.
84 WO 26/5, p. 289.
85 SP 44/41, p. 57.
86 SP 44/60, p. 38.
87 WO 26/2, p. 418.
88 *APC*, vol. 1, no. 623.
89 WO 26/1, p. 95.
90 *Ibid.*, p. 36.
91 *CSPD, 1683*, p. 344; WO 5/1, p. 4.
92 WO 26/1, p. 342.
93 WO 26/2, p. 62.
94 *CSPD, 1670*, pp. 233–4, 343.
95 Cobbett, *State Trials*, vol. 6, p. 879.
96 *CSPV, 1669–70*, p. 29, 15 March 1669.
97 WO 26/2, p. 172.
98 WO 26/5, p. 130.
99 *CSPD, 1684–5*, p. 92, 10 July 1684.
100 Lucy Hutchinson, *Memoirs of the Life of Colonel Hutchinson*, ed. C. H. Firth, London, 1906, pp. 369–70.
101 Mackinnon, *Coldstream Guards*, vol. 1, p. 114.
102 Magolotti, *Cosmo's Travels*, p. 310.
103 AO 1/149/Roll 21 (PRO), Exchequer and Audit Department, Pipe Office, Declared Accounts for the Army, 21 September 1672 to 20 September 1673.
104 WO 26/1, pp. 420–23.
105 Mackinnon, *Coldstream Guards*, vol. 1, p. 140.
106 *Ibid.*, vol. 1, p. 114.
107 SP 44/52, pp. 49/50.

108 CO 279/30, ff. 358–9, 'The True State of Tangier, or Tangier Improveable' (1682).

109 SP 29/29, f. 47, Establishment, 26 January 1661.

110 *CSPD, 1678*, p. 149; *CSPD, 1667–8*, p. 395.

111 *CSPD, 1670*, p. 697. Commission to John Knight, Sergeant-Surgeon, to be Surgeon-General of all the Forces in England and Wales.

112 WO 26/2, pp. 71–2, 21 January 1678.

113 *CSPD, 1678*, p. 509, 8 November 1678.

114 SP 29/403, f. 165, 4 May 1678. The government offered an additional 2*s* 8*d*, on top of establishment pay of 4*s* 0*d* a day, to each new surgeon.

Chapter IV Discipline and the Law

1 E. R. Adair, 'The Petition of Right', *History*, 1920–1, vol. 5, pp. 99–103.

2 Throughout this chapter, the 'common law' refers to all the laws of England, as passed by Parliament, which applied to civilians in peacetime, i.e. all law that was non-military.

3 From the Petition of Right. Quoted in Cobbett, *Parliamentary History*, vol. 2, pp. 376–7.

4 Firth, *Cromwell's Army*, pp. 179–82, 216–19.

5 K. H. D. Haley, *The First Earl of Shaftesbury*, Oxford, 1968, pp. 304–5.

6 SP 30/Case F, 'Articles and Rules for the Better Government of his Majesty's Forces by Land during this Present War'; *Williamson's Letters*, vol. 1, p. 42.

7 Charles Hatton to Viscount Hatton, 8 July 1673, *Hatton Correspondence*, vol. 1, p. 111.

8 Robert Yard to Joseph Williamson, 4 August 1673, *Williamson's Letters*, vol. 1, p. 143.

9 C. M. Clode, *The Military Forces of the Crown: Their Administration and Government*, London, 1869, vol. 1, p. 55.

10 See Appendix F.

11 SP 29/153, f. 56, 9 April 1966, 'Orders and Articles of War'.

12 Clarendon State Papers, vol. 80, ff. 175–6.

13 *CJ*, vol. 8, p. 628.

14 PC 2/64, p. 394, 1 March 1675.

15 WO 4/1, p. 4, 13 June 1684.

16 Grey, *Debates*, vol. 2, p. 206; *CJ*, vol. 9, p. 285.

17 PC 2/64, p. 137, 21 November 1673.

18 *Ibid.*, p. 191, 13 March 1674.

19 *HMC*, Bath MSS, vol. 2, p. 166, Henry Saville to the Earl of Rochester, 2 July 1678.

20 WO 92/1, 1666–1704.

21 WO 89/1, pp. 54–66.

22 7 Henry VII, c. 1.

23 3 Henry VIII, c. 5.

24 1 William and Mary, c. 5, *SR*, vol. 6, p. 55.

25 See Appendix F.

26 SP 29/29, ff. 86, 86i.

27 *Ibid.*, f. 47, Establishment, 1661.

28 *CSPD, 1682*, p. 69, 10 February 1682.

29 For the earlier history of the Provost-Marshal see: A. Vaughan Lovell-Knight, *The History of the Office of Provost-Marshall and the Corps of Military Police*, London, 1943; L. Boynton, 'The Tudor Provost-Marshall', *EHR*, 1962, vol. 77, pp. 437–55.

30 WO 24/5, Establishment, 1680. This was a reduction. In 1668, the Marshall of the Horse received 9*s* a day with an extra half-a-crown for a servant.

31 *CSPD, 1678*, p. 387. The officer appointed was Thomas Sherburne.

32 SP 30/Case F, 'Articles and Rules for the Better Government of his Majesty's Forces by Land during this Present War', 1673.

33 BM, Sloane MSS, nos. 1957, 1959, 1960, 3498, 3514. Minutes of courts martial at Tangier.

34 SP 29/140, f. 94, December 1665.

35 SP 29/187, f. 337, 1666.

36 Sir John Talbot to Arlington, *CSPD, 1673*, p. 174.

37 SP 29/363, f. 175, 1674.

38 WO 30/48, 'Abstract of a Particular Account of all the Inns, Ale Houses, etc, in England, with their Stable-Room and Bedding. In the Year 1686'.

39 *CSPV, 1664–6*, p. 178.

40 *LJ*, vol. 11, p. 345.

41 Grey, *Debates*, vol. 2, pp. 201, 215–16; Walton, *Standing Army*, pp. 711–12.

42 PC 2/63, p. 73, 13 September 1671.

43 Grey, *Debates*, vol. 2, p. 205, 31 October 1673.

44 *Ibid.*, pp. 215–16.

45 PC 2/56, p. 678, 13 January 1663.

46 *CSPD, 1673*, p. 136, April 1673.

47 Grey, *Debates*, vol. 5, pp. 325–6.

48 31 Charles II, c. 1; *SR*, vol. 5, p. 934.

Chapter V The Staff and Administration

1 SP 29/272, f. 87, 21 January 1670.

2 F. S. Allen, 'Towards a Theory of Civil-Military Control in England, 1670–80', *JSAHR*, 1962, vol. 40, p. 96.

3 The members of the Committee were: the Duke of York, the Duke of Monmouth, the Earl of Oxford, the Earl of Craven, John Russell, Sir Philip Howard, Marquis de Blanquefort, Sir Walter Vane and Sir Charles Littleton.

4 BM, Add. MSS, no. 10,115, Sir Joseph Williamson's State Papers, 1677–8, relative to the preparations for the projected War with France.

5 WO 26/3, pp. 204–5, 7 September 1676.

6 Gumble, *Life of Monck*, p. 423.

7 The Secretary at War's pay was:

1661–9 — 10*s* 0*d* a day.
1670–80—£1 0*s* 0*d* a day.
1680–5 —£2 0*s* 0*d* a day.

8 WO 26/2, pp. 342–3.

9 G. A. Jacobsen, *William Blathwayt, a late Seventeenth Century English Administrator*, New Haven, London and Oxford, 1932, pp. 210–11.

10 *CSPD, 1676–7*, p. 316.

11 Grey, *Debates*, vol. 6, p. 219.

12 *Ibid.*, pp. 210–20.

13 *Ibid.*, p. 222.

14 *Ibid.*, pp. 224–5.

15 *CSPD, 1683*, p. 334. Locke, an Irishman, was a distant relative of Sir Robert Southwell. Southwell was a patron of Blathwayt.

16 Blathwayt continued as Secretary at War until 1704.

17 Correlli Barnett, *Britain and Her Army, 1509–1970*, London, 1970, p. 131.

18 WO 26/1–6, Entry Books of Warrants and Precedents. Orders were given under the Sign Manual by the Secretaries of State until 1683. After this date Blathwayt's signature appears.

19 Independent garrison companies did remain on one station all the while and suffered from most of the faults mentioned above. See A. Browning, *The Memoirs of Sir John Reresby*, Glasgow, 1936.

20 SP 44/52, p. 100. Sunday was always a rest-day.

21 Edye, *Royal Marines*, vol. 1, p. 18.

22 SP 78/115, ff. 147–8, 1660.

23 CO 279/1, ff. 99–110. This was the code in force in Tangier.

24 BM, Add. MSS, no. 38,694, ff. 20–1. War Office Correspondence.

25 Life Guards
Royal Horse Guards } The Horse was always senior to the foot.
1st Foot Guards.
Coldstream Guards.
Admiral's Regiment.
Holland Regiment.

26 SP 29/260, f. 21, 10 May 1669.

27 SP 29/335, f. 229, 28 May 1673.

28 WO 26/4, p. 396, 20 July 1678, 'For preventing all Disputes that may arise concerning the Ranks of Companies within any of his Majesty's Garrisons'.

29 WO 24/3, Establishment, England, 1673.

30 Walton, *History of the British Standing Army*, p. 644.

31 C. G. Cruickshank, *Elizabeth's Army*, Oxford, 1968, pp. 144–5.

32 Firth, *Cromwell's Army*, p. 44. There certainly were complaints about agents in the time of Charles II and James II. 'Richard Thurloe, Agent to Colonel Kirk's and Colonel Trelawney's Regiments, and Clerk to Colonel Cornewell's Troop in Lord Oxford's Regiment, ran away with Regimental Money. 40 guineas reward offered for his apprehension' (*London Gazette*, 29 October 1685).

33 Eighteen Deputy-Commissaries in 1668; 12 in 1673; 8 in 1684.

34 Only one example of a muster-roll for Charles II's reign has been discovered. It is for the Duke of York's independent company in the Portsmouth Garrison for 10 August 1661. BM, Add. MSS, no. 18,764, f. 36.

35 Succeeded as the 5th Earl in 1691.

36 SP 29/29, ff. 81 and 81a, 17 March 1663; WO 26/5, pp. 293–295.

37 Pepys, *Diary*, 13 October 1663.

38 Cruickshank, *Elizabeth's Army*, pp. 140–2.

39 C. G. Cruickshank, *Army Royal*, Oxford, 1969, p. 69.

40 Turner, *Pallas Armata*, p. 197.

41 WO 26/1, pp. 42, 84.

42 Henry Ball to Joseph Williamson, 13 June 1673, *Williamson's Letters*, vol. 1, p. 42.

43 Hutchinson, *Memoirs*, pp. 364–5.

44 WO 89/1, pp. 67–8.

45 SP 29/367, f. 107, 23 January 1674.

46 For the Flanders Expedition of 1678, bread was provided for the soldiers at the daily cost of one quarter of a farthing per man. This sum was deducted from the subsistence money (SP 44/41,

p. 162). The Government also laid on supplies of 'butter, cheese, and biscuit', but these had to be purchased individually by the men (SP 44/52, p. 34).

47 SP 29/443, f. 3.

48 Hamilton, *Grenadier Guards*, vol. 1, p. 192.

49 WO 24/5, f. 10, Establishment 1680.

50 SP 29/236, f. 193, Establishment 1668.

Part Two

Chapter VI The Garrison of Tangier

1 Sir Hugh Cholmley, *The Memoirs of Sir Hugh Cholmley, Knt. and Bart.*, 1837, printed privately, pp. 16–17; CO 279/1, f. 98.

2 CO 279/33, ff. 134–7, 142–4.

3 C. H. Firth, 'Royalist and Cromwellian Armies in Flanders, 1657–62', *TRHS*, 1903, vol. 17, p. 105.

4 WO 24/1, ff. 9–19; CO 279/1, f. 156.

5 CO 279/1, f. 19; Cholmley, *Memoirs*, pp. 17–19.

6 CO 279/1, f. 156.

7 Routh, *Tangier*, p. 310; Lancelot Addison, *A Discourse of Tangier under the Government of the Earl of Teviot*, London, 1685, pp. 5–6.

8 C. S. S. Higham, *The Development of the Leeward Islands under the Restoration, 1660–1688*, Cambridge, 1921, p. 50; D. W. Rannie, 'Cromwell's Major-Generals', *EHR*, 1895, vol. 10, p. 478; Firth and Davies, *Cromwell's Army*, vol. 1, p. 305.

9 SP 71/13, f. 109; WO 24/1, ff. 4–5.

10 CO 279/6, ff. 44–5; SP 44/20, pp. 138, 138a.

11 SP 29/236, f. 193.

12 BM, Sloane MSS, no. 3509, ff. 230–1.

13 SP 44/30, p. 52.

14 BM, Sloane MSS, no. 1952, ff. 42–7.

15 CO 279/19, f. 371.

16 CO 279/22, f. 20, Fairborne to Williamson, 10 January 1678.

17 WO 26/5, p. 338.

18 Samuel Pepys, *Tangier Papers*, ed. E. Chappell, 'Notes on Tangier', pp. 89–90.

19 *Ibid.*

20 *CSPD, 1663–4*, p. 419.

21 CO 279/3, ff. 36, 63; Dalton, *Army Lists*, vol. 1, p. 37.

22 Routh, *Tangier*, p. 26.

23 Colonel of the 2nd Tangier Regiment (Plymouth's) in 1681. Major General under William III.
24 *CSPD, 1663–4*, p. 419.
25 CO 279/22, f. 110, Fairborne to Williamson, 1 March 1678.
26 CO 279/21, f. 44, Fairborne to Williamson, 28 July 1677.
27 *CSPV, 1661–4*, p. 54, 14 October 1661.
28 Cholmley, *Memoirs*, pp. 17–19.
29 *Ibid.*
30 *CSPD, 1679–80*, pp. 97–8, 101, 121.
31 BM, Sloane MSS, no. 3509, ff. 220, 254.
32 BM, Sloane MSS, no. 3496, f. 16, and no. 3509, ff. 220, 254. Ensigns John Herbert, Henry Size and William Whitaker. Stafford Fairborne, eldest son of Sir Palmes, and John Mackenny, son of Captain Alexander Mackenny, also received pay as reformadoes.
33 BM, Sloane MSS, no. 3510, f. 215.
34 CO 279/29, f. 220.
35 CO 279/33, f. 126. The Governor sends a list of officers absent on leave in England, requesting that they be ordered to return to Tangier: 2 majors, 11 captains, 1 lieutenant, 1 ensign, 1 cornet. CO 279/29, f. 220, 18 May 1682. Another list of absent officers: 1 lieutenant-colonel, 2 majors, 16 captains, 16 lieutenants and 10 ensigns.
36 Routh, *Tangier*, p. 315.
37 *CSPD, 1671–2*, p. 250, 29 March 1672; CO 279/21, f. 124.
38 CO 279/26, ff. 296–7, 11 August 1680, 'Notes taken from My Lord Craven's mouth relating to Tangier'.
39 BM, Sloane MSS, no. 1956, f. 9.
40 CO 279/16, f. 287, 5 February 1673. Tangier was used as a naval station for squadrons patrolling the western Mediterranean. Whenever ships put into Tangier they provisioned out of the garrison stores. This was a major contribution to the army's food shortage.
41 CO 279/10, f. 84, 17 October 1668. A fine of £2 10*s* was imposed on any person boarding a ship which had not been passed by the quarantine officials.
42 CO 279/30, ff. 358–9, 'The True State of Tangier, or Tangier Improveable'.
43 CO 279/32, f. 138, Dartmouth to Jenkins, 16 September 1683.
44 CO 279/22, f. 45.
45 SP 71/13, f. 109; BM, Sloane MSS, no. 3509, ff. 230–1; CO 279/3, f. 225. The weekly allowance of provisions (7 days) purchased with the 6*d* was: 5lbs of biscuit, 2lbs of wheat, 2lbs of salt beef, 2lbs of salt pork, 4 pints of dried peas, 3 pints of oatmeal, 4 ounces of oil, ½lb of butter. Cheese is mentioned in some later accounts.

46 CO 279/3, ff. 266–7: arrears of 3 months in August 1664; CO 279/14, f. 243: arrears of 12 months in 1671; CO 279/16, f. 58: arrears of 2 years in August 1674; CO 279/20, f. 252: arrears of 2 years 6 months in April 1677.

47 BM, Sloane MSS, no. 3510, ff. 96–7.

48 CO 279/4, ff. 50–3, Cholmley to the Lords Commissioners for Tangier, 28 February 1665.

49 *Calendar of Treasury Books* vols. 1 and 2.

50 *Ibid.*, vol. 2, pp. 425–6.

51 CO 279/6, f. 73, Letter from Witham, 31 May 1666.

52 CO 279/18, ff. 329–31, Fairborne to Lords Commissioners, 19 May 1679.

53 CO 279/30, ff. 358–9.

54 Pepys, *Tangier Papers*, 'Notes on Tangier', p. 96.

55 BM, Sloane MSS, nos. 1957, 1959, 1960, 3498, 3514, Minutes of Courts Martial at Tangier, 1662 to 1674.

56 CO 279/31, f. 308, Kirke to Jenkins, 17 May 1683.

57 BM, Sloane MSS, no. 3512, ff. 238–41; CO 279/18, f. 363.

58 CO 279/20, f. 252, 18 April 1677.

59 CO 279/21, f. 364, 24 December 1677.

60 *The Rules of Civility*, London, 1678.

61 CO 279/3, ff. 299–300, Letter from Edward Witham, 29 October 1664.

62 The court of the Corporation of Tangier.

63 In the courts martial records, it is stated frequently that punishments must be carried out in front of, or in 'the face of the parade'. This was intended to serve as an example to all would-be offenders.

64 Cowper, *The King's Own*, vol. 1, pp. 18–20; Routh, *Tangier*, p. 284.

65 Cholmley, *Memoirs*, p. 130; Pepys, *Diary*, 15 December 1662; Davis, *Second Queen's Royal Regiment*, vol. 1, p. 36; CO 279/17, 8 March 1675. The garrison church was also the parish church for protestant civilians, with the right-hand side reserved for the military, and the left-hand side for civilians.

66 BM, Sloane MSS, no. 3509, ff. 139–40, 196.

67 CO 279/27, f. 68, 28 January 1681; CO 279/28, f. 249, 5 October 1681.

68 CO 279/33, f. 371, 'An Abstract of the State of the City and Garrison of Tangier on a Survey taken thereof the 30th of December, 1676'.

69 CO 279/33, f. 58, Dartmouth to Jenkins, 5 January 1684.

Chapter VII The Fight for Tangier

1 *The Present Interest of Tangier*, London, 1680, pp. 3–4.

2 L. Addison, *A Discourse of Tangier under the Government of the Earl of Teviot*, London, 1685, p. 3.

3 Cholmley, *Memoirs*, pp. 39–41.

4 CO 279/2, f. 104, Mr Rudyer's account of the late action at Tangier.

5 'Galtraps' and 'Crows' Feet' were spiked, iron tripods, placed on the ground to injure the soft part of a horse's hoof.

6 SP 89/6, f. 180, Sir Richard Fanshawe to Secretary Bennet, 18 July 1663, Lisbon.

7 CO 279/3, ff. 4, 41.

8 CO 279/3, ff. 32–3, 41.

9 CO 279/3, f. 43, Teviot to Martin Wescombe, consul at Cadiz, 25 April 1664.

10 SP 89/6, f. 31, 11 February 1663.

11 CO 279/3, f. 36.

12 *HMC*, Heathcote MSS, pp. 156–7, Alsopp to Sir Richard Fanshawe, 13 June 1664.

13 CO 279/3, f. 63.

14 CO 279/3, ff. 45, 63. The casualties, all presumed dead, for the action on 4 May 1663 were: the Governor, 19 commissioned officers, 16 gentleman volunteers, and 396 other ranks. Seventy-four privates were known to have been captured.

15 CO 279/6, ff. 43–6, 2 April 1666.

16 CO 279/3, ff. 323–4, 'A Memorandum of the method of the new Fortifications as they are to be made in his Majesty's City and Castle of Tangier'.

17 CO 279/12, f. 158, Fairborne to Williamson, 3 July 1669.

18 CO 279/14, f. 121, Cholmley to Williamson, 14 August 1671.

19 CO 279/32, ff. 156–66, 2 October 1683.

20 CO 279/17, f. 112, 19 September 1675, 'A True Narration of Sir Palmes Fairborne's, Major, deportment against the Moors on the 19th of September, 1675, at nine a clock at night, to three the next morning'.

21 CO 279/17, unnumbered, 25 September 1675.

22 CO 279/17, unnumbered, Lords Commissioners to Inchiquin, 8 November 1675.

23 CO 279/18, f. 363, Fairborne to Lords Commissioners, 31 May 1676.

24 BM, Sloane MSS, no. 1952, ff. 20–1.

25 PRO. MP/H/1, Maps and Plans of Tangier.

26 *The Present Danger of Tangier or an Account of its being attempted by a Great Army of the Moors by Land, and under some Apprehensions of the French by Sea.* Printed, being A Letter from Cadiz to a Friend in England, 29 July 1679.

27 *London Gazette*, no. 1488.

28 *A Second Journal of the Siege of Tangier, from 25th March, 1680, to 22nd May, 1680*, London, 1680.

29 *An Exact Journal of the Siege of Tangier, from the First Sitting Down of the Moors Before it on March 25th, 1680, to the Late Truce, May 19th, following*, London, 1680.

30 *Second Journal.*

31 CO 279/25, ff. 211–12, Fairborne to Jenkins, 17 May 1680.

32 CO 279/25, f. 209, Fairborne to Jenkins, 11 May 1680.

33 Casualties. Average of figures from various sources:
Forts Charles and Henrietta—160 killed, 53 prisoners.
Boynton's Force —15 killed, 'several' wounded.
Devil's Drop (Giles Fort) —11 prisoners.

34 CO 279/25, ff. 211–12.

35 CO 279/25, f. 217, Fairborne to Jenkins, 21 May 1680.

36 *A Particular Relation of the Late Success of his Majesty's Forces at Tangier against the Moors*, Published by Authority, London, 1680.

37 'A Short and True Account of the most remarkable things that passed during the late Wars with the Moors at Tangier during the year 1680, and the Treaty of Peace betwixt Alcad Domar and Lt. Colonel Sackville. By Sir James Halkett commander of 16 Companies and Major of the E. of Dumbarton's Regiment there', ed. H. M. McCance, *JSAHR*, 1922, vol. 1, Special Number; CO 279/26, ff. 78–9, 'Account of what passed at Tangier from the 15th to the 23rd Sept. '80'.

38 Three troops of horse had been hired from Spain in the absence of cavalry reinforcements from England. However, three troops of English horse arrived just before the action. Fairborne had been adamant that a large body of horse must support the sally if it was to be successful.

39 CO 279/26, f. 183, Beckman to Sunderland, 29 October 1680.

Chapter VIII The Colonies

1 SP 29/52, f. 152, Pamphlet by 'J.B.' (John Brydall), 1662.

2 PRO, State Papers Foreign, Treaty Papers, vol. 57, nos. 107, 116, 128, 228.

3 *JSAHR*, 1928, vol. 27, pp. 139–41; W. Foster, *The English Factories in India, 1661–64*, Oxford, 1923, pp. 128–9.

4 *Oxford Gazette*, 16–20 November 1665.

5 W. Foster, *The English Factories in India, 1665–67*, Oxford, 1925, p. 300.

6 *JSAHR*, 1928, vol. 27, pp. 139–41; *Calendar of Treasury Books*, vol. 11, p. 441.

7 Firth and Davies, *The Regimental History of Cromwell's Army*, vol. 1, p. 36, vol. 2, pp. 699–702.

8 *CSPC, 1681–5*, no. 208.

9 See C. S. S. Higham, *The Development of the Leeward Islands under the Restoration, 1660–1688*, Cambridge, 1921; A. P. Newton, *The European Nations in the West Indies, 1493–1688*, Cambridge, 1933; V. T. Harlow, *A History of Barbados, 1625–1685*, Oxford, 1926.

10 Dalton, *Army Lists*, vol. 1, p. 115; H. R. Knight, *The Historical Records of the Buffs*, London, 1905, vol. 1, pp. 130–1.

11 *CSPC, 1661–8*, no. 1524, Narration of the Fight on St Christophers on 8 June 1667, by Major John Scott.

12 The casualties of the landing party were: 506 killed, 284 wounded, 210 prisoners.

13 *CSPC, 1661–8*, no. 1524.

14 *APC*, vol. 1, no. 786, 28 July 1668.

15 WO 26/1, Warrants and Precedents, p. 179.

16 *APC*, vol. 1, nos. 993, 995, 1001, 1240.

17 *CSPC, 1681–5*, no. 291.

18 *CSPC, 1661–8*, no. 1362; SP 44/35a, p. 88, 30 May 1674.

19 *CSPC, 1660–74*, no. 1030.

20 *CSPC, 1675–6*, no. 964, William Sherwood to Williamson, 28 June 1676.

21 SP 29/366, f. 237, Notes by Williamson; WO 26/3, pp. 215–224, 229–30.

22 SP 29/359, ff. 39–42, 9 October 1676.

23 SP 29/386, f. 206, John Gibbons to Williamson, 6 November 1676.

24 *CSPD, 1677–8*, p. 115, 6 May 1677.

25 *Ibid.*, p. 180, 7 June 1677.

26 WO 26/4, p. 177. Each company had 200 men on embarkation in 1676. Their musters on return in 1678 were:

Colonel Herbert Jeffreys's Company—69 privates, 7 NCOs, 1 lieutenant.

Lt Colonel Edward Pict's Company—67 privates, 7 NCOs, 1 ensign.

Major John Mutlowe's Company—69 privates, 7 NCOs, 1 lieutenant.

Captain Charles Middleton's Company—56 privates.

Captain Edward Meole's Company—66 privates.

27 WO 26/5, p. 112, 31 December 1678.

28 *CSPC, 1677–80*, no. 591.

Chapter IX Foreign Service

1 Burnet, *History of His Own Time*, vol. 1, pp. 294–5.

2 *CSPD, 1661–2*, p. 251; *Calendar of Clarendon State Papers*, vol. 5, p. 192.

3 Firth and Davies, *Regimental History of Cromwell's Army*, vol. 2, pp. 499–500; *CSPV, 1661–4*, pp. 141, 152.

4 SP 44/2, p. 27; *HMC*, Heathcote MSS, p. 29; *CSPD, 1661–2*, pp. 331, 344.

5 *Calendar of Clarendon State Papers*, vol. 5, pp. 242–3.

6 For a list of the British regiments in Portugal see Appendix B.

7 SP 89/6, f. 44, 31 October 1662.

8 *HMC*, Heathcote MSS, pp. 55–6, Dempsey to Sir Richard Fanshawe, 4 January 1663.

9 SP 89/6, ff. 7–10, Fanshawe to Charles II, 6 February 1663.

10 *Calendar of Clarendon State Papers*, vol. 5, pp. 410–11.

11 SP 89/6, ff. 257–8.

12 SP 89/7, f. 156, 2 April 1666.

13 SP 89/9, f. 32.

14 CO 279/10, f. 111, Norwood to Arlington, 24 September 1668.

15 The Battle of Ameixial, or El Canal, 8 June 1663.

16 *HMC*, Heathcote MSS, pp. 101–5, A Relation by Colonel James Apsley of events from 7 to 8 June 1663. Casualties at the battle were:

The two foot regiments—Captains Atkinson and Goudinge killed. Forty other ranks killed and wounded.

The horse regiment—Colonel Dongan, Captain Paulinge and Cornet Wharton killed. One hundred other ranks killed and wounded.

17 SP 29/75, f. 33, John Pitt to Samuel Pepys, 7 June 1663.

18 Pepys, *Diary*, 4 July 1663.

19 Valencia de Alcantara, 40 miles north of Badajoz.

20 SP 89/6, f. 293, 1 July 1664. Nine officers killed, 14 wounded, 250 other ranks killed and wounded.

21 *Calendar of Clarendon State Papers*, vol. 5, pp. 442–3.

22 SP 89/7, f. 46. The Battle of Montes Claros.

23 SP 89/7, ff. 48–52, 'Relation of last summer's Campaign in the Kingdom of Portugal, 1665', by le Conde de Castelmelhor; *ibid.*, f. 46,

Thomas Maynard to Arlington, 14 June 1665. Five officers killed, 11 officers wounded, 150 other ranks killed and wounded.

24 SP 89/7, f. 63, Maynard to Bennet, 3 August 1665.

25 *Oxford Gazette*, 14–18 December 1665.

26 For Army Lists of the brigade in Portugal see Appendix B.

27 SP 89/6, f. 23, 'Articles against Colonel Guy Molesworth'.

28 *CSPD, 1668–9*, p. 90.

29 PC 2/62, p. 21.

30 *An Historical Account of the British Regiments employed since the Reign of Queen Elizabeth and King James I in the formation and defence of the Dutch Republic, particularly of the Scotch Brigade*, London, 1795, p. 6.

31 For the Army Lists of the Anglo-Dutch Brigade see Appendix C.

32 See Appendix C.

33 John Bernardi, *A Short History of the Life of Major John Bernardi*, London, 1729, p. 13.

34 One new Scottish regiment was formed under Henry Graham in 1674. This was added to the two 'ancient' Scottish regiments already in the Dutch service.

35 *CSPD, 1679–80*, pp. 10–11; SP 77/52, f. 108, Sir Richard Bulstrode, English Resident at Brussels, to Williamson, 25 February 1679.

36 *A Particular Account of this Last Siege of Maestricht, with the sundry remarkable circumstances thereunto relating, together with a List of the Officers killed and Wounded in the Three English Regiments and the Scotch Regiment: Being the substance of a Letter written out of Holland by a Friend to a Person of Quality in London, Sept. 5. 1676, Stylo Novo*, London, 1676.

37 For an account of the Scots in the Russian service, see J. W. Barnhill and P. Dukes, 'North-east Scots in Muscovy in the Seventeenth Century', *Northern Scotland*, 1972, vol. 1, pp. 49–64.

38 13 Charles II, c. 6, 'An Act for declaring the sole Right of the Militia to be in the King and for the present ordering and disposing the same'.

39 PC 2/60, p. 178, 12 February 1668.

40 *Ibid.*, p. 180; Add. MSS, no. 38,694, f. 7, War Office Correspondence.

41 C. T. Atkinson, 'Charles II's Regiments in France, 1672–1678', *JSAHR*, 1946, vol. 24, p. 55.

42 *CJ*, vol. 9, p. 7.

43 For the Army Lists of the regiments in France see Appendix D. An account of the services of the British troops is to be found in

Atkinson, 'Charles II's Regiments in France', pp. 53–65, 129–36, 161–72.

44 SP 29/390, f. 59, 'A Proclamation: Discharging the levying and transporting any Men for the Wars beyond the Seas', 18 January 1677.

45 *CJ*, vol. 9, p. 362; *LJ*, vol. 13, p. 10a.

46 Burnet, *History of His Own Time*, vol. 2, pp. 114–15.

47 *CJ*, vol. 9, p. 426.

48 WO 26/4, p. 259; *CSPD, 1677–8*, p. 593; Hamilton, *Grenadier Guards*, vol. 1, p. 191.

49 SP 104/17, p. 28, Foreign Entry Book, France, 2 October 1672.

50 SP 44/37, p. 49; SP 78/132, f. 132, William Perwick to Williamson, 20 December 1671.

51 *CSPV, 1673–5*, p. 168.

52 See Appendix D, under *Services*.

53 Sir Charles Littleton to Viscount Hatton, 7 October 1671, *Hatton Correspondence*, vol. 1, p. 71.

54 Robert Yard to Joseph Williamson, 3 October 1673, *Williamson's Letters*, vol. 2, p. 32.

55 Yard to Williamson, 21 November 1673, *Williamson's Letters*, vol. 2, p. 81.

56 SP 44/41, p. 17.

57 SP 44/41, pp. 33, 63–5.

58 SP 29/167, ff. 1, 69.

59 SP 29/205, f. 74, John Conny to Williamson, 14 June 1667.

60 This humiliation on the Medway had considerable repercussions in England, and during the Third Dutch War special measures were taken to ensure that the same thing did not happen again. On 3 February 1674 Arlington sent orders to Sir Charles Littleton, Colonel of the Duke of York's Regiment and commander of the Rochester District, outlining contingency plans for the location of forces should the Dutch make another attempt on the Medway. Littleton was given twenty-five companies to cover his region, principally based at Rochester, Dartford, Chatham, Upnor, Gillingham and the Isle of Sheppey (WO 26/2, pp. 109–10).

61 SP 29/208, f. 105.

62 SP 29/208, ff. 28, 55.

63 SP 77/42, f. 6, Unsigned letter from Antwerp, 4 January 1673.

64 Sir Thomas Player to Williamson, *Williamson's Letters*, vol. 1, p. 69.

65 *CSPD, 1673*, pp. 448, 455.

Chapter X Flanders 1678

1 Burnet, *History of His Own Time*, vol. 2, p. 123.

2 *CSPD, 1678*, pp. 182–3.

3 SP 8/1, King William's Chest, f. 18, Danby to William of Orange, 1 July 1678.

4 SP 84/207, f. 21, 9 July 1678.

5 SP 77/52, f. 66, Sir Richard Bulstrode to Williamson, 17 December 1678.

6 The Royal English, Dumbarton's, Dongan's.

7 Add. MSS, no. 10,115, f. 3.

8 For a list of the new regiments of 1678 see Appendix E.

9 WO 26/4, p. 138, 16 March 1678; see Appendix E.

10 A battalion of foot consisted of eight companies of 100 men each, making 800 in all. A squadron of horse numbered 180. A squadron of dragoons numbered 160.

11 The bread wagons were drawn by four horses and cost 5 francs a day to hire. Ammunition wagons were pulled by only three horses and cost 3 francs.

12 SP 44/52, pp. 52–5.

13 SP 44/41, p. 162.

14 SP 44/52, p. 34.

15 *HMC*, Ormonde MSS, n.s. vol. 4, p. 158, Earl of Arran to Ormonde, 29 June 1678.

16 *CSPD, 1678*, p. 34.

17 *Ibid.*, p. 26, 9 March 1678.

18 Sir Charles Littleton to Viscount Hatton, 18 March 1678, *Hatton Correspondence*, vol. 1, p. 161.

19 Add. MSS, no. 29,587, f. 67, Hatton–Finch Papers.

20 SP 77/52, f. 8, Letter from Thomas Musgrave, 29 May 1678.

21 SP 44/52, pp. 63–75, Journal of the Duke of Monmouth's Travels in Flanders, 1678, written by James Vernon.

22 *CSPD, 1678*, p. 343.

23 Peace was signed between France and the United Provinces at Nymwegen on 31 July 1678.

24 SP 77/52, f. 8, Letter from Thomas Musgrave, 29 May 1678.

25 SP 44/52, p. 30, July 1678.

26 SP 77/52, f. 26, Bulstrode to Sir Leoline Jenkins, 15 August 1678.

27 *Ibid.*, ff. 28, 31.

28 SP 44/41, pp. 170–2.

29 SP 77/52, f. 8.

30 *Ibid.*, f. 7, 26 March 1678.

31 *HMC*, Dartmouth MSS, vol. 5, p. 27.

32 SP 44/52, p. 31, Monmouth to Sir Samuel Clarke, 30 July 1678.

33 SP 77/52, f. 108, Bulstrode to Williamson, 25 February 1679.

34 SP 44/52, p. 167, 23 December 1678.

35 SP 77/52, f. 84, Bulstrode to Williamson, 10 January 1679.

36 *Ibid.*, f. 86, 14 January 1679.

37 Add. MSS, no. 23,642, f. 2, Tyrawly Papers, 'Abstract of the Forces in the Year 1680'; WO 24/5; SP 44/58, pp. 21–2, 31 May 1679.

38 SP 44/48, p. 65.

Chapter XI Scotland and Ireland

1 PRO. SP 57/3, Scottish Warrant Books, pp. 36–7, 118–19.

2 SP 57/5, pp. 19–24, 19 October 1678.

3 The Scottish £ was of a lower value than the £ sterling. Pay rates above are given in £ sterling.

4 *CSPD, 1677–8*, pp. 6–7, 4 March 1677.

5 *CSPD, 1682*, pp. 593–4, 28 December 1682.

6 *CSPD, 1678*, pp. 484–5.

7 Both sides numbered about 800 at the beginning of the action.

8 *CSPD, 1677–8*, pp. 322–3f.

9 SP 57/4, pp. 325–8, King to the Scottish Privy Council, 11 December 1677.

10 *CSPD, 1677–8*, pp. 597–8; Burnet, *History of His Own Time*, vol. 2, p. 134.

11 *CSPD, 1678*, p. 184.

12 SP 44/41, pp. 133–4, 28 May 1678.

13 PC 2/68, p. 104.

14 Sidney, *Diary*, vol. 1, p. 5.

15 The officers who served with the regiment in France were Lieutenant-Colonel Edward Mayne, and Captains Coy, Nedby and Langton.

16 Colonel, the Earl of Feversham; Lieutenant-Colonel, Percy Kirke; Major, Theophilus Oglethorpe.

17 These were the three troops of horse grenadiers attached to the Life Guard: Captains Henry Carr, John Staples and Thomas Rowe.

18 Rutherglen, some 10 miles from Glasgow.

19 SP 29/411, f. 150.

20 The future Earl of Dundee. Killed at the Battle of Killiecrankie in 1689.

21 *An Exact Relation of the Defeat of the Rebels at Bothwell Bridge*,

London, 1679. The Scottish army consisted of two regiments of foot, four troops of horse, and three companies of dragoons.

22 C. Dalton, *The Scots Army, 1661–1688*, London and Edinburgh, 1909, p. 56–7. Monmouth had four guns and one gunner, 'besides three men that were pressed from Leith who proved very unfit for that service'.

23 *London Gazette*, no. 1419.

24 *A Further and More Particular Account of the Total Defeat of the Rebels of Scotland*, Edinburgh, 1679.

25 *London Gazette*, no. 1534.

26 *HMC*, Ormonde MSS, vol. 2, p. 186; *Mercurius Publicus*, no. 21.

27 C. Dalton, *The Irish Army Lists, 1661–1685*, London, 1907; Firth and Davies, *Regimental History of Cromwell's Army*, vol. 2, p. 587f.

28 WO 26/2, pp. 54, 67, 137.

29 Before the end of 1678 this regiment of twenty-one companies each of fifty men was taken over by Justin Macarty, and once in France it formed the basis of the future Irish Brigade. See C. Duffy, *The Wild Goose and the Eagle*, London, 1964; J. C. O'Callaghan, *History of the Irish Brigades in the Service of France*, Glasgow, 1870.

30 PRO. SP 63/337, State Papers Ireland, f. 17.

31 SP 63/332, f. 122, 31 March 1672; SP 63/331, ff. 58, 58i.

32 *CSPD, 1672–3*, p. 77.

33 SP 63/309, f. 284, 15 April 1671.

34 *CSPD, 1673–5*, p. 161.

35 Add. MSS, no. 14,286, Sir William Clarke's Public Diary of 1666, f. 8.

36 PRO. SO 1/9, Signet Office, Irish Letter Books, pp. 103–4, 9 May 1674.

37 SP 63/337, f. 39, 23 June 1676.

38 *Oxford Gazette*, no. 15, 21 December 1665.

39 Essex to Coventry, 17 June 1676, *Essex Papers*, p. 54.

40 SP 63/331, f. 130, Essex to Arlington, 20 August 1672.

41 *Essex Papers*, p. 43.

42 SP 63/338, f. 41, Rawdon to Conway, 13 February 1678.

43 *CSPD, 1673–5*, p. 10.

44 *HMC*, Ormonde MSS, vol. 5, p. 17.

45 SO 1/10, p. 512, 19 April 1681.

Part Three

Chapter XII Society, the Army and Parliament

1 SP 29/160, f. 104, 30 June 1666.

2 *HMC*, Bath MSS, vol. 2, pp. 161–2, Savile to Rochester, 2 June 1678.

3 SP 29/412, f. 8, 21 July 1679.

4 SP 29/411, f. 24. The *Courant* was a manuscript news-sheet circulated in London during the time of the Popish Plot. It was a highly unreliable document filled with rumour and cheap scandal, but it reflected the then current emotions and prejudices.

5 Charles Hatton to Viscount Hatton, 11 July 1678, *Hatton Correspondence*, vol. 1, p. 167.

6 WO 26/5, p. 6.

7 *CSPD, 1679–80*, pp. 97–8, 101.

8 William Harbord to the Earl of Essex, 7 April 1674, *Essex Papers*, vol. 1, p. 208.

9 SP 29/219, f. 144, 12 October 1667.

10 SP 29/220, f. 2, 13 October 1667.

11 PC 2/62, p. 224, 20 July 1670.

12 Henry Ball to Williamson, 4 July 1673, *Williamson's Letters*, vol. 1, pp. 87–8.

13 Ball to Williamson, 20 June 1673, *Williamson's Letters*, vol. 1, p. 52.

14 Grey, *Debates*, vol. 5, pp. 287–8.

15 J. S. Omond, *Parliament and the Army, 1642–1904*, Cambridge, 1933, p. 14.

16 13 Charles II, c. 6, in *SR*, vol. 5, pp. 308–9.

17 Grey, *Debates*, vol. 5, p. 325.

18 Cobbett, *Parliamentary History*, vol. 4, p. 145.

19 Thomas Trenchard, *A Short History of Standing Armies in England*, London, 1698, p. 15.

20 C. Robbins, ed., *The Diary of John Milward Esq, Member of Parliament for Derbyshire, September 1666, to May 1668*, Cambridge, 1938, pp. 83–4.

21 SP 29/360, f. 40, 15 January 1674, The Answer of the Earl of Arlington to the Charges against him in the House of Commons.

22 *CJ*, vol. 9, pp. 276–7; Grey, *Debates*, vol. 2, pp. 161–3.

23 Robert Yard to Williamson, 30 June 1673, *Williamson's Letters*, vol. 1, p. 79.

24 B. D. Henning, ed., *The Parliamentary Diary of Sir Edmund*

Dering, 1670–1673, New Haven, 1940, p. 160; Grey, *Debates*, vol. 2, pp. 215–16.

25 Grey, *Debates*, vol. 2, pp. 220–1.

26 *CJ*, vol. 9, p. 7.

27 *Ibid.*, pp. 425–6.

28 *LJ*, vol. 13, p. 130.

29 Grey, *Debates*, vol. 5, p. 111.

30 *CJ*, vol. 9, p. 435.

31 *Ibid.*, p. 441.

32 Grey, *Debates*, vol. 5, p. 286.

33 SP 29/403, f. 183, 7 May 1678, 'Notes on Parliamentary Business'.

34 *LJ*, vol. 12, pp. 221–2, 23 May 1678.

35 *CJ*, vol. 9, p. 483.

36 30 Charles II, c. 1; Burnet, *History of His Own Time*, vol. 2, p. 144.

37 *LJ*, vol. 12, p. 293.

38 Grey, *Debates*, vol. 6, p. 279.

39 31 Charles II, c. 1.

40 WO 33/19, f. 338.

41 Sir John Dalrymple, *Memoirs of Great Britain and Ireland*, Edinburgh, 1771, vol. 1, p. 59; Leopold von Ranke, *A History of England*, Oxford, 1875, vol. 4, p. 129; H. C. Foxcroft, *A Character of the Trimmer*, Cambridge, 1946, p. 134.

42 *HMC*, Portland MSS, vol. 7, p. 16.

43 CO 279/32, ff. 156–66, 2 October 1683.

44 *CJ*, vol. 9, p. 581, 1 April 1679.

Select Bibliography

Manuscript Sources

Public Record Office

AO 1/48–53, Exchequer and Audit Department, Declared Accounts for the Army.
CO 279/1–33, Colonial Office Papers relating to Tangier.
CO 5, Colonial Office Papers relating to North America and the West Indies.
E 351/344–5, Exchequer, Declared Accounts for Dunkirk, 1660–2.
MP H/1, Maps and Plans of Tangier, 1661–84.
PC 2, Registers and Minutes of the Privy Council.
SO 1, Irish Letter Books of the Signet Office.
SP 29 and 30, State Papers Domestic, Charles II.
SP 44, State Papers Domestic, Entry Books of the Secretaries of State.
SP 57, Scottish Warrant Books.
SP 63, State Papers Ireland.
SP 71, State Papers Foreign, Barbary States.
SP 77, State Papers Foreign, Flanders.
SP 78, State Papers Foreign, France.
SP 84, State Papers Foreign, Dutch Republic.
SP 89, State Papers Foreign, Portugal.
SP 101/91, State Papers Foreign, Entry Book of newsletters from Portugal.
SP 104, State Papers Foreign, Entry Books of the Secretaries of State.

WO, War Office Collection.
WO 4/1, Secretary at War, Out-Letters.
WO 5/1, Marching Orders, 1683–5.
WO 9/1, Miscellaneous Accounts and Returns.

WO 24/1–7, Establishments.
WO 25, Commission Book, 2 vols.
WO 30, War Office Miscellanea.
WO 55, Ordnance Office Miscellanea.
WO 71/121, General Courts Martial, Proceedings.
WO 89/1, General Courts Martial, 1666–97.
WO 92/1, General Courts Martial, Register (fragment).
WO 93, War Office Miscellanea.
WO 94, Records of the Constable's Office in the Tower of London.

The principal source of manuscripts relating to the army of Charles II is the State Papers Domestic. The War Office Collection commences in earnest in 1683, after Blathwayt's assumption of office. In general there is no one primary source for the history of the British army in this period. Information has to be gleaned from a wide variety of manuscript collections.

The British Museum (*British Library*)

As with the Public Record Office, the British Museum does not provide a central source for army history. Various classes of documents provide small amounts of information, although two are of vital importance: the Sloane Manuscripts which cover Tangier, and Williamson's State Papers concerning the Flanders Expedition of 1678. The Blathwayt Papers are now housed in the British Museum, but as with the War Office Collection in the PRO, these are of little use before 1683.

Add. MSS nos:
5,759, Register of Petitions, 1660–70.
10,115, Sir Joseph Williamson's State Papers, 1677–8, relative to the Preparations for the Projected War with France.
14,286, Public Diary of Sir William Clarke, April to June 1666, with news of the Second Dutch War and other Military Matters.
18,764, Muster Roll of a Company in the Portsmouth Garrison for 1661.
23,642, Tyrawly Papers, Miscellaneous, 1679–1759.
28,082, Army Establishments in 17th and 18th centuries.
29,587, Hatton–Finch Papers.
36,781, Lists of the Civil and Military Establishments in 1661.
38,694, War Office Correspondence, vol. 1.

Sloane Manuscripts nos:
1,952, Tangier Papers, General Correspondence.
1,956, Proceedings at Tangier, 1661.

1,958, Earl of Middleton's negotiations and correspondence at Tangier, 1671–2.
1,961, Papers relating to Tangier, 1665–6.
3,299, Letters and Warrants relating to Tangier.
3,496, Proceedings at Tangier, 1665–6.
3,499, Correspondence of Lord Bellasise and Colonel Henry Norwood at Tangier, 1665 and 1668–9.
3,509–12, General Papers relating to Tangier, 1660–80.
1,957, 1,959, 1,960, 3,498, 3,514: Minutes of Courts Martial at Tangier, 1661–74.

National Army Museum, London

A disappointing source for primary material on seventeenth-century military history. Only four items proved of value.
Papers of the 1st Marquis of Anglesey.
Certificate of Militia Training, 15 August 1661, MSS nos. 6112–490.
Buckley, Francis, *Notebook on Military Affairs from 1680–1720*.
Sumner, Percy, *Notebook, 1665–1759*.

Dorset County Record Office, Dorchester

Public Papers of Sir Stephen Fox.
This collection contains the records of Fox's services as Paymaster-General of the Guards and Garrisons under Charles II, and as Head of the Board of Green Cloth. Under the former are his account book and ledgers, interest accounts, numerous establishments, and many other papers relating to military finance. These documents are the basis for any study of army finance under the Restoration.

Printed Sources

1 *Reports of the Historical Manuscripts Commission*

Bath Manuscripts, 1907, Series 58, 2 vols.
Manuscripts of the Earl of Dartmouth, 1887, 11th Report, Appendix 5.
Heathcote Manuscripts, 1899, Series 50.
Manuscripts of the Marquess of Ormonde, 1902, Series 36, New Series, vols 1–7.

2 *Calendars of State and other Official Papers*

Acts of the Privy Council, Colonial Series, Hereford, 1908, vol. 1.
Calendar of Clarendon State Papers, 1660–1726, ed. F. J. Routledge, Oxford, 1970, vol. 5.
Calendar of State Papers Colonial, America and the West Indies, 1661–1685.
Calendar of State Papers Domestic, Charles II, 1660–85.
Calendar of State Papers Venetian, 1659–75, vols 31–8.
Calendar of Treasury Books, 1661–85, vols 1–7.

3 *Records of Parliament*

BOND, M. F., *Guide to the Records of Parliament*, London, 1971.
COBBETT, W., *Parliamentary History of England*, London, 1808, vol. 4.
GREY, ANCHITEL, *Debates of the House of Commons*, London, 1769, 9 vols.
The History and Proceedings of the House of Commons from the Restoration to the Present Time, London, 1742, vols 1–2.
The History and Proceedings of the House of Lords from the Restoration in 1660 to the Present Time, London, 1742, vol. 1.
Journals of the House of Commons, vols 8–9.
Journals of the House of Lords, vols 11–13.
Public and General Acts, vols 12–32.
Returns of Members of Parliament, London, 1878, vol. 1.
Statutes of the Realm, London, 1810–22, vols 1–11.

4 *General*

ADDISON, LANCELOT, *A Discourse of Tangier under the Government of the Earl of Teviot*, London, 1685.
ANDROS, SIR EDMUND, *The Andros Tracts*, ed. W. H. Whitmore, Boston, 1868–74, 3 vols.
BLUNDELL, WILLIAM, 'The Military Diary of Captain William Blundell from 1660–80', in *Crosby Records: A Cavalier's Notebook*, ed. T. E. Gibson, London, 1880.
BROOKS, NATHAN, *A General and Complete List Military of Every Commission Officer of Horse and Foot now commanding in his Majesty's Land Forces of England*, London, 1684.
BROWNING, ANDREW, *English Historical Documents, 1660–1714*, London, 1953.
BULSTRODE, SIR RICHARD, *Memoirs of the Reign of Charles II*, London, 1721.

CHOLMLEY, SIR HUGH, *The Memoirs of Sir Hugh Cholmley, Knt. and Bart.*, 1837.

CLARKE, SIR WILLIAM, *The Clarke Papers: Selections from the Papers of Sir William Clarke*, ed. C. H. Firth, Camden Society, 1891–1901, 4 vols.

COBBETT, W., *State Trials*, London, 1809–26, 33 vols.

DALRYMPLE, SIR JOHN, *Memoirs of Great Britain and Ireland*, Edinburgh, 1771.

ESSEX, ARTHUR CAPEL, EARL OF, *Selections from the Correspondence of Arthur Capel, Earl of Essex, 1675–1677*, ed. C. E. Pike, Camden Society, 1913.

EVELYN, JOHN, *Diary of John Evelyn*, ed. E. S. de Beer, Oxford, 1955, 6 vols.

An Exact Journal of the Siege of Tangier, from the First Sitting Down of the Moors Before it on March 25th, 1680, to the Late Truce, May 19th, following, London, 1680.

An Exact Relation of the Defeat of the Rebels at Bothwell Bridge, London, 1679.

A Further and More Particular Account of the Total Defeat of the Rebels in Scotland, London and Edinburgh, 1679.

GWYNNE, JOHN, *Military Memoirs of the Great Civil War, being the Military Memoirs of John Gwynne*, Edinburgh, 1822.

HALKETT, SIR JAMES, 'A Short and True Account of the most remarkable things that passed during the late Wars with the Moors at Tangier in the year 1680 etc.', ed. H. M. McCance, *JSAHR*, 1922, Special Number.

HATTON, FAMILY OF, *Correspondence of the Family of Hatton*, ed. E. M. Thompson, Camden Society, 1878, 2 vols.

HUTCHINSON, LUCY, *Memoirs of the Life of Colonel Hutchinson*, ed. C. H. Firth, London, 1906.

JAMES II, *The Memoirs of James II, his Campaigns as Duke of York, 1652–1660*, ed. A. Lytton Sells, London, 1962.

A Letter from Tangier Bay, London, 1680.

A List of the Officers claiming to the Sixty Thousand Pounds etc. granted by his Sacred Majesty for the relief of his Truly Loyal and Indigent Party, London, 1663.

London Gazette.

LUDLOW, EDMUND, *The Memoirs of Edmund Ludlow*, ed. C. H. Firth, Oxford, 1894, 2 vols.

LUTTRELL, NARCISSUS, *A Brief Historical Relation of State Affairs*, Oxford, 1857, vol. 1.

MAGOLOTTI, COUNT LORENZO, *The Travels of Cosmo the Third, Grand*

Duke of Tuscany, through England during the Reign of King Charles the Second, 1669, London, 1821.

MILWARD, JOHN, *The Diary of John Milward, Esq., Member of Parliament for Derbyshire, September, 1666, to May, 1668*, ed. C. Robbins, Cambridge, 1938.

A Particular Relation of a Great Engagement between the Garrison of Tangier and the Moors, London, 1680.

A Particular Relation of the Late Success of his Majesty's Forces at Tangier against the Moors, London, 1680.

PEPYS, SAMUEL, *Diary*, ed. H. B. Wheatley, London, 1904–5, 8 vols.

—— *The Tangier Papers of Samuel Pepys*, ed. E. Chappell, Navy Records Society, 1935.

The Present Interest of Tangier, London, 1680.

RERESBY, SIR JOHN, *The Memoirs of Sir John Reresby*, ed. A. Browning, Glasgow, 1936.

A Second Journal of the Siege of Tangier, from 25th March, 1680, to 22nd May, 1680, London, 1680.

SIDNEY, HENRY, *Diary of the Times of Charles the Second*, ed. H. W. Blencowe, London, 1843, 2 vols.

TEMPLE, SIR WILLIAM, *Memoirs of What past in Christendom from the War begun in 1672 to the Peace concluded in 1679*, London, 1692.

WILLIAMSON, SIR JOSEPH, *Letters addressed to Sir Joseph Williamson from London*, ed. W. D. Christie, Camden Society, 1874, 2 vols.

Secondary Books and Articles

ALLEN, F. S., 'Towards a Theory of Civil-Military Control in England, 1670–80', *JSAHR*, 1962, vol. 40.

ASHMOLE, ELIAS, *Memoirs of the Life of that Learned Antiquary Elias Ashmole Esq.*, London, 1717.

ATKINSON, C. T., 'Charles II's Regiments in France, 1672–1678', *JSAHR*, 1946, vol. 24.

—— *History of the Royal Dragoons, 1661–1934*, Glasgow, 1934.

—— *Marlborough and the Rise of the British Army*, London, 1921.

BARNETT, CORRELLI, *Britain and Her Army, 1509–1970*, London, 1970.

BAXTER, S. B., *William III*, London, 1966.

BERNARDI, JOHN, *A Short History of the Life of Major John Bernardi*, London, 1729.

BLOMFIELD, SIR REGINALD, *Sebastien le Prestre de Vauban, 1633–1707*, London, 1938.

BOYLE, ROGER, EARL OF ORRERY, *A Treatise of the Art of War*, London, 1677.

BOYNTON, L., 'The Tudor Provost-Marshall', *EHR*, 1962, vol. 77.

BRACKENBURY, HENRY, *The Nearest Guard: a History of her Majesty's Body Guard of the Honourable Corps of Gentlemen-at-Arms*, London, 1892.

BROWNING, ANDREW, *Thomas Osborne, Earl of Danby*, Glasgow, 1944–1951, 3 vols.

BRYANT, ARTHUR, *King Charles II*, London, 1934.

BURNET, GILBERT, *History of His Own Time*, Oxford, 1823, 4 vols.

CALVERT, E. M. and R. T. C., *Serjeant-Surgeon John Knight*, London, 1939.

CANNON, RICHARD, *Historical Record of the First or Royal Regiment of Foot*, London, 1847.

—— *Historical Record of the Life Guards*, London, 1835.

—— *Historical Record of the Marine Corps*, London, 1850.

—— *Historical Record of the Sixth, or Royal First Warwickshire Regiment of Foot*, London, 1839.

CHAMBERLAYNE, EDWARD, *Angliae Notitia: or the Present State of England*, London, 1671, 1679, 1684.

CHILDS, JOHN, 'Monmouth and the Army in Flanders', *JSAHR*, 1974, vol. 52.

CHURCHILL, SIR W. S., *Marlborough: His Life and Times*, London, 1933–8, 4 vols.

CLARK, SIR GEORGE, *War and Society in the Seventeenth Century*, Cambridge, 1958.

CLODE, C. M., *The Military Forces of the Crown: Their Administration and Government*, London, 1869, 2 vols.

CORBETT, JULIAN, *Monk*, London, 1889.

COWPER, L. I., *The King's Own, the Story of a Royal Regiment*, Oxford, 1939, 2 vols.

CRUICKSHANK, C. G., *Army Royal, Henry VIII's Invasion of France, 1513*, Oxford, 1969.

—— *Elizabeth's Army*, Oxford, 1968.

DALTON, CHARLES, *English Army Lists and Commission Registers, 1661–1714*, London, 1892, vol. 1.

—— *Irish Army Lists, 1661–1685*, London, 1907.

—— *The Scots Army, 1661–1688*, London and Edinburgh, 1909.

DAVIES, GODFREY, *The Early History of the Coldstream Guards*, Oxford, 1924.

DAVIES, J. D. G., *Honest George Monck*, London, 1936.

DAVIS, JOHN, *The History of the Second Queen's Royal Regiment*, London, 1887, vol. 1.

DEAN, C. G. T., *The Royal Hospital Chelsea*, London, 1949.

DOYLE, J. E., *The Official Baronage of England*, London, 1886, 3 vols.

DUFFY, C., *The Wild Goose and the Eagle, a Life of Marshall von Browne, 1705–1757*, London, 1964.

EDYE, L., *The Historical Records of the Royal Marines*, London, 1893, 2 vols.

ELTON, RICHARD, *The Complete Body of the Art Military*, London, 1668.

FIRTH, C. H., *Cromwell's Army*, London, 1962.

—— 'Royalist and Cromwellian Armies in Flanders, 1657–62', *TRHS*, 1903, vol. 17.

FIRTH, C. H., and DAVIES, GODFREY, *The Regimental History of Cromwell's Army*, Oxford, 1940, 2 vols.

FORTESCUE, J. W., *A History of the British Army*, London, 1910–30, 13 vols.

FOSTER, SIR WILLIAM, *The English Factories in India, 1661–64*, Oxford, 1923.

—— *The English Factories in India, 1665–67*, Oxford, 1925.

G.E.C., *The Complete Baronetage*, Exeter, 1900–6, 5 vols.

—— *The Complete Peerage*, London, 1910–59, 12 vols.

GORDON, HAMPDEN, *The War Office*, London, 1935.

GROSE, FRANCIS, *Military Antiquities respecting a History of the English Army*, London, 1812, 2 vols.

GUMBLE, THOMAS, *The Life of General Monck, Duke of Albemarle*, London, 1671.

HALEY, K. H. D., *The First Earl of Shaftesbury*, Oxford, 1968.

HAMILTON, SIR F. W., *The Origin and History of the First or Grenadier Guards*, London, 1874, 2 vols.

HARDACRE, P. H., *The Royalists during the Puritan Revolution*, The Hague, 1956.

HARLOW, V. T., *A History of Barbados, 1625–1685*, Oxford, 1926.

Het Staatsche Leger, 1568–1795, The Hague, 1911–59, 8 vols.

HIGHAM, C. S. S., *The Development of the Leeward Islands under the Restoration, 1660–1688*, Cambridge, 1921.

JACOBSEN, G. A., *William Blathwayt, a late Seventeenth Century Administrator*, London and New Haven, 1932.

KAUFMAN, H. A., *Conscientious Cavalier: Colonel Bullen Reymes, M.P., F.R.S., 1613–72*, London, 1962.

KENYON, J. P., *The Popish Plot*, London, 1972.

KNIGHT, H. R., *Historical Records of the Buffs*, London, 1905, 2 vols.

LILLY, WILLIAM, *Mr William Lilly's History of his Life and Times, from the year 1602 to 1681*, London, 1715.

LOVELL-KNIGHT, A. V., *The History of the Office of Provost-Marshall and the Corps of Military Police*, London, 1943.

LYNCH, K. M., *Roger Boyle, First Earl of Orrery*, Knoxville, 1965.

MACKINNON, DANIEL, *Origin and Services of the Coldstream Guards*, London, 1833, 2 vols.

MATHEWS, WILLIAM, *British Diaries: An Annotated Bibliography of British Diaries written between 1442 and 1942*, London, 1950.

MEAKIN, J. E. B., *The Moorish Empire*, London, 1899.

MILLER, JOHN, 'Catholic Officers in the Later Stuart Army', *EHR*, 1973, vol. 88.

MUIR, AUGUSTUS, *The First of Foot: The History of the Royal Scots*, Edinburgh, 1961.

NEWTON, A. P., *The European Nations in the West Indies, 1493–1688*, Cambridge, 1933.

NYE, N., *The Art of Gunnery*, London, 1670.

OMAN, SIR CHARLES, 'The British Army and Royal Jubilees', *JSAHR*, 1935, vol. 14.

OMOND, J. S., *Parliament and the Army, 1642–1904*, Cambridge, 1933.

RANNIE, D. W., 'Cromwell's Major-Generals', *EHR*, 1895, vol. 10.

ROUTH, E. M. G., *Tangier: England's Lost Atlantic Outpost, 1661–1684*, London, 1912.

The Rules of Civility, London, 1678.

SACKFIELD, JOHN, *Memoirs of the Life of Sir Stephen Fox Kt, from his First Entrance upon the Stage of Action under the Lord Piercy, till his Decease*, London, 1717.

SCOULLER, R. E., *The Armies of Queen Anne*, Oxford, 1966.

TRENCHARD, THOMAS, *A Short History of Standing Armies in England*, London, 1698.

TURNER, F. C., *James II*, London, 1949.

TURNER, SIR JAMES, *Pallas Armata: Military Essays of the Ancient Greek, Roman, and Modern Art of War*, London, 1683.

UNDERDOWN, D., *Royalist Conspiracy in England, 1649–60*, New Haven, 1960.

WALKER, H. M., *A History of the Northumberland Fusiliers, 1674–1902*, London, 1919.

WALTON, CLIFFORD, *History of the British Standing Army, 1660–1700*, London, 1894.

WESTERN, J. R., *The English Militia in the Eighteenth Century*, London, 1965.

WEYGAND, M., *Turenne, Marshal of France*, London, 1930.

WIFFEN, J. H., *Historical Memoirs of the House of Russell*, London, 1833, 2 vols.

WOLF, J. B., *Louis XIV*, London, 1968.

ZANTHIER, F. W. VON, *Feldzüge des Vicomte Turenne*, Leipzig, 1779.

Index

STUDIES IN SOCIAL HISTORY

Editor: HAROLD PERKIN

Professor of Social History, University of Lancaster

Assistant Editor: ERIC J. EVANS

Lecturer in History, University of Lancaster

ANCIENT CRETE: A Social History from Early Times until the Roman Occupation	R. F. Willetts
CHILDREN IN ENGLISH SOCIETY, VOL. I: From Tudor Times to the Eighteenth Century	I. Pinchbeck & M. Hewitt
CHILDREN IN ENGLISH SOCIETY, VOL. II: From the Eighteenth Century to the Children Act 1948	I. Pinchbeck & M. Hewitt
CHURCHES AND THE WORKING CLASSES IN VICTORIAN ENGLAND	K. S. Inglis
EDUCATION IN RENAISSANCE ENGLAND	Kenneth Charlton
ENGLISH LANDED SOCIETY in the Eighteenth Century	G. E. Mingay
ENGLISH LANDED SOCIETY in the Nineteenth Century	F. M. L. Thompson
ENGLISH PARISH CLERGY ON THE EVE OF THE REFORMATION	P. Heath
FROM CHARITY TO SOCIAL WORK in England and the United States	Kathleen Woodroofe
HEAVENS BELOW: Utopian Experiments in England, 1560–1960	W. H. G. Armytage
A HISTORY OF SHOPPING	Dorothy Davis
THE IMPACT OF RAILWAYS ON VICTORIAN CITIES	J. R. Kellett
THE ORIGINS OF MODERN ENGLISH SOCIETY, 1780–1880	H. Perkin